W9-BND-759

THE BIRTH OF CHINA

A BRONZE RITUAL VESSEL OF SHANG TYPE, OF THE FORM *CHIA*
Reproduced by courtesy of Mr. P. C. Huang, Peiping.

THE BIRTH OF CHINA

A Study of the Formative Period of Chinese Civilization

By
HERRLEE GLESSNER CREEL
Professor of Early Chinese Literature and Institutions
The University of Chicago

FREDERICK UNGAR PUBLISHING CO.
NEW YORK

Printed in the United States of America

Sixth Printing, 1967

Library of Congress Catalog Card No. 54-5633

CONTENTS

CONTENTS

BOOK III—CHOU

ILLUSTRATIONS

ILLUSTRATIONS

INTRODUCTION

The outstanding importance of Dr. Creel's study of the Chinese civilization in its earlier aspects has already received recognition among specialists and scholars everywhere. The result of his labors in this field he has now made available to the general public also, in his latest book, *The Birth of China*.

It has not been so long since our newspaper men used to say, "China news is no news." Now the press, as we all know, mirrors only too faithfully the interests and feelings of the great mass of its readers. We could therefore scarcely have better proof (if indeed any were needed) that a similar attitude of indifference toward China formerly characterized the minds of most people.

Today all this has changed. China is now a subject of interest to everyone. Recent books about her have attained the rank of "best sellers." Her history, her civilization, her language—all that concerns her, in fact—are receiving a steadily growing amount of attention in our universities, our colleges, and our high schools. We find collections of Chinese art in all our larger and many of our smaller cities. The Library of Congress at Washington houses one of the most important assemblages of Chinese books to be found anywhere in the world. No longer, in short, do we think of the Chinese people, when we think of them at all, as quaint, curious, and somehow different from the rest of civilized mankind; as doing everything backward, and with manners and customs unchanging, stereotyped, fixed for all time. On the contrary, we are beginning to realize that the development of China has been as eventful and variegated and picturesque as that of any country on earth.

INTRODUCTION

We used to ask ourselves, Whence did the Chinese people come? Upon this question recent researches and excavations have shed a flood of new light. We now know that the Chinese did not reach China as immigrants from some other land, bringing with them their civilization ready-made; but that they have instead been living for thousands of years—as far back, in fact, as we are yet able to trace them—just where we find them today. It has been in China itself that they have slowly worked their way upward from primitive savagery through exactly the same successive stages of development as have all civilized folk. Like ourselves, for example, so they too passed through their Stone Ages, Old and New; then through their Bronze Age; until finally they entered upon their Age of Iron.

About the Old Stone Age of the Chinese we have as yet comparatively little information, although we know that it existed. In regard to their New Stone Age we have learned considerably more. During its course, we find, their way of living was only a little more advanced than that of the American Indians of the Atlantic seaboard before the days of Columbus. Not until they had acquired a knowledge of bronze does the real history of the Chinese people commence. It is of the earlier portions of their Bronze Age—of that colorful, still half-barbaric period when they were laying the foundations of that great historical civilization which the world has known as Chinese—that Dr. Creel paints such an illuminating picture in the present volume.

Many of the fundamental elements of its ancient culture China shared with those other great river-valley civilizations of antiquity which arose in the basins of the Euphrates and the Tigris, of the Indus and the Nile. These all had in common certain basic traits whose gradual development alone made possible their emergence from barbarism. Among these were the idea of writing; the building of towns; the casting of bronze; the use of the wheel in transport; the possession of domestic animals; and the practice of true agriculture on a large scale.

In spite, however, of these and other resemblances to the ancient civilizations of the West—resemblances pointing unmistakably to contacts of some sort during prehistoric times—the type of culture existing in the valley of the Yellow River some three thousand years ago was essentially and characteristically Chinese. Whatever ideas and inventions and techniques may have come to it from without had been thoroughly naturalized in their new environment before written history began. China thus in time became a focus of cultural diffusion not dissimilar in function from that other which had arisen considerably earlier in the Near East. In the spread of civilization, China has played a part in southeastern Asia comparable in many ways to the rôle assumed in the Occident by Babylonia and Egypt, Greece and Rome. This fact—the existence in the Ancient World of not one but two centers of progress—is not the least interesting of the many points that Dr. Creel has so clearly brought out in his new book.

As we have already remarked, until quite lately we have known very little about the initial phases of that process which culminated in the formation of the historical Chinese civilization. During the past few years, however, much has been brought to light. Not a little has been learned in regard to the religious beliefs, the social organization, the methods of warfare, the architecture, and the art of that remote period. The results of these most interesting of recent discoveries have however been published hitherto almost exclusively in Chinese. For this reason they have remained quite inaccessible to the great majority of us Occidentals, and little is generally known about them.

Most fortunate is it, therefore, that a scholar so thoroughly qualified in every way as is Dr. Creel should have been willing to make available to the English-reading public everywhere this great body of new knowledge. In the performance of this task he has laid under contribution all possible sources of information. Among these have been the classical Chinese literature; recent scientific publications in Chinese as well as other languages; archaic inscriptions on bronze and tortoise-shell and bone; objects dug up from ancient sites; and detailed personal examination of the sites themselves. The facts thus obtained Dr. Creel has collated and analyzed and correlated with painstaking care and great acumen. He has then discussed them exhaustively with other investigators, principally in China but also in Europe and America. The result of all this research he has now set down for us in a volume of truly absorbing interest. *The Birth of China* is by far the best, the most comprehensive, and the most pleasantly readable account yet published of the Chinese people at the very threshold of their long history. It is certain of a welcome as wide as it will be well-deserved.

CARL WHITING BISHOP.

FREER GALLERY OF ART,
SMITHSONIAN INSTITUTION,
WASHINGTON, D. C.
12 FEBRUARY, 1937.

PREFACE

This book is not written for specialists. It does not take for granted a knowledge of the Chinese language, or even of Chinese history. My aim, in writing it, has been to make it readable, and as interesting as possible, for the general intelligent reading public. To this extent it partakes of the nature of a 'popular' book.

But there are certain connotations which sometimes go with the term 'popular' which do not apply to this book. It has not been written hastily, nor in any sense at second hand. This book summarizes the results of four years of full-time, concentrated research on nothing but the history of Chinese culture during the period of approximately 1400-600 B.C. I have studied virtually every current document from that period, including many thousands of inscriptions on bone and hundreds of bronze inscriptions which have never before been utilized in a study of this kind. All of these documents have been studied in the most original form in which they now exist; inscriptions in the original or in photostatic facsimile, and transmitted documents, such as the Classics, in the oldest and best texts now existent—the Han Stone Classics, in so far as they are preserved, and similar texts. I have read all of the reports of excavations, chiefly in Chinese, and a large proportion of the very voluminous critical work which is constantly being produced by Chinese scholars. I have visited all the chief archæological sites, covering the ground traversed by the Chou conquest and other such movements, and handled and examined a considerable share of the tens of thousands of objects of this period excavated in recent years. I have discussed the various problems involved, on the sites of excavation and elsewhere, with the excavators and many other Chinese scholars in innumerable conversations.

In writing, I have placed accuracy above every other consideration. This does not mean that there are no mistakes in this book—such a claim would be absurd—but it does mean that it does not contain hasty and careless generalization. I have written it with the same care that I put into the most meticulously documented technical paper for a scholarly journal. Whenever I have referred to a bone or bronze inscription, the facsimile of the original has lain before me on my desk. References to Chinese books have been made with the best existent Chinese text before my eyes. Each page of this book represents an average of about twenty-five separate entries in my notes which have been consulted at the moment of writing.

None of my research has been based on translations. But where, in the text of this book, it was desired to quote from Chinese works, I have quoted from the standard translations into English where these existed and where my understanding of the passage agreed with that of the translator. Where this was not the case, I have myself translated completely or modified the quoted translation. For the convenience of readers desirous of identifying quotations I have given, in the notes, the location of quoted passages in standard English translations. It is to be remembered, however, that reference to a translation does not necessarily mean that the translator's rendering has been reproduced in this book, although in most cases I have altered it only slightly if at all. I have not burdened the notes with references to works of which there is no standard translation, since these would be of use only to sinologists.

In the Selected Bibliography a number of works in English have been included for the Stone Ages, because it happens that a great deal of the fundamental archæological work in this period has been done by Occidental scholars. For the later periods, with the exception of translations, no works in any language but Chinese have been listed. Nevertheless, a number of articles, some popular and some serious, have been published, particularly concerning the Shang discoveries, in recent years. They have not been included for two reasons. In the first place, none of the research on which this book depends is based on any of these articles. Secondly, the discoveries of the last year have been so revolutionary, and have made necessary such a complete re-orientation of our conception of Shang culture, that all previous publications in Western languages, including my own, are rendered more or less obsolete.

In writing a book like this one it is impossible to give complete demonstration of proof on every point without boring the general reader hopelessly. In many cases, therefore, I have had to present as casual flat statements propositions which the specialists in this field may consider startling, or even untrue and incapable of demonstration. In discussing human sacrifice, for instance, I have spoken of the name of the tribe of *ch'iang* and the surname of a Chou noble family, *Chiang*, as if they were the same character. They are, as a matter of fact, two forms of the same character, as bronze inscriptions and literary evidence show. But to go into this evidence would have been tedious and of no interest to most readers. Specialists, who desire full proof and meticulous documentation for the material treated in this book, will find them in my technical work, *Studies in Early Chinese Culture*, of which the first volume is completed, and now in process of publication.

The interpretation of the events surrounding and succeeding the Chou conquest, given here, differs considerably from the traditional accounts of Chinese and Western historians. In part it is in agreement with the interpretation of contemporary Chinese historians and in part it is original with myself. It is based in large measure on textual criticism depending on comparisons, made by myself, of bone and bronze inscriptions with the transmitted literature. The details of this research will be found in my technical work mentioned above.

Even to mention all of those who have been of material assistance in this investigation is impossible. My wife's share in the making of this book is recorded in the dedication. I cannot forbear to mention the late Dr. Berthold Laufer, even though circumstances made it impossible to have his aid and criticism in this particular undertaking, because it was directly due to his kindness that I was given the opportunity to prosecute this research. Mr. Carl W. Bishop has aided me in many ways, but especially by his counsel and criticism in person and by letter.

Without the generous assistance of the many Chinese scholars who have helped me in a great many ways I should certainly have been able to accomplish only a fraction of the results which they have made possible during these years in China. Professor Mei Kuang-ti and Professor Liu Chieh must be mentioned specially, for each of them gave me hours of his time, for two years, in unravelling the many problems which arose, without any sort of return. To Mr. Chang Tsung-ch'ien I am also indebted more deeply than I can express.

The officials of the National Research Institute have aided me in many ways. I wish especially to acknowledge my obligation to Dr. Fu Ssŭ-nien, Dr. Li Chi, Mr. Tung Tso-pin, Mr. Liang Ssŭ-yung, Mr. Kuo Pao-chün and Mr. Hsü Chung-shu.

Among the many other Chinese scholars who have assisted me very materially are Mr. Chang P'êng-i, Chairman of the Shensi Archæological Association; Professor Ch'ên Yin-k'ê of National Tsing Hua University; Professor Hu Kuang-wei of National Central University; Professor Jung Kêng of Yenching University; Professor Ku Chieh-kang of Yenching University; Mr. Kuan Pai-i, Director of the Honan Provincial Museum; Professor Li I-shao of National Central University; Mr. Liu I-chêng, Director of the Kiangsu Provincial Sinological Library; Mr. Lo Mou-tê of the Shensi Archæological Association; Professor Miu Fêng-lin of National Central University; Professor Shang Ch'êng-tso of Chinling University; Mr. Sun

Hai-po, author of the *Chia Ku Wên Pien*; Professor T'ang Lan of the National University of Peking and National Tsinghua University; Professor T'ang Yung-t'ung of the National University of Peking; Dr. C. C. Young of the Geological Survey of China; and Mr. T. L. Yuan, Director of the National Library of Peiping.

For help of various kinds I am indebted to Dr. Otto Burchard, of Berlin and Peiping; Mr. Mortimer Graves of the American Council of Learned Societies; Mr. P. C. Huang of the Tsun Ku Chai, Peiping; Mr. Orvar Karlbeck of the Museum of Far Eastern Antiquities, Stockholm; Dr. Nils Palmgren, Curator of H.R.H. the Crown Prince of Sweden's Collections; Mr. Laurence C. S. Sickman, Curator of Far Eastern Art in the William Rockhill Nelson Gallery of Art, Kansas City; and H.E. Dr. Oskar P. Trautmann, German Ambassador to China.

My thanks are due to Mrs. W. J. Calhoun, Mrs. Dagny Carter, Colonel and Mrs. Walter Scott Drysdale, Mrs. Wirth Stewart Dunham, H.E. Mr. Nelson Trusler Johnson, American Ambassador to China, and Mr. Owen Lattimore, for their kindness in reading the manuscript and criticizing it from various points of view.

To the American Council of Learned Societies and the Harvard-Yenching Institute I am indebted for appointment to the research fellowships which have made this investigation possible.

HERRLEE GLESSNER CREEL

PEIPING,
16th August 1935

BOOK I

DISCOVERY

CHAPTER I

THE ORACLE BONES

MORE than three thousand years ago there flourished on the plains of North China one of the most interesting and important peoples the world has ever known. Their civilization was equal in many respects, and superior in some, to that of any other people in the world of their time. It was the ancestor of the civilization of most of the Far East, or about one-fourth of mankind.

Unfortunately most of the things used by these people, which might have come down to us as evidence of their culture, were very perishable. Their great temples were built with pillars of wood. Their books were written on tablets of wood or bamboo. In the wet climate of China such materials decay quickly. Even their wonderful marble sculptures, perfectly preserved though they were, were buried thirty to forty feet deep in great tombs which concealed them effectually, so that, until 1934, the very existence of the art which produced them was hardly suspected. For these reasons we have had to depend chiefly on tradition and legend for our knowledge of these people, and tradition and legend have been none too trustworthy. Only within the last seven years have we come to possess definite historical records and actual objects used by them which make it possible now, for the first time, to give a reasonably detailed picture of their life and some connected account of their history, based on fact rather than conjecture. Indeed, some of the most important facts have been known for less than six months.

All of the new evidence for this ancient civilization comes

from the site of one city. Like many great archæological discoveries, this one was led up to by events so casual and made possible by clues so slight as to be almost absurd. In fact it might never have been made but for the peculiar tastes of the modern Chinese in medicine.

The site of this ancient city includes the tiny modern village of Hsiao T'un, in the district of Anyang in northern Honan Province. It is some eighty miles north of the Yellow River, three hundred miles west from the sea. Its latitude is approximately that of Gibraltar. Farmers noticed that in their fields on the bank of the Huan River, directly north of the village, after a rain or after ploughing, bones of a very peculiar sort came to the surface. Most of them were broken pieces, yet some of their edges showed an uncommon smoothness and finish. The surfaces of some were polished until they gleamed like glass. Most of them had queer oval notches on their backs, and T-shaped cracks. A thrifty farmer named Li decided that they must be dragon bones, since dragon bones are used in Chinese medicine and therefore worth money. He collected as many as he could find and marketed them.

A few of the bones, about one out of ten, had even more mystifying markings—rows of geometric designs and small pictures. These, the druggists thought, would hardly be found on the bones of even the most whimsical dragon. So they were scraped off before the bones were sold. This process went on for several decades, with old-fashioned Chinese physicians prescribing a bit of the bone, pounded in a mortar, to be fed to the ailing. It was thought especially good for nervous disorders. But in 1899 some of these bones still bearing their markings came into the hands of Chinese antiquaries skilled in the most ancient known forms of Chinese writing, who recognized that this must be a still older form.

With this event an entirely new epoch in our understanding of the history of man in the Far East was begun. These fragments of bone are at present our sole remnant of the written

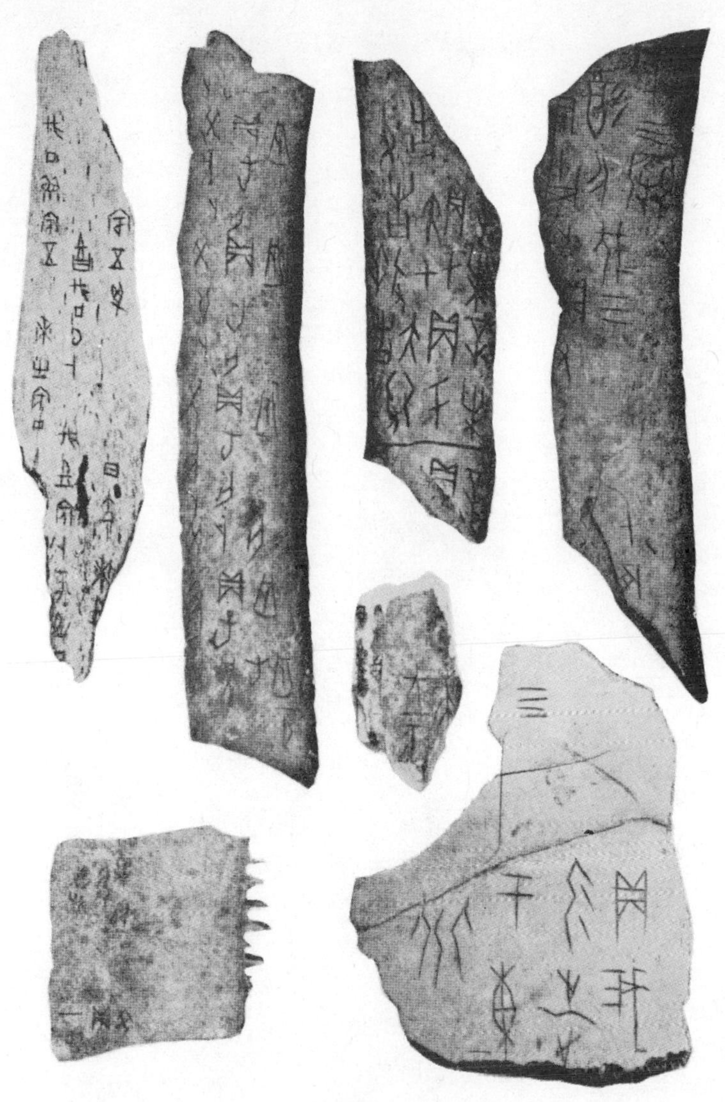

PLATE I

SHANG ORACLE BONES

SPECIMENS OF THE MANY THOUSANDS OF PIECES OF INSCRIBED BONE AND TORTOISE-SHELL FROM WHICH IT IS POSSIBLE TO RECONSTRUCT MUCH OF THE LIFE OF SHANG TIMES. IN THE UPPER LEFT-HAND CORNER IS AN EXAMPLE OF THE FORGED INSCRIPTIONS CARVED FOR SALE TO THE UNWARY. THE INSCRIPTION IN THE UPPER RIGHT-HAND CORNER APPARENTLY HAD TO DO WITH THE SACRIFICE OF THREE HUMAN BEINGS. THE PIECE IN THE LOWER RIGHT-HAND CORNER IS IN THE COLLECTION OF DR. CYRUS PEAKE, THE REMAINDER IN A PRIVATE COLLECTION.

Reproduced by kind permission.

records of most ancient eastern Asia. There is much talk of the four thousand years of Chinese history, but actually we knew virtually nothing of the period before 1122 B.C. until they were discovered. Already they have revolutionized our whole conception of ancient China.

They are a part of the royal archives of the latter portion of the Shang (sometimes called Yin) dynasty to which Chinese tradition assigns the dates 1765-1123 B.C. This fact in itself makes them precious as historical material. Yet they are very brief. The longest inscriptions barely exceed sixty words, and most of them contain not more than ten or twelve. If they were ordinary documents, such as records of trading or memoranda of debts, they might tell us very little of the people who produced them. Fortunately they are of far more illuminating character.

These bone fragments contain records of questions which the people of that time put to their ancestors and their gods. The Shang people used these bones much as the Greeks used the Delphic Oracle, except that they divined much more frequently and casually than the Greeks sent to Delphi for guidance. In the beginning, no doubt, the Shang people, too, asked for advice only on the most momentous matters. But later, when we know them, they used their oracle more in the manner in which some people to-day use a ouija board or confer with a spiritualistic medium daily, asking for supernatural guidance in even the smallest matters. There was good reason for them to do this. The spirits they consulted were believed to be able to help men powerfully if they wished, but they also harmed them most terribly if they were displeased. They might send swift-raiding enemies, who fell upon their victims without warning and carried off as many as they could capture to slavery or death. They might send plagues of disease. They might appear in one's dreams, as ghosts, and frighten one almost out of one's senses. For all of these reasons it was better to take no action of any possible importance without first asking what they thought about it. And it was better to take care to give them sacrifices regularly, and sacrifices of just the things they preferred; to know what would please them most—this was divined about, too.

To learn the will of the spirits they used the scapula or leg bones of cattle, or the shell of the tortoise. The leg bones were split, so as to make flat or slightly rounded pieces of bone. The tortoise-shells, at least, were probably prepared with much ceremony and laid away carefully until they were needed. The divination itself probably took place in the ancestral temple. The diviner asked a question, such as 'So-and-so is ill; if this fact is announced to the spirit of Grandfather Ting (will he aid him to recover)?' Heat was applied to the back of the shell or bone, and this caused a T-shaped crack to appear on its face. From this crack the diviner decided whether the answer of the spirits was favourable or unfavourable, and announced the result to the king or other person for whom he was divining.

In many cases, though not always, the diviner wrote the question, inscribing it with some sort of stylus, on the bone beside the cracks which answered it. These questions, covering a wide range of subjects, give us archæological material of a sort not often found. They make it possible to form a picture of the men who asked them such as no materials less intimate could possibly do. And it must be noted that these inscriptions have a reliability which history, and many inscriptions, do not have. For they are not history, and they were not written for posterity or for anyone save the writer and perhaps his colleagues to read. To exaggerate, then, would have been without point. For this reason it is highly probable that when we read 'It is asked, "Shall an army of five thousand men be raised?"' for a certain campaign, there actually were just about that number of men involved. In contrast to this we find an inscription on a bronze of a few centuries later which tells us that a general who conducted an expedition against some barbarians in the West captured thirteen thousand and eighty-one living men, in addition to the number slain. This figure seems quite unbelievable. His whole army could hardly have been so large, to say nothing of its being able to take so many captives. But this bronze was cast as a souvenir of his prowess, to be left to his admiring posterity. We should expect him to boast in such an inscription. It cannot possibly have the same value, as historical evidence, as is possessed by the oracle bone inscriptions.

It is not to be supposed that once these bits of bone reached the hands of scholars they were deciphered easily. At first, even Chinese palæographers could make out no more than a word here and there, while the very nature of the inscriptions remained a mystery. Even to-day they contain many problems which still await solution, but the main outlines of their content have been wrested from them. This has required thirty-five years of constant effort by many scholars, and some of the most important discoveries have been made during the last two years. This adventure in scholarship has been as thrilling and in many ways as notable an achievement as the decipherment of the Egyptian Hieroglyphics. A few foreigners have contributed to it, but they have been less than a handful. Most of this work has been done by Chinese scholars who speak no other language and have had no Western training.

These bone inscriptions had hardly become known to the world of scholarship before it was declared by some that they were forged. There are a few Chinese scholars and perhaps a few Western sinologists who still believe that not one of them is genuine. They had good reason, as a matter of fact, for their scepticism. The Chinese are masters at counterfeiting antiquities, and they began counterfeiting these inscribed bones almost as soon as it was learned that archæologists would pay for them. Thousands of them have been turned out, most of them quite near to the site where the genuine ones are found. The fakers use the bones without writing (90 per cent. of those found), which are practically valueless, for their work, and some of it is very good indeed.

A number of these fakes were shipped abroad and some of them have been given places of honour as genuine inscriptions. One sometimes hears the fallacy that bones bought within a few years of the first discovery must be genuine, but it is more likely that the opposite of this is true. For at that time there had been little digging, and genuine bones were very scarce. The market value was high, and very few persons could tell the genuine writing from the counterfeit. Mr. James M. Menzies, one of the few foreigners who has contributed to the deciphering of the inscriptions, lived within a few miles of the Anyang site, and bought his bones in the very fields from which they were dug up. Yet he has written that all the large and fine pieces which he bought early proved later to be forgeries.[1] To-day one rarely finds large genuine pieces, with complete inscriptions, for sale. I recently went to an antique shop in Peiping which I knew had some, and asked to see them. They showed me a considerable number. After a brief examination I told the proprietor, rather indignantly, that every one was a fake.

'Quite true,' he said. 'Did you want to see the genuine ones? We keep them in the back room.'

Nevertheless, the great majority of the bones used by Chinese scholars in their work are unquestionably genuine. The grooves carved in many of them contain a mineral deposit which can be formed only during many years of lying in the soil. And a final proof has been furnished by the excavation of the site at Anyang. Thousands of these bones have been found by scientists many feet underground, in undisturbed soil, surrounded by other relics of the Shang dynasty. The writing on these bones is identical with that of others which had previously been determined, by other means, to be genuine.

At present many more than one hundred thousand pieces of these oracle bones are in the hands of collectors. Facsimiles of almost fifteen thousand pieces, including nearly all of the larger and more important ones, have been published, so that they are generally available for study.

CHAPTER II

EXCAVATION

HAD the Shang oracle bones been discovered in Europe or America, scientific excavation of the spot on which they were found would probably have started within the year. In China it was not begun until the autumn of 1928, almost thirty years after the original discovery. This fact sums up much of the reason why we have not known more about the ancient history of China.

There is a general and deep-rooted antipathy to archæological excavation in China, and even to extensive digging of any sort. Cutting into the earth is believed to disturb the magical influences of the region in which it is done. And it is impossible to do any great amount of digging in China proper without disturbing one or more graves. The Chinese do not ordinarily bury in communal cemeteries as we do, though the graves of a single family may be together. But the spot for the grave, or the family tombs, is selected after complicated investigations into the magical influences to be found in various proposed locations. A good site for a grave may bring prosperity to the whole family; a bad one may cause quick disaster. And what is a good location for one person is not necessarily so for another. Thus we find graves in all sorts of places in the countryside. They dot the fields, which are carefully cultivated up to the very mounds, a few feet in diameter, which cover the graves. But they must not be disturbed. This would be disrespect to the honoured dead, it would anger the spirits, and it might well bring misfortune on the whole family by destroying the delicate balance of magical influences. This was learned, to their sorrow, by the men who laid out railroads in China.

We can all understand and sympathize with the very human dislike of having the graves of one's ancestors disturbed. But in China ancestor-worship has raised this feeling to a pitch it does not reach elsewhere. We read in Chinese history that on one occasion a besieged city was in very sore straits, completely surrounded, without hope of outside help, out of food and almost out of water. The people were reduced to cannibalism. There were no alternatives save surrender or extinction. The general of the beleaguered city knew that there were spies among his men. To one of them he said: 'I only hope that the enemy will not think of digging up the graves of the people's ancestors. That would force us to surrender.' That night this information was smuggled out of the city. The next day the enemy began digging up graves, in full view of the city walls. The people of the besieged city rose as one man, poured through the gates and fell like raging lions upon the attacking army. It was completely routed.

This feeling extends even to very ancient graves. At present the National Research Institute of History and Philology, a Chinese government institution, is carrying on excavations at various points. Yet, in April 1934, the chairman of the Examination Yüan, one of the highest officials of the Chinese government, sent a circular telegram to various leaders urging that the government prohibit the excavation of ancient tombs at once. He pointed out that grave-robbing was formerly punished by cutting the offender into thin slices. Why, he asked, should those who practise this crime be exempted from punishment, and even paid salaries by the government, merely because they call themselves 'scientists'?

But graves have been robbed, of course, in China as elsewhere. Men all over the world have tried to prevent such desecration by setting up the severest penalties, by traps and poisons secreted in tombs, by the most awe-inspiring curses written above the coffin. All these have had little effect. Practically everywhere that objects of value have been buried there have been men with the hardiness to dig them up.

The same reverence for the past which causes the Chinese to oppose the excavation of ancient tombs gives them an avid passion for the collection of antiquities. This is catered to by the grave-robbers, who sell their spoils through antique or (as they are known in Peiping) 'curio' shops. This gives us the paradox that in China we find an unusual wealth of ancient objects, while almost nothing is known about their origin. The grave-robbers are naturally not going to attach their names to the objects they sell, and the dealer in such things, who usually has only a financial interest in them, often gives them such a history as he thinks will most enhance their value.

This situation is very perplexing to the archæologist of Western training, who has learned to distrust all materials which have not been excavated under scientific conditions by men whose reputations he knows and respects. It is impossible to maintain such an attitude in working with Chinese materials. One sees a beautiful and most interesting piece of bronze. One asks, 'Where did it come from?' 'Who knows?' is often the only answer. 'It turned up on the Peiping market.' It is useless, in such a situation, to refuse to study the object further. All one can do is to subject it to the most rigid analysis and compare it, where this is possible, with similar objects which have been excavated scientifically. But such materials for comparison are all too rare.

Because it has given a wealth of such comparative materials as well as a flood of new light on ancient Chinese civilization, the excavation of the Shang capital at Anyang has an importance which can hardly be exaggerated. The inception of this work is closely connected with American archæology. Mr. Carl Whiting Bishop, Associate Curator of the Freer Gallery of Art of the Smithsonian Institution, had long had the intention of excavating this site when the necessary arrangements could be made. Dr. Li Chi, who has had general charge of the excavation, was connected with the Freer Gallery of Art until 1930, and is a graduate of the Department of Anthropology of Harvard University. A small preliminary excavation of seventeen days' duration was made by the Chinese National Research Institute in the autumn of 1928. In 1929 the work was begun on a larger scale and continued for two months in the spring and two months in the autumn under the joint auspices of the Freer Gallery of Art and the National Research Institute. In 1930 excavation was impossible because of civil war. Beginning with 1931 the work has been carried on with little interruption by the Chinese organization. Four volumes of reports of these excavations have been issued,[1] entirely in Chinese save for one brief paper on the microscopic analysis of bronzes found, written by Sir H. C. H. Carpenter.[2]

Many difficulties, apart from the fundamental one of Chinese opposition to digging, beset the excavators. The winters and summers are too cold and too hot for work, which must be done in the spring and autumn. But these are the windy seasons, when much of the time the yellow dust flies so thickly that one cannot see twenty feet ahead. As one stands on the brink of an excavation thirty feet deep the wind nearly lifts him from his feet and plunges him to the bottom. Under such conditions, wearing goggles, eight scholars directed the work of some three hundred workmen in 1935, and kept detailed archæological records. This is anything but easy.

Because of the danger of bandits the archæologists must pay a great deal of attention to guarding their finds and themselves. The Anyang region is especially bad in this respect. Across the mountains to the west, in Shansi, banditry is almost unknown. But Honan, and the Anyang district in particular, is filled with poverty-stricken peasants, some of whom are ready to turn to banditry in sheer desperation whenever the opportunity offers. They have crude home-made pistols which can be bought for three dollars local currency, equal to a little more than one

U.S. dollar. A few of them have made fortunes from digging up the antiquities with which the region abounds. These rich unfortunates go in terror of their lives, for they are carried off for ransom at the least opportunity. For one such captive bandits recently asked a half-million dollars, probably more than twice as much as all of the farmers of the region together have received for all of the antiques they have sold.

This private digging interferes with the work of the excavators, by destroying material before they can reach it, far more than the bandits do. Soldiers and police are on hand to prevent it, and the National Research Institute keeps a man on the spot all the year round to maintain the watch. But the area to be supervised is a very large one, since the finest bronzes and other objects were buried in graves, and these graves seem to be scattered over the whole countryside. As a result of the official ban on digging, the grave-robbers have now developed a method of nocturnal operation, according to officers of the Institute. To prevent them from prospecting in the daytime is almost impossible. They use an instrument something like a post-hole digger, and when this brings up a peculiar type of 'pounded earth,' they know that they have located an ancient grave. In preparation for digging they assemble fifty or sixty men, all with the greatest secrecy. After nightfall this band, all armed with guns, proceeds to the chosen spot. A few of them dig; the rest, taking advantage of any natural cover, or devising some slight protection, form an armed ring about the scene of operations. Work proceeds feverishly and the entire tomb is gutted before morning. As compared with their abject poverty there is a fortune for each of these peasants at stake in their enterprise. If any attempt is made to interfere with them they will shoot to kill, resisting with the utmost stubbornness. In such circumstances it is almost impossible to prevent digging. To do so one must know in advance where and when digging is planned. Given this information, one must have at his disposal a large body of soldiers or police ready and willing to walk into a nocturnal ambush of armed, desperate men.

Under these conditions it is surprising that any headway has been made in the task of preventing such digging. But if one may judge by the lessening in the stream of antiquities which appear on the Peiping market, and by the resentment of the peasants in the Anyang region, the attempts at suppression have met with some success. The National Research Institute rents the ground it digs, at the rate of one hundred and eighty Mexican dollars per acre per year; this is much more than the farmer can realize by sowing the same ground. But the people are bitter, feeling that they are being cheated of a rightful source of revenue. It is said that they have formed a defence association, with the object of assassinating the director of the excavations.

These threats have not materialized, but great and irreparable damage has already been done by private digging. It is estimated that as many as fifty Shang bronze vessels of good quality have been appearing every year on the Peiping market alone, to say nothing of those sold elsewhere or of other things such as inscribed bones and ornamental objects. A large proportion of them go abroad to museums and private collectors. They are not, of course, lost to science, for they are still available for study, though it does seem rather unfair for Chinese scholars to have to go abroad to study their own antiquities. But far more serious is the fact that in the process of digging up these objects the grave-robbers heedlessly destroy the most valuable and irreplaceable archæological evidences. Chariot fittings come on to the market, with wood still adhering to them. If they had been excavated by trained archæologists, the decayed wooden parts of the chariot could probably have been strengthened with shellac or some similar substance, and a great deal of the original form of the Shang chariot preserved. The grave robbers wrench off the saleable bronze and toss the wood aside. Until the autumn of 1934, not a single skeleton

PLATE II

EXCAVATING A 3000-YEAR-OLD CAPITAL UNDER THE EAVES OF A MODERN VILLAGE

ARCHAEOLOGISTS OF THE NATIONAL RESEARCH INSTITUTE RECOVERING ORACLE BONES AND OTHER RELICS OF SHANG CIVILIZATION IN THE VILLAGE OF HSIAO T'UN, WHICH STANDS ON THE RUINS OF THE ANCIENT CAPITAL. AS THE REGION HAS ITS FULL SHARE OF BANDITS, THE EXCAVATORS WORK UNDER ARMED GUARD AT ALL TIMES, AS SHOWN HERE.

Official photograph, reproduced by courtesy of Dr. Li Chi, Director of the Archæological Section of the National Research Institute of History and Philology.

which could be dated absolutely as Shang had been found, and not a single tomb of indisputably Shang date had been excavated scientifically. Yet we knew that many, probably hundreds, of Shang tombs had been looted of their bronzes and other valuable articles by men who deliberately break up the skeletons they encounter and scatter the bones in order to prevent the dead from taking vengeance.

It is easy to say that this destruction of historical materials could be stopped if foreigners would cease buying Chinese bronzes, but this is not quite true. Chinese collectors were encouraging this practice before the foreigners began buying, although the present high prices were then unknown. The problem is a complex one. According to Chinese law all ancient articles dug out of the earth belong to the nation, rather than to the individual who holds the title to the surface of the ground. The justice of this position has been disputed. But it is in accordance with the established principles of Chinese law, and it is difficult to see how a man who bought a piece of land in ignorance that they were there can claim title to articles buried under it three thousand years ago. On the other hand, however just the present laws may be, it is almost impossible to enforce them strictly. And they make it almost impossible for a law-abiding foreign student of ancient Chinese culture to obtain even a modest amount of study material.

Ideally, proper government supervision in China should be supplemented by action of foreign governments forbidding their nationals to engage in this illicit traffic. The Chinese government should enforce strict laws forbidding any but qualified archæologists to excavate ancient objects; at the same time, as a practical measure, a reasonable reward could be paid to the man from whose lands they were removed. It would then be a simple matter for the Chinese government to arrange the exchange or sale of antiquities not required for Chinese museums to foreign governments, museums, and cultural organizations. It should even be possible to provide for the interests of legitimate dealers and private collectors, for these objects are very numerous, and there could be no objection to the sale of pieces of which there are a great many examples, if they had been excavated in such a manner as to preserve the archæological record. If this were done, the chief losers would be the bandits, who eventually get the peasants' money, while the gain to science would be enormous. But such steps will not be taken. It would be impossible to get all of the nations concerned to agree on such steps, and those who profit by the existing situation, in China and in other countries, are too many and too powerful.

The sites excavated were found to be dotted with the pits, about three feet square, made by private digging. They are quite clear in the walls of the larger excavations as shafts of loose earth occurring perhaps every ten feet. At a small but important supplementary dwelling-site, discovered in the spring of 1934, seven large and complete inscribed tortoise-shells were found; six inches to the north of them was a pit dug by a peasant. These inscribed shells dated several buildings found on this spot, showed the nature of the new site, and have added much to our knowledge in several ways; had the peasant dug his pit six inches farther to the south, their connection with the place would have been for ever unknown.

For years there was a very real danger that this private digging, destroying the evidence at so rapid a rate, would cut off for ever our chances of gaining very vital information concerning the Shang people. The oracle bones told us much about them, and careful excavation of the site of the capital had added greatly to that knowledge. But until the autumn of 1934 not a single tomb which could be dated as certainly Shang had been excavated. The least important consequence was that we knew very little about burial customs of the period, and lacked such light as they might throw on the religion. Moreover, not a single Shang bronze ritual vessel had been scientifically excavated under satisfactory circumstances. This meant that for all of the marvellous bronzes which had been dug up by grave-robbers, and which we felt quite certain for various reasons were Shang, we had not a single unquestionable piece which could be used as a 'control,' for comparison. Most important of all, we had virtually no reliable data on the racial characteristics of the Shang people. Hundreds of accurately datable skeletons had been destroyed ruthlessly; not one had been preserved. Were the bronze-using Shang aristocrats Mongoloid, descendants of the Neolithic inhabitants of north-east China? Or were they, as some maintained, alien invaders from the West? We could not say. And the pillars of the grave-robbing industry sent word to the excavators saying that while their activities in the dwelling-sites (which yield little that is saleable) had been tolerated, one attempt to go beyond this and excavate tombs would be the signal for a quiet shot in the back for each of the scholars directing the work.

Officials of the National Research Institute laid the situation before the leaders of the national government. They acted promptly and effectively. In the early autumn of 1934 a strongly worded telegram, signed by Chiang Kai-shek and Wang Ching-wei, was dispatched to the regional authorities at Anyang. It directed that all necessary measures were to be used to prohibit private digging, and give adequate protection to the archæologists. The effect of this order was apparent in an immediate dwindling of the articles from Anyang coming into the Peiping market.

Backed by this support, the excavators located a large grave field, increased their force to three hundred labourers, and commenced operations on an unprecedented scale. The results have been almost incredible, even to those of us who have watched the work for years and predicted a portion of the recent finds. Up to the close of excavation in June 1935, something more than eleven hundred datable skeletons from the Shang period have been recovered, many of them in an excellent state of preservation. More than three hundred Shang tombs, four of them undoubtedly royal tombs of huge proportions, had been scientifically excavated. They have yielded a wealth of new data of every sort concerning Shang culture. Bronze ritual vessels, of the finest quality, were found by the score. And an almost unsuspected art of Shang sculpture is attested by a large number of pieces of marble statuary of an excellence which is altogether breath-taking.

*

Beginning with the next chapter we shall be concerned with an account, more or less chronological, of the development of early Chinese culture. It is inevitable that the unpleasant subject of dates be mentioned at this point.

The relative chronology of ancient China is unusually clear and complete. That is to say, there is very little difference of opinion as to the sequence of events and the order of the reigns of kings. But the absolute chronology is very uncertain. Thus the traditional chronology assigns to the Shang dynasty the dates of 1765-1123 B.C., but another system of chronology[3] places the same dynasty at 1558-1051 B.C. The two chronologies agree after 841 B.C.

It is altogether probable that the traditional chronology includes some degree of error, but the other chronology is based on a work which scholars generally agree to be a forgery. This does not prove the chronology to be false, but it robs it of authenticity unless that can be given to it by outside evidence. The new discoveries, both the oracle inscriptions and the excavations, give us no evidence whatever for absolute chronology.

As matters stand, one is faced with two alternatives. He may retain the traditional chronology for practical reasons, frankly acknowledging that it probably involves a degree of error. If so, he will be able to avail himself of carefully worked-out tables of events, giving their relative chronology, but based on the traditional dates. Or he may renounce all this, instead taking up a chronology which, while it may be nearer the truth, has little real claim to accuracy. If he does this he must take upon himself the task of working out the dates of minor events by means of calculations which require much time and always involve an element of conjecture.

As between these two courses I have had no hesitation in choosing the former. Dates are given in this book as infrequently as possible, but where they are given they agree with the traditional chronology. This is given solely as a matter of convenience, in order to assist the reader to keep events in their proper sequence. But he must remember that the dates given for events prior to 841 B.C. involve a possible error of something more or less than a century, that is, the events may have occurred something like a century later than the date given for them.

CHAPTER III

ORIGINS OF CHINESE CIVILIZATION*

THE question of the origin of Chinese civilization is one which has been debated almost as long as foreigners have taken a serious interest in China. For the traditionally minded Chinese there is, of course, no question; his civilization was developed by the great Chinese sages of the past. For the foreigner who is intent on maintaining the superiority of the white race there is no question; anything of real value in Chinese civilization must have been imported from the West.

These positions are equally unscientific, but the latter one in particular has had tremendous influence on most discussion of the subject by Occidentals. Thus a whole literature has grown up, suggesting various places, chiefly Egypt and Babylon, as the points from which either the Chinese people or their civilization began a migration to China. Chinese writing has been compared with both Egyptian and Babylonian, with the conclusion that it was certainly borrowed from one or the other. Unfortunately most of the persons who made these comparisons were handicapped by the fact that they had no complete understanding either of Chinese, on the one hand, or of Babylonian or Egyptian on the other. Despite this fact, such works enjoyed a great popularity during the latter half of the nineteenth century.

With the collaboration of an expert Egyptologist, I have myself been able to point out certain very interesting parellel-

* This chapter is necessarily more technical than the remainder of the book; it may be omitted by the reader who is not interested in the prehistory of Chinese culture, since it is not essential to the understanding of that which follows.

isms between the structure of Chinese and Egyptian hieroglyphic writing. But although they are very instructive these similarities do not exceed what we might reasonably expect in two entirely independent systems having in common the ideographic principle. At the present time theories seeking to prove an Egyptian or Mesopotamian background for Chinese culture on the ground of very hasty generalization have happily passed out of fashion. This is not to say that it is not possible that someone may, in the future, prove such affinities on the basis of sound and thorough study. But it has not yet been done, and as we find more and more that is distinctive in early Chinese civilization it seems increasingly unlikely that it will or can be done.

To ask: 'What is the origin of Chinese culture?' is to state the question improperly. No civilization has a single origin. No people has originated in a state of isolation from all contacts with other peoples. Writers seeking to show the innate superiority of the white race used to try to demonstrate that all of the beginnings of Chinese culture were borrowed, and thus that the yellow race was permanently inferior, lacking in originality. This betrays a mistaken understanding of the nature of the development of cultures. History shows that wherever we find a particularly high civilization we are likely to find that it developed from the contact and cross-fertilization of several cultures. Mesopotamia, Palestine, Asia Minor, Greece, are all cases in point.

Instead of asking what was the origin of Chinese civilization we should rather inquire what were the origins of the various cultural elements which figured most prominently in its development. We are still unable to trace the origin of some of these individual elements, but recent excavation and study have advanced us far on the road toward the ultimate solutions.

It used to be, and in some quarters still is, customary to take for granted that the Chinese migrated to the region of the lower Yellow River valley from an earlier home elsewhere, probably to the west. It is still said with all seriousness that this theory is supported by Chinese traditions of such a migration. But qualified scholars have been pointing out for twenty years that there is no mention of such a tradition in genuinely early Chinese literature or inscriptions[1] and that stories of such a migration, led by the mythical Yellow Emperor, appear only in relatively late literature of a speculative character. Nevertheless, until about fifteen years ago those who held to this view could point out that there was no certain evidence that men had lived in China even as early as the New Stone Age, to say nothing of a still earlier time. But recent excavation has changed all that.

The earliest man-like inhabitant of the Chinese area known to us is the Peking Man, or *Sinanthropus pekinensis*. Considerable skeletal remains of this early relative of modern man were found in the Chou K'ou Tien cave, some thirty miles southwest of Peiping, by palæontologists of the Geological Survey of China, under the general direction of J. G. Andersson.[2] The earliest certain finds were made in 1927. The several individuals found on this spot are believed to have lived in early Pleistocene times, and to represent an off-shoot from the human family tree somewhat later, and more human, than *Pithecanthropus erectus*, and somewhat earlier than Neanderthal Man. Along with the bones were found rocks which have been accepted by Abbé Breuil and other authorities as purposely shaped, if crude, stone implements. China, then, ranks with almost any other part of the world in the antiquity of the time at which it can be proved to have been inhabited by man-like beings.

Early investigators considered *Sinanthropus* to be an offshoot from the main line of man's ancestry before the differentiation of modern races, so that they did not consider him to be an ancestor of modern man. But Professor Franz Weidenreich, of the Cenozoic Research Laboratory of the Geological Survey of China, after prolonged study of this material, has declared that 'nothing contradicts the assumption that Sinanthropus is a direct ancestor of recent man.' Even more important, he states that a peculiar thickening of the jaw bones, and the conformation of the teeth, indicate 'direct genetic relations between Sinanthropus and the Mongolian group of recent mankind.' Indeed, *Sinanthropus* seems to be related not merely to the Mongolian peoples, but to the Chinese specifically. Weidenreich says that the observed peculiarities 'in Chinese skulls at my disposal . . . are not only found in prehistoric (æneolithic) but also in modern jaws in exactly the same formation and variability as in Sinanthropus.'[3]

The significance of this for the history of Chinese culture is tremendous. It will frequently be pointed out, in the course of this book, that many aspects of Chinese culture are unique, seeming to represent a cultural tradition developed in and peculiar to the Chinese area. This must seem strange if, as has commonly been assumed, the Chinese migrated to their present home at a late date, when their culture had reached something very like its present form. But if further investigation should substantiate that ancestors of the modern Chinese have been living in China since early Pleistocene times, some 500,000 years or more ago, then this strongly individual and local genius of their culture is perfectly natural.

Whether China has been inhabited continuously by man-like and human beings from the time of *Sinanthropus* to the present is a question which cannot be answered with absolute certainty at this time. Professor Weidenreich believes that it has. But because of the absence of positive evidence, many have held that China has been uninhabited during long periods. Such negative argument has little validity in China. The study of such questions, even in Europe, is largely a matter of the last hundred years, and in China it has barely begun. In Europe and America excavation is widespread, and there is a very general interest in these problems and an eagerness, even among the laity, to bring unusual finds to the attention of scientists; in China both of these conditions have only begun to obtain in the last decades. Even after numerous Neolithic sites had been excavated in China, it was held that men had not lived here in the Old Stone Age. It is now recognized that *Sinanthropus* himself represents an early Palæolithic culture. Reconnaissance by French and Chinese scholars, at various times from 1922 to 1929, has shown that not only the Ordos region to the north-west, but also the valley of the Yellow River between modern Shensi and Shansi, were inhabited by Palæolithic man. His weapons, resembling those of the Palæolithic Age in Europe, and remains of his camp-fires have been found, but these sites yielded no skeletal remains save a single tooth which may have belonged to him.

But a number of Palæolithic skeletons were found in 1933 and 1934, in a small cave adjoining the one inhabited by Peking Man. From the tools and ornamental objects found with them, these people are considered to have had a late Old Stone Age Culture. But here again we get one of the perplexities which make Chinese archæology so interesting. For whereas *Sinanthropus* is said to show definite Mongoloid characteristics, these late Palæolithic people who lived on the site of his former home are not Mongolian in physical type, but rather resemble the Palæolithic Europeans. Weidenreich suggests that they may have been a tribe of wanderers, on their way to the sea. We know that the Chinese are racially complex, and that time after time other people have come in and been absorbed by the local population. These possibly alien visitors to the region of Peking suggest that this process was already under way in the Old Stone Age.

After the Palæolithic there is another gap in our record. Scores of Neolithic sites have been located in north China, and dozens have been excavated, but all of them date from late Neolithic times. Whether China was uninhabited by man during the early and middle Neolithic periods, or whether we have simply failed as yet to discover his traces, is a moot point. Time and future investigation must decide.

The first of the excavations of Neolithic material was made in 1921 by the Geological Survey of China, the work being under the direction of J. G. Andersson. A large number of sites were excavated by this organization in successive years. Much of this work was financed by a Swedish organization headed by H.R.H. the Crown Prince of Sweden. One site was excavated by collaboration between the Freer Gallery of Art and Tsing Hua University, and a number have been excavated by the Honan Archæological Association and the National Research Institute.

Speaking in the most general terms, we can divide late Neolithic culture in north China into three types. The first has comparatively little to distinguish it from that basic type of Neolithic civilization which spread itself, so widely and so mysteriously, over most of the known world, including America as well as Eurasia. The men of this civilization hunted and fished, but they were primarily agriculturalists. They raised millet, and possibly other grains and vegetables. They made meal, grinding it on 'mealing-stones.' The pig and the dog are the only domestic animals which they knew in the earlier period; large numbers of both were raised for their meat. Like Neolithic men everywhere they made tools and weapons, chiefly knives and axes, of stone which they ground to a smooth surface and polished. They used the bow and arrow, wove baskets and cloth, and sewed with bone needles. They made a great deal of pottery. In the earlier period most of it was of rather poor quality and greyish in colour; designs, sometimes of no little beauty, were often pressed into the wet clay.

Even in this earliest known phase of Neolithic culture in China we see the first trace of an extremely significant regional differentiation. The regions which are relatively best known through the excavation of Neolithic sites include the modern provinces of Kansu to the north-west, and Honan and Shantung which occupy an eastern and somewhat northerly position. There has also been some excavation in Shensi, Shansi, and

Fêngtien. Excavation in Honan has been chiefly in the northern part of the province. The Honan-Shantung area has constituted, as we shall see, something of a cultural unit. These provinces belong to north China, and are definitely eastern; with regard to the great historic theatre of Chinese civilization they occupy a north-easterly position. When a 'north-eastern culture area' is mentioned it will be understood that it is this general Honan-Shantung region which is indicated, and not the still more north-eastern provinces of Jehol, Fêngtien, Kirin, and Heilungkiang.

In the earliest known stage of the Neolithic in China we find one of the distinctive peculiarities of Chinese culture in the north-eastern region. This is the *li* tripod. Two examples of this vessel are illustrated at the top of Plate IV. Andersson has suggested that it originated in the leaning of three pots with pointed bottoms together over a fire; someone then had the idea of making the three in one piece.[4] The bulging legs bring the food in the pot into close contact with the heat. In so far as is known, this form and others developed from it are typically Chinese, unknown in other parts of the world. A close relative of the *li* is the *hsien* 'steamer.' This vessel consists of a *li* surmounted by another vessel which has a perforated bottom, like a colander. Water is placed in the lower part and turned into steam which passes through the holes and cooks the food in the upper chamber. Beautifully executed specimens of both the *li* and the *hsien* are found in the north-eastern area during the earliest Neolithic period known, but they do not occur at all to the west, in Kansu, during that period. On the other hand, a very small amount of painted pottery, along with the prevailing monochrome ware, is found in Kansu but not in the north-east at that stage.

The next age is that of painted pottery. This Neolithic culture is called, from the type site at Yang Shao in north-western Honan, the Yang Shao culture. The pottery is a new type, of finer quality, painted with strikingly beautiful designs in various colours. The best examples of this ware, as produced in Kansu and in Honan, are said to be among the very finest works of Neolithic art the world over.

We have seen that this art appears in north-western China, in Kansu, somewhat earlier than in the north-east. Not only this, but it persisted much longer in Kansu than it did in the north-east. Andersson has distinguished six stages in his sites excavated in Kansu.[5] In even the first of them, before the Yang Shao period, there was a little of the painted ware, and it continued even down into the latest Iron Age[6] sites, which he has tentatively dated at 600-100 B.C.[7] But in the north-east it was only at a time corresponding to the second, or Yang Shao stage, that painted pottery was made, according to our present evidence. We have an abundance of later Neolithic sites, but not only do they lack the painted pottery technique but its very influence seems to have vanished. The beautiful motifs, and the very spirit of the painted pottery art, disappeared from the north-eastern area at the end of Yang Shao times, and they have never reappeared, in the art of that region, to this day. Why?

It is an axiom of anthropology that a given technique will spread, normally, in a widening circle, like the ripples caused by a pebble dropped into a pool. It will appear earliest, and its influence will be strongest near its point of origin. Therefore it is altogether probable that the north-eastern region was farther from the point of origin of the painted pottery technique than was Kansu. This whole theory is strengthened by the circumstance that this pottery is declared to show very strong resemblances to wares produced to the west of China, in places of which some are as remote as the Near East. It seems plausible then to suppose the painted pottery technique to be an intrusion from the West. But how far west it is impossible to say; it might even be argued that its origin was in far north-western China, but the whole matter is uncertain.

There seems to be another reason for the early disappearance of the painted pottery technique in the north-east. It has frequently been assumed that recent civilization is due entirely to impulses radiating from a single centre, probably in Mesopotamia, spreading their influence over all Eurasia and northern Africa. But recent discoveries indicate clearly that there was at least one other centre of creativeness, originating cultural impulses of its own, somewhere in the Pacific area. And it is altogether possible that that centre was located in the region of north-east China. Our most striking evidence of it is in the highly developed, strongly original genius of Chinese culture as we find it in Shang times, but we can find its traces earlier than this, and discover what seems to be the same general influence outside the Chinese area. Its most important aspects were probably intangibles, such as ideas of religion and social organization. But we must trace it by means of more solid, if less intriguing, clues.

It is very generally accepted by anthropologists that the American Indian peoples represent migrations from Asia which began some time after the close of the last glacial epoch. In excavating in America we distinguish Indian skulls just as Mongoloid skulls are distinguished in China, by their 'shovel-shaped incisors.' Various scholars have published more or less tentative comparisons between American Indian and Asiatic languages, social organization, mythology, and art, tending to establish similarities. There is a type of stone knife, sometimes rectangular and sometimes half-moon shaped, 'semi-lunar,' which is found in China in all the Neolithic stages and in Shang culture, and which persists in iron examples in China to the present day. Such knives are said not to occur in the Near East or in Europe. But they are found among northern Asiatic tribes and among the Eskimos, and Andersson has even suggested that knives from prehistoric South America should perhaps be placed in this same group.[8] The 'composite' bow and clothing with sleeves, known to anthropologists as 'tailored clothing,' were common to the ancient Chinese and some of the aboriginal inhabitants of America. Many have suggested that there are strong resemblances between the art of ancient China, of some of the Pacific islands, and of some of the American Indians, particularly the Aztecs and the Mayas. I have been able to point out, as will be shown in detail later, certain definite and close resemblances between Shang design and the decorative art of certain North American Indians.

It would be easy to cite a number of vague resemblances in the various cultures of the Pacific area and to draw glowing generalizations from them. But for such comparisons to be of any scientific value they must be made with the utmost care, by persons who possess specialized knowledge of each of the cultures studied. As I am not an expert in the Oceanic and American fields, I am unable to draw any definite conclusion from the facts which have been mentioned. But this much can be said: that there is a very considerable likelihood that somewhere in the Pacific area there was a centre from which cultural influences radiated to affect a very large proportion of that region. And it was probably somewhere on the Pacific side of Asia, for if it had been located anywhere else it could hardly have affected all of the areas which it seems to have affected.

That a cultural centre did exist in north-east China is provable fact, but whether this centre had anything to do with a larger, Pacific culture area is not yet wholly clear. But in any case it seems altogether possible that one of the reasons for the disappearance of the western influence represented by painted pottery from the region of north-eastern China was that it came into conflict with this eastern type of culture.

We have seen that the *li* tripod has been found only in the north-eastern area in sites older than the painted pottery age. The same is true of the painted pottery time. The *li* does not occur in Kansu, in fact, until the fifth of the six stages, long after painted pottery had disappeared from the north-east. There are two sites, one in north-western Honan and one in south-western Shansi, which illustrate the situation very well. The Honan site is earlier than the painted pottery time, while the Shansi site has thick painted pottery deposits. The Shansi site must be many centuries later than that of Honan, and the two are only forty miles apart. Yet the *li*, very common in the Honan site, does not occur at all in the Shansi remains. It is as if a magic circle had been drawn about the Honan-Shantung area, forbidding the *li* to leave it. The painted pottery did invade the territory of the *li*, and the two are found together in some sites—but not for long. In the end the culture represented by the *li* triumphed. This picture of the circumstances may be altered somewhat by future discoveries, of course. But in general it seems to be a true portrayal of the situation.

In the third and last great phase of the Neolithic the *li* tripod is in full possession of the north-east, and the painted ware is gone. The latest Neolithic culture is also the most recently discovered. Its type site, Ch'êng Tzŭ Yai, east of Tsinan in Shantung, was excavated by the National Research Institute in 1930 and 1931. It is called a 'black pottery culture,' from a distinctive sort of glossy black wheel-made pottery, sometimes less than a millimetre in the thickness. Needless to say, not every Neolithic culture which has pottery which is black is a 'black pottery culture' in this sense.

That this culture is later than the painted pottery and earlier than Shang culture is proved by sites where the remains of the various cultures lie in clear stratification. The black pottery people were relatively advanced, and their culture included many factors not found in other Neolithic remains in China. Their city at Ch'êng Tzŭ Yai was surrounded by a mile of walls, built of 'pounded earth,' which still stand, in places, ten feet high and more than thirty feet wide at the base, showing that they must have been much higher originally. Like all the inhabitants of the north-eastern area in Neolithic times, they seem to have been more warlike than their neighbours to the west. Where other Neolithic peoples were quite without the ox and the horse, bones of both of these animals are found in the black pottery excavations. The cattle may well have been domesticated; they were apparently of the same species as those raised by the Shang people. Whether or not the horses were domesticated cannot be determined from their skeletons, but there is some reason to believe they were; no vehicles have been found, but they would have rotted away in any case, for since metal was not known to these people they would have been made entirely of wood. These people also made a kind of white pottery out of porcelain clay, and practised scapulomancy, divination by means of cracks produced by scorching the scapular bones of animals. While it probably originated in the north-eastern area, this culture seems to have penetrated west into Shensi.

The earliest civilization known to us, historically and archæologically, which can be called 'Chinese' in a cultural sense, is that of the Shang people living at Anyang in the fourteenth century B.C. One of the most important questions in Chinese history is: what is the relation between this historic Chinese culture and the Neolithic culture which preceded it in northeast China?

There has been a definite tendency among Western scholars, and even among some of the Chinese, to represent the Chinese culture of the Bronze Age as having little direct relation with the preceding Neolithic culture. Some have gone so far as to conceive of a set of invaders from the West, coming in with bronze, horses and chariots, cattle, and an entirely new culture, settling down as the overlords of an enslaved Neolithic population, and becoming the historic Chinese aristocracy. Picturesque though this undoubtedly is, it finds little support from the facts as we now know them.

The basic technique of manufacturing and casting bronze was probably imported to China from the West. But it was vastly improved in north-eastern China, as will be shown.

Shang bronze sacrificial vessels were cast in the form of the *li* tripod and related shapes, and occupied an important place in Shang religion. Religion is normally conservative, and Chinese religion is especially so. If the Shang aristocrats are held to have been invaders, then we must believe that they brought with them the process of making bronze, but cast vessels for sacrificing to their gods in patterns copied from the cooking pots of the Neolithic inhabitants they had enslaved. Furthermore, they decorated those sacrificial vessels with elaborate designs which have been found nowhere outside the Chinese area. From what we know of invading conquerors in India and elsewhere, such a course is unthinkable.

All of our present evidence tends to disprove this theory. The data on the black pottery culture were not published until June, 1935, and when they are generally known the 'invasion theory' will probably be abandoned. For this culture is the hitherto missing link between earlier Neolithic cultures and Chinese civilization. The *li* tripod is one of its commonest ceramic types, and the whole culture obviously belongs to the north-eastern area. And its resemblances to Shang culture are extremely close. Pounded earth walls, horses, cattle, white pottery made of porcelain clay, divination bone—all aspects which this culture does not share with other Neolithic cultures —*are* shared with Shang culture. The cattle are probably the same species. The divination bone was prepared and used by a complicated process involving several steps which are identical in the black pottery and Shang cultures; the latter simply carried it to a further degree of refinement. Most important of all is the statement of Mr. Liang Ssŭ-yung, a specialist in pottery trained at Harvard University, who has studied both potteries exhaustively. He says that the Shang pottery technique is beyond doubt a continuation of the pottery technique of the black pottery culture.

Nor does the theory that Chinese culture was brought in by an invading or migratory group fare better from an examination of skeletal material. For this side of the case there are regrettable gaps in our evidence, but for the painted pottery period in the north-east and for this and later periods in Kansu there is abundant material. After careful examination of all of it the late Davidson Black, foremost authority in this field, concluded that 'the prehistoric populations were essentially Oriental in physical character. Further, the resemblances between these prehistoric and recent north China populations would appear to be such that the term "proto-Chinese" may with some propriety be applied to the former.'[9] To date we have not, unfortunately, any skeletons of the black pottery people. More than eleven hundred skeletons of Shang date have been excavated scientifically during the past ten months, but sufficient time has not yet elapsed for careful study of them. Mr. Liang Ssŭ-yung has kindly acquainted me, however, with the results of the examination of a small number of skulls, selected to be as representative as possible. Of the individuals examined, every one had clearly marked 'shovel-shaped incisors,' indicating that all of them belonged to the Mongoloid division of mankind. Some of these skulls undoubtedly belonged to Shang aristocrats. We may conclude, then, that all of the evidence so far available shows the inhabitants of north China, from Neolithic times to the present, to belong to a single general racial type, and that there is no skeletal evidence of an invasion of the area by people of any other type.

Chinese civilization was not imported wholesale from the West, nor was it developed in complete isolation by the East. As a matter of fact, its origins are much more complex than this brief sketch has suggested, for some of its elements, such as rice, apparently came from still another centre of culture, in the south. Certain of its fundamental techniques, the raw materials as it were of civilization, did filter in from time to time from the West, and it may be that groups of people came with them, being quickly absorbed into the general Chinese population. Others of its essentials were developed entirely in eastern Asia. The resultant civilization was neither Western nor Pacific, but Chinese.

It must be emphasized that this resultant Chinese culture was not merely a blend of various elements gathered from east, west, and south. It was no more this than a lily is a mere mixture of water, earth, and fertilizer; the product possesses characteristics not present in any of the raw materials. This is especially true when we turn from the material side of Chinese civilization to the non-material aspects of her culture. Chinese art, religion, political theory and practice, philosophy—these are peculiarly distinctive of China, borrowed from and like nothing else in the world.

*

According to tradition, Chinese history began with a number of rulers who reigned before the establishment of the first dynasty. Some of them are represented as culture heroes, who personally invented agriculture and other fundamental techniques and taught them to the people. The number and the order of these rulers vary in different accounts; this in itself would make us suspect, what is abundantly evident, that they are purely legendary. The same is true of Yao and Shun, who did not leave their thrones to their sons, but chose the most able man in the empire to succeed them. Professor Ku Chieh-kang has pointed out that these rulers are mentioned little or not at all in the earliest literature, but that their traditions grow in importance and circumstance in later works, composed by men beginning to speculate about early times. Many of these late books were falsely attributed to early dates, of course.

But the so-called Hsia dynasty, the first Chinese dynasty according to tradition, cannot be dismissed as wholly fictitious. It was certainly not a dynasty in the sense that it ruled all or even a great portion of the territory we know as China, but neither was the Shang, in all probability. And certainly the Hsia tradition was greatly elaborated, for purposes of deliberate political propaganda, in early Chou times. It seems quite probable, in fact, that the whole genealogy of the Hsia rulers and every detailed circumstance of Hsia tradition which has come down to us is a falsification of later times. But it also seems certain that there was in early China a state of the name of Hsia. It was probably endowed with a relatively high degree of culture, and may have been, like the Shang state which came after it, a cultural if not political leader in the north Chinese area. But there is not yet a scrap of archæological evidence concerning the Hsia people. Many attempts have been made to link them with excavated Neolithic sites, but so far without success. From the archæological and scientific point of view, the curtain rises on Chinese history with the Shang people living at Anyang in the fourteenth century B.C.

BOOK II

SHANG

CHAPTER IV

THE GREAT CITY SHANG

A TRADITION which is supported by archæology tells us that shortly after 1400 B.C. a powerful ruler named P'an Kêng moved his people to Anyang and built a city on the banks of the Huan River. This city was called 'the Great City Shang.' Its people are the first Chinese known to history; the kingdom which they ruled from this spot is known to the Chinese as the Shang dynasty.

But it was no emperor, at whose slightest command 'all within the four seas' trembled and hastened to do his bidding, who moved his subjects with their animals and other possessions into this region. He was rather a king, whose military prestige served to keep the surrounding kings peaceful and even submissive until such time as they felt powerful enough to attack him.

A tradition which is not very trustworthy tells us that these people had moved their capital city five times in the previous four centuries. From this it has been supposed that they were pastoral nomads, following their flocks and herds. But this is hardly likely, since we know that they were in the habit of building complicated permanent houses. Some of them did follow the flocks and herds of sheep and cattle, but in the main they were town-dwellers and agriculturists. If these moves really took place at all, they were more probably caused by the raids of enemies, which we know were frequent. A few disastrous attacks on a poor location would soon show the necessity of seeking a more strategic situation.

From the point of view of the men of that day the location at Anyang must have been almost ideal. In the first place the soil was loess, the yellow, finely divided loam which is one of the richest of soils for farming. As one travels through this country to-day, and sees mile after mile of perfectly level plain stretching beyond the horizon, covered with unbelievably vivid green, it seems a peculiarly lush region. Trees do not grow in great numbers on these plains, so that it was probably unnecessary to clear land for planting. Beyond the area which they wished to cultivate lay broad pasture lands, with the river providing water for their cattle and sheep.

These advantages must have been obtainable in many places in this part of China. But Anyang has others. The site on which the city of Shang was located is easily defended. A bend in the river forms a promontory, so that the city had a natural moat on the north, the east, and a portion of its western front. The remainder of the west and the south were probably defended by an earthen wall, although no remains of it have yet been found. The general region could not be easily attacked by a large force from the west (where some of their chief enemies were located) since a range of mountains west of the city extends for about a hundred miles to the north and more than fifty miles southward. They are not wholly impassable, but they must have afforded some protection.

From the oracle inscriptions it seems that it was surprise attacks which were chiefly feared. Laying siege to a city would have required a large army, an organization of supply and transport service, and a command of the lines of communication which would have been difficult for the Shang people themselves. For their enemies to have carried such operations into the territory controlled by the Shangs would ordinarily have been impossible. On the other hand, swift raids by small bodies of highly mobile troops were common. Such attacks depend for their success on the element of surprise. On a broad level plain like that at Anyang, where one can see for miles and where the war chariots used by the Shangs could be marshalled with ease, it must have been very difficult to take them by surprise or even to attack them with impunity. They had many outlying settlements, too, which kept them warned of the approach of enemies.

Yet another element contributed to the convenience of the Anyang site. It was on a level plain, which was necessary; it was also within seventeen miles of the foothills of an eastward-jutting spur of mountains, which was highly desirable. In their building they depended chiefly on wood, and the plain can hardly have provided an adequate supply of large beams and pillars; these had to be brought from the mountains. Further, these men of Shang were great hunters, and much of the game they sought was much more plentiful in the mountain region than on the plain. At Anyang, then, they could live in an easily defended city, surrounded by fertile fields and rich pasture land, with a river at hand to supply water and aid in defence, while a short ride in a chariot would take them into the mountains for timber or for hunting. And in the hot and moist summers the kings and nobles of that day doubtless sought relief from the heat in those mountains, much as the later emperors and the modern residents of Peking go to the Western Hills.

The men of Shang were not the first to realize the advantages of this location. Like most things worth having, it was probably fought for more than once. Two miles east and south of the main Shang site the Huan River makes another bend forming a similar but smaller promontory. Many centuries before the coming of the first Shangs it was selected as a village site by Neolithic men of the painted pottery culture, whose civilization, as we have seen, had Western affinities; they left behind them painted pottery of a rather primitive sort. They moved away and the place was unoccupied for a time. After that, men of the black pottery Neolithic culture, more eastern in its character, moved in and built a much larger settlement. They probably realized that this location was a prize which others would take from them if they could, for they built a defensive wall of imposing proportions. Excavation has shown that it was at least twelve feet broad at the base, so that it must have reached a considerable height. Accumulated arrow-heads at the foot of the wall tell the story of its defence.

These latest Neolithic settlers may still have been in possession when the Shang people arrived. They may have resisted and been defeated, or have submitted without a struggle. In either case they would undoubtedly have been reduced to the status of virtual slaves, and made to do as much as possible of the work of building the new city.

The houses, constructed by the Neolithic settlers, which were in this location when the Shangs came, were of a type used by Neolithic men all over north China. They were beehive-shaped pits, dug in the ground, some ten feet in diameter and about the height of a man or considerably deeper. They were roofed over with timbers and these were covered with sod or thatch. Entrance was through a door in the top. Such houses were fairly practicable, especially owing to the peculiar tendency of loess soil to stand in vertical walls without falling. Dwellings dug in the loess, by tunnelling horizontally into a standing bank, are common in China to the present day. I have seen uncounted thousands of them in Honan, Shensi, and Shansi; the number of people who pass their whole lives in such cave-dwellings must number some millions. Some of these homes are surprisingly elaborate, with well-fitted doors which can be locked.

But the pit-dwellings dug by the Neolithic inhabitants are surprisingly crude. They are not even regularly square or rectangular in shape; far worse, it is rarely that they have so much as a level floor. It is hard to understand how Neolithic men, with their rather good weapons and pottery, could have refrained from preparing for themselves more comfortable habitations when it would have been so easy. Andersson thinks that they were used only as storage pits; it may be that they were used as dwellings only during the coldest weather. Some students of the Shang dynasty think that the Chinese newcomers themselves occupied such pit-dwellings for many years after they took possession of this spot, but that seems quite inconceivable. A people who possessed a highly developed system of writing, a literature, and a decorative art of no mean pretensions, who were mechanics enough to build chariots and who knew how to erect buildings of complicated construction —such a people would never have been content to live in these wretched pits, unless as a purely temporary shelter until their regular houses were completed. They did use such pits for storage purposes throughout their history, much as we use cellars; one 'treasure-pit' was found containing more than five thousand articles. It has been suggested that they used them as dungeons, for captives of war and other unfortunates. Doubtless they were the dwellings of slaves, servants, and perhaps the least important of the Shang people themselves. But the men of position occupied houses of quite another sort.

These houses are interesting because in their chief structural details they are almost identical with the Chinese house of to-day—with the house, in fact, in which this is being written. The typical house of the present is built on a raised terrace or platform of earth which is faced with brick to make the floor. In Shang times they had no brick; instead, the earthen terrace was beaten. A board frame like a mould for concrete was made to hold in the earth on the sides; loose earth was piled into this frame and pounded down, layer after layer, until the desired height was reached.

We have seen that this technique of pounding earth was used in the black pottery Neolithic culture; it is still used in China to-day. On the very site of the city of Shang is a village surrounded by walls made by this very method; by using it they manage to make a mud wall two feet thick stand eleven or twelve feet in height. The only difference is in the quality of the work; the modern walls will not last more than a few decades, while the platforms of the Shangs have resisted the rains of three thousand years. Some of their pounded earth is still so hard that it almost rings when struck.

The platform was made a little larger than the outline of the completed house. Sometimes a small projection was made in front of the place where the door was to be, as a sort of step or extended threshold (see Figure 1). On this platform the house was erected; it was essentially a gabled roof supported on three rows of pillars. Obviously no earth, no matter how well pounded, could resist the constant pressure and grinding of the ends of these pillars during many years of high winds and heavy rain. A base had to be provided, therefore, to keep the pillar from sinking down into the foundation earth. Usually this was merely a large rock, rolled and smoothed by water, looking like an over-sized ostrich egg, which was sunk into the earthen platform below the pillar. But in a few cases the pillar bases were large dome-shaped bronze discs.

These terraces, pillar bases, and the charred stump of one pillar are all that remain to us. The city may have been destroyed by the enemies of the Shangs when they were finally conquered; whatever was left has been obliterated by time and the anti-historical Chinese climate. But despite the efforts of all these destroyers we can easily tell how the Shang people built their houses. One of the characters found in the oracle bone inscriptions is ; its exact meaning is not clear, but from the way it is used we can be quite certain that it is a pictograph of one of their large buildings, probably a temple, as seen from the end. This convenient picture shows us the earthen platform on which the building stood, the end wall of the building itself, and the gabled roof. From the arrangement of the pillar bases (see Figure 1) we know that there were three rows of pillars, one at either side under the eaves and one in the middle under the ridge-pole. The middle pillars were spaced farther apart than those at the sides, to leave as much clear space in the centre as possible. In modern Chinese buildings they are eliminated, that is to say they do not come down to the floor but rest on horizontal beams which are supported by the side pillars. This is perhaps the only major structural change in three thousand years. The walls of modern Chinese

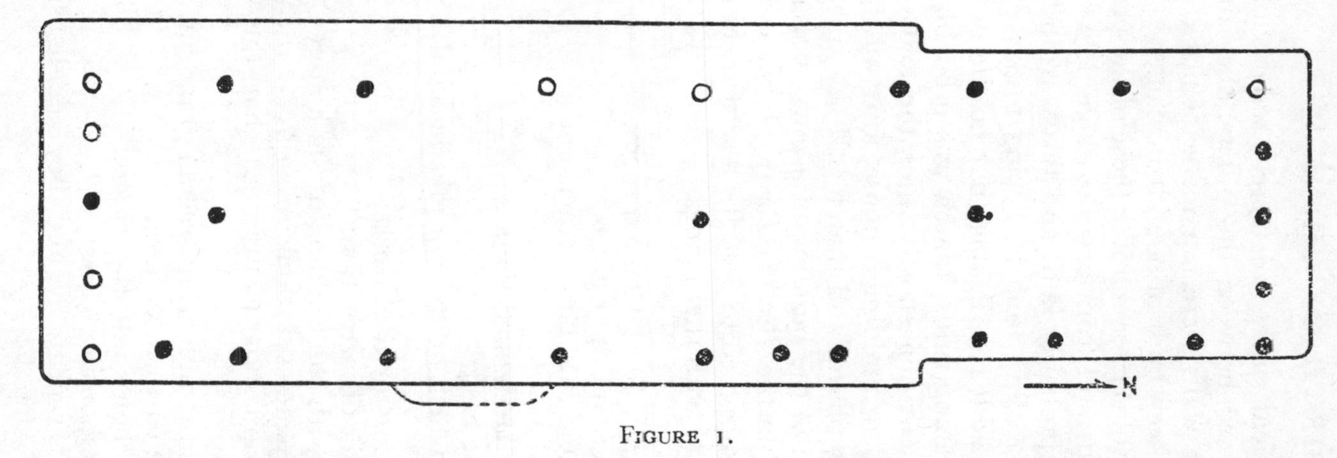

FIGURE 1.

Plan of the largest building foundation excavated at Anyang, twenty-six feet wide and ninety-two feet long. The black circles indicate the points at which stones, used as pillar bases, were found in place ; the outlined circles mark places where the prints of such stones were found, but the stones themselves were missing. Some movement in the soil during three thousand years appears to have shifted these stones slightly to the eastward. After the reports of the National Research Institute.

houses, as of these ancient ones, are merely screens of one material or another placed between the pillars; they do not support the roof. These walls were not made of brick, as at present; they may have been built of pounded earth.

The roofs were probably very much like those of the present. First light poles had to be laid from eaves to ridge-pole. Over these rush matting was probably laid, and this was no doubt plastered with mud, just as is done in Peking to-day. After this tiles are commonly added in Peking, but no tile or brick has been found in the Shang ruins; thatch was probably substituted for it. A book written shortly after the end of the Shang dynasty says that 'in building a house, after all the toil on its walls, they have to plaster and thatch it.'[1]

We have a description of the building of a town, not unlike this 'Great City Shang,' in the *Book of Poetry*. It was written at a later date, but it is supposed to describe a settlement made by a people contemporary with the Shangs.

'He encouraged the people and settled them;
Here on the left, there on the right.
He divided the ground into larger tracts and
  smaller portions;
He dug the ditches; he defined the acres;
From the west to the east,
There was nothing which he did not take in hand.

He called his superintendent of works;
He called his minister of instruction;
And charged them with the building of the houses.
With the line they made everything straight;
They bound the frame-boards tight, so that they
  should rise regularly.
Up rose the ancestral temple in its solemn grandeur.
Crowds brought the earth in baskets;
They threw it with shouts into the frames;
They beat it with responsive blows;
They pared the walls repeatedly, and they sounded strong.

Five thousand cubits of them arose together.
So that the roll of the great drum did not overpower
(the noise of the builders).'[2]

Another description of the building of a palace, also from a later period, tells us:

'By the graceful sweep of these banks,
With the southern hill so calm in the distance,
(Has the palace arisen), firm as the roots of a clump
of bamboos,
(With its roof) like the luxuriant head of a pine tree. . . .
Having entered into the inheritance of his ancestors,
He has built his chambers, five thousand cubits of walls,
With their doors to the west and to the south.
Here will he reside; here will he sit;
Here will he laugh; here will he talk.

They bound the frames for the earth, exactly over
one another;
T'o-t'o went the pounding;—
Impervious to wind and rain,
Offering no cranny to bird or rat,
A grand dwelling is it for our noble lord. . . .
Level and smooth is the courtyard,
And lofty are the pillars around it.
Pleasant is the exposure of the chamber to the light,
And deep and wide are its recesses;—
Here will our noble lord repose.'[3]

These buildings were not small even in Shang times. The largest hall found to date measures twenty-six feet wide by ninety-two feet long. From the arrangement of its pillars (see Figure 1) we can see that the ridge-pole over the clear middle section must have been made of a single wooden beam about thirty-two feet in length.

It was suggested above that such beams, and the pillars on which they rested, were probably carried to the city of Shang from mountains near by. This is indicated by another poem, which also appears in the *Book of Poetry*. It was written by the descendants of the Shang people, who continued their line in the state of Sung after the Shang dynasty had been extinguished.

> 'We ascended the Ching mountain,
> Where the pines and cypresses grew symmetrical.
> We cut them down, and conveyed them here;
> We reverently hewed them square.
> Long are the projecting beams of pine;
> Large are the many pillars.
> The temple was completed—a resting place (for his spirit).'[4]

The pride taken in 'long projecting beams' and 'many pillars' has not died out in modern Chinese design. Chinese architecture is uncompromisingly 'structural.' It takes pride in showing the massive beams and well-shaped pillars which are the actual framework of the building. On the outside of the house, especially, these beams and pillars are decorated with pictures of flowers, books, old vases and bronzes, bats and peaches, landscapes, and similar motifs, in gay colours. One would expect these to look garish, but actually the effect is thoroughly dignified and pleasing. We can hardly suppose that the men of Shang times used exactly the same type of decoration as is used to-day. We do know, however, that they decorated walls, at least, with polychrome painting. We have evidence that beams and pillars were decorated with pictures by the time of Confucius,[5] and that much attention was paid to their appearance before his time.

Concerning the interior decoration of these buildings we have little direct evidence. But even if we had none it would be safe to infer that the creators of the Shang bronzes and sculptures did not leave their halls of state and temples without suitable adornment. Whether they made much use of sculptures for this purpose is uncertain. One small fragment of a sculptured figure, found in the ruins of the city, is thought to be

PLATE III

ONE OF THE OLDEST PIECES OF CHINESE SCULPTURE KNOWN, EXCAVATED BY THE NATIONAL RESEARCH INSTITUTE ON THE SITE OF THE SHANG CAPITAL OF ANYANG

FROM LEFT TO RIGHT AND TOP TO BOTTOM, THESE SHOW THE RIGHT SIDE, LEFT SIDE, FRONT, AND BACK. NOTE THE UBIQUITOUS CHINESE EYE, RUNNING VERTICALLY ACROSS EACH FOREARM. FOR DESCRIPTION SEE PAGE 106.

Official Photographs of the National Research Institute, reproduced by courtesy of Dr. Li Chi.

part of a stone pillar-base, but if sculptures were used generally they must have been carried away when the site was abandoned. From the paintings found in the tombs, it seems quite probable that walls of buildings were similarly decorated. To visualize what these may have been like it is only necessary to look at the illustrations of Shang bronzes and imagine their motifs, many times magnified, executed as polychrome murals. From the very fine wood-carving of the tombs we may be quite sure that the woodwork of buildings was similarly decorated. Some of it was also inlaid with carved pieces of boar's-tusk ivory; many of these have been found in the ruined city. Altogether, the interior of a Shang palace was probably a sight worth the seeing.

We have seen that the character [character] is an end view of a Shang building. Comparison of this with the façade of the typical Greek temple shows interesting similarities. The earthen terrace of the Chinese temple is paralleled by a stone terrace in the Greek. The gabled roof and even the pediment are common to both. The slight narrowing of the north end of the building platform illustrated in Figure 1 indicates that it may have had an open portico like that of the Greek temples. I am not suggesting, of course, that the Greek temple was borrowed from that of the Shangs, but merely that the Chinese and the Greeks solved some of their architectural problems similarly.

An obvious difference between Greek and Chinese architecture is that the Greek buildings we know are built of stone, a medium which the ancient Chinese did not use at all and which is used extremely little in native Chinese architecture to this day. The reason for this is not clear. Stone is certainly available, and it has been used for pavements, tablets, statues, balustrades, and so forth, but scarcely at all in building. A Chinese authority on their architecture has said that the Chinese have never properly understood the structural use of stone; instead they have employed it, if at all, as if it were another kind of wood, using mortises and other devices quite inappropriate to the fact that it has little tensile strength. Apparently it has merely never occurred to the Chinese to make their public buildings of stone—just as it never occurred to Europeans to print instead of writing until long after printing had been invented by the Chinese.

The arrangement of the houses and public buildings in the city of Shang is a subject on which little can be said as yet. But it is quite certain that buildings of any size were laid out, in relation to each other, according to a definite plan, and not merely allowed to grow up helter-skelter as in some modern Western cities. The excavators have pointed out that all of the buildings of size square with magnetic north, deducing from this that the Shang people probably knew the lodestone and used it as a compass. It has long been known that this invention was made in China, but it has not been supposed to be so ancient. To what extent the direction of magnetic north has altered in the last three thousand years, and what effect this would have on the probabilities in this regard, I do not know. It is quite possible that the Shangs had courtyards like the modern Chinese 'compound' arrangement around their buildings. We know that this existed at about the end of the Shang dynasty, and the finding of a wall three feet thick and eight feet high within the city suggests such courtyards.

One of the excavated areas, about sixteen acres in extent, is completely covered with the foundations of buildings of considerable size. This is supposed by some to be the royal palace area. Adjacent to this is a district which seems to have been given over entirely to the work of various types of artisans, whose productions may have been a royal monopoly. One section of this district has yielded a great deal of the by-products of bronze manufacture—ash from furnaces, slag, bits of ore, charcoal, and broken moulds. An idea of the extent of the activity of this 'bronze quarter' may be gained from the fact that at least one house foundation has been found, in this section, which was composed almost entirely of these waste materials. Another section of this manufacturing area specialized in work in stone, making knives and other utensils and producing articles of more artistic interest from fresh-water mother-of-pearl, stones of various sorts, and varieties of jade. Still another section produced bone utensils; arrowheads, ladles, hairpins, and other beautifully carved bone objects come from this locality.

The excavators think that they have found the treasuries of the Shang kings in still another location. It is quite probable, of course, that the most valuable articles were carried away, either by conquerors who looted the city, or by the Shang people themselves. What sort of treasure-rooms they may have had above ground we do not know, but it is quite certain that they, like modern banks, found it convenient to construct vaults underground. In one treasure pit there were five thousand eight hundred and one articles, including pottery, bone, mother-of-pearl, tortoise-shell, cowries (probably shell money), bronze, gold, and varieties of jade. Evidence indicates that fabrics, possibly including silk, were stored here, although they had long since rotted away.

No defensive wall surrounding the city has yet been found, but it certainly existed. Excavation has been concentrated rather on the central areas than on the fringes of the city where we should look for the wall. Even if this wall is never found, this will not prove that it did not exist, for there was no necessity for a surrounding wall to have such hardness as was required for house foundations, which were to be walked on constantly and had to support the weight of buildings. This wall might have been made, therefore, of comparatively loosely packed earth, like village walls in the same locality to-day. Such walls would hardly have had to withstand battering-rams and siege operations since, as we have seen, a real siege was rather unlikely. What was needed was merely a rampart which would stop the first rush of the chariots and men of a surprise raiding party. A wall quite adequate for this purpose might have been washed away by the centuries, leaving but little trace of its existence. It might also have been razed by the eventual conquerors.

It is my belief, however, that a very durable pounded earth wall surrounded the city and that it is still there waiting to be excavated. We have seen that such a wall, of great size, was built by the black pottery people in Shantung, and that men of the same culture built a wall of this type at Anyang, which must have been clearly visible when the Shangs moved in. And we know that such walls were a standard feature of Chinese culture in the early Chou period. It is unthinkable, therefore, that the Shang people did not build such a wall to protect their capital.

The modern Chinese word meaning 'capital' is 京. This is the 'king' element in Peking (North Capital) and Nanking (South Capital). On the Shang oracle bones we find this word in the form . Various explanations have been given for its origin. To me it seems quite evidently a drawing of a gate in a city wall; the gate has two leaves, and a tower surmounts it. This ancient Chinese character has a striking resemblance to some small gates which one sees in China at the present time; it could have been drawn directly from some of the gates in the wall of the so-called 'Chinese City' in Peiping. These gate towers are among the most picturesque features of the Chinese landscape, but they were not originally built for their beauty. Their usefulness is obvious. They provide, first of all, a watch tower from which it is possible to see if an enemy is coming, and so to close the gates against him long before he arrives. If he attacks the gate, the most vulnerable point in a walled city, the tower provides a protected place from which to rain arrows, rocks, and other missiles upon him. The word shown above, which now means 'capital,' seems to have been used by the men of Shang for at least one city other than their own; in those days it perhaps meant only 'a walled city large enough to have towers above its gates.' It would seem, then, that Shang was not the only walled city in that part of China at that time. The word which the Shang people used most in speaking of their own city was . The upper half of this character represents an enclosure, the lower half is a man sitting on his haunches. The whole means 'an enclosed place where men dwell,' that is, a city.

We have an account of the walling of a city south of the Yellow River, using the pounded-earth method, in 598 B.C. We read that 'the superintendent of the work . . . estimated the labour to be done, and the number of days; gave out all the money that was necessary for it; adjusted the frames, and provided the baskets and stampers, and other articles for raising the walls; apportioned equally their tasks, according to the distance of the labourers from the place; marked out the foundations; supplied the provisions; and determined the inspectors. The work was completed in thirty days, exactly in accordance with the previous calculations.'[6] Whether the city of Shang had a moat on the sides not protected by the river we do not know, but a moat is mentioned in a book of about the end of the Shang period.

Excavation has revealed several outlying settlements of the Shang people in the immediate neighbourhood of their city. One of these, found in 1934, is of especial interest. It is across the Huan River, north and west of the main site, not far from the more recently discovered Shang tombs. Foundations of buildings and seven large inscribed tortoise-shells, used for divination, were found there. The divinations were made for the king, and concern hunting, from which it is supposed that this may have been the site of a royal hunting-lodge. It may also have been a part of the outlying defences of the city.

CHAPTER V

LIVELIHOOD

THE men of the Great City Shang depended primarily on agriculture for their living. They raised domestic animals and went hunting, but these activities were more productive of luxuries than of the fundamental necessities of existence. Bishop says that even in the Neolithic period in north China 'hunting and fishing played a very subordinate part to planting,' and other authorities are of the same opinion.

Hunting and trapping did provide one very practical item, namely, skins for making fur coats. The summers are hot at Anyang, but the winters are very cold, and such garments are needed. The game provided by hunting no doubt supplemented the diet in a welcome and sometimes necessary way. But there was also a large element of sport in hunting expeditions. We read in the *Book of Poetry:*

'Shu has gone hunting,
Mounted in his chariot and four.
The reins are in his grasp like ribbons,
While the two outside horses move (with
regular steps), as dancers do.
Shu is at the marshy ground.
The fire flames out all at once,
And with bared arms he seizes a tiger
And presents it before the Duke.
O Shu, try not (such sport) again;
Beware lest you be injured.'[1]

The fire referred to is that of the blazing grass, burned off to start the animals from their coverts.

Hunting parties were also used as an opportunity at once to review and to train the army. The *Book of Poetry* gives us more than one account of royal hunting expeditions, though all of them date from a period later than Shang. The following is a good example:

'Our chariots were strong,
Our horses were well matched;
And with four steeds (for each), sleek and large,
We yoked and proceeded to the east. . . .

With their four-horsed chariots (they came),
Forming a long train,
In their red knee-covers and gold-adorned slippers,
Like the crowd of an occasional or a general audience.

The bowstring thimbles and armlets were fitted on;
The bows and arrows were adjusted to one another;
The archers acted in unison,
Helping us to rear up a pile of game.

Of the four yellow horses of each chariot,
The two outsiders inclined not to either side.
No error in driving was committed,
And the arrows went forth like downright blows.'[2]

This translation is Legge's. Here he has not been as successful as usual in the difficult task of rendering the spirit as well as the letter of Chinese poetry into English. The Chinese original, with four words to a line, breathes a martial spirit like vapour spurting from the nostrils of an impatient steed on a frosty morning; in its tempo one can fairly hear the *rat-a-tat-tat* of the galloping horses. Here is another hunting poem, from the same book:

'A lucky day was *kêng-wu*.
We had selected our horses;

The haunts of the animals,
Where the does and stags lay numerous,
The grounds by the Ch'i and the Chu,—
That was the place for the Son of Heaven
(to hunt). . . .

We have bent our bows;
We have our arrows on the string.
Here is a small boar transfixed;
There is a large rhinoceros [?] killed.
The spoil will be presented to the visitors and
guests,
Along with the cup of sweet liquor.'[3]

The Shangs did not call their king 'Son of Heaven'; with this exception these poems might almost equally well describe hunting expeditions of the earlier period. The Shang kings hunted a great deal, as we know from the oracle bones. It is possible that in certain sacrifices they had to present animals which they had personally procured; we find survivals of such a custom at a later day.

The bag enumerated for some of the Shang hunts certainly justifies description as 'a pile of game.' One bone inscription tells us of a total of three hundred and forty-eight animals taken on one occasion. Another list includes one hundred and sixty-two deer, one hundred and fourteen of some other animal, ten boars, and one rabbit. Pheasants are commonly included among the game. Horses were caught, but this may have been capture alive, for domestication. Very rarely, we find elephants enumerated among the bag of the hunt.

This is surprising, because elephants are not native to that part of China to-day. One would suppose that the climate, as far north as Anyang at any rate, would be much too cold for the elephant. But there is some indication that the climate of ancient China was rather warmer than that of to-day, for we find bamboo, the water-buffalo, and certain wild animals thriving much farther to the north than they can live at present. A scholar of the National Research Institute has shown that, as a matter of fact, elephants have lived in China as far north as the Yangtse River until the last two hundred years. Even during the first part of the last dynasty they existed in the wild state, as is shown by records of their capture, and tame elephants were used to compose a section of the Imperial Chinese armies. This was not merely a late and brief intrusion of the elephant into China, for it is also mentioned from time to time in works covering China's whole history. Wild elephants are said to live in Yünnan Province to-day.

Elephant bones have been excavated at Anyang. They are not numerous, but apparently represent more than one individual. Whether elephants were tamed by the Shang people is not certain. That they were is strongly indicated by a character found on the oracle bones, which is the present verb 'to be' and therefore one of the most frequent characters in the written language. It is , quite clearly an elephant with a human hand on its trunk, leading it. (It is said that one must employ some sort of 'elephant hook' for this purpose, but we can hardly expect such completeness in a pictograph.) How this word came to have the meaning of 'to be' and 'to do' we can only conjecture. But certainly in an age without machines one who could enlist the aid of an elephant could 'do' many things at an unparalleled rate of speed. If the Shangs made their buildings lofty, as they may have, the assistance of elephants in moving the great timbers used for pillars would have been invaluable. Whether the Shangs tamed the elephant or not, we can be quite sure that some of the ancient Chinese knew him well. For we find bronzes, cast in the shape of elephants and decorated with their pictures, which are amazingly realistic.

Pere Teilhard de Chardin and Dr. C. C. Young have identified the bones of the following animals among the Anyang finds: dog (two kinds), bear (two kinds), badger, tiger, panther, whale, common rat, bamboo rat, hare, tapir, horse, pig (two kinds), deer (two kinds), sheep, goat, ox, water-buffalo, elephant, and monkey. Of these, they suggest that the following were domesticated: dog, pig, sheep, goat, and possibly one variety of deer, the ox, the water-buffalo, and the monkey. The whalebone must have been either captured or traded from tribes living on the sea coast. To the statement that the ox, as judged by its remains, may have been domesticated, we can add the testimony of the oracle inscriptions, which show that it certainly was.

Teilhard and Young did not include the horse in their list of domestic animals because they did not have access to the latest finds. From these, as well as from the bone inscriptions, it is absolutely certain that the Shang people kept horses in large numbers and drove them to chariots.

Only the horse can be proved to have been used as a draft animal in Shang times. But the horse and chariot as used by early men in Eurasia generally was primarily an instrument of war. In the *Book of Changes*, a work on divination which dates from about the end of the Shang period,[4] we find reference to carts drawn by cattle, and it is quite probable that oxen and water-buffalo were used for purposes of heavy hauling by the Shang people.

The domestic animals used for food by the Shangs include cattle, pig, sheep, dog, and chicken. Bishop says that 'There is no sign that the domestic fowl was yet known in China during the Neolithic, although it may already have been present in the south.'[5] The fowl is clearly depicted in the oracle inscriptions, and chicken bones have been excavated at Anyang, but not in any great quantity. From this it would seem that the domestic fowl was a recent acquisition in Shang times. A little later it took and kept an important place in the ancient Chinese economy.

Bones of a species of dog were found with the remains of the Peking Man, associated with those of other animals considered to belong to the early Pleistocene or an even more remote period. The dog and the pig were the most important food animals of Neolithic China. At Anyang the dog was less important than the pig, but was eaten and sacrificed in considerable numbers. At a later period in ancient China we find the dog as the *pièce de résistance* of ceremonial banquets. Even to-day the meat of the dog is eaten regularly in some parts of China. The prejudice among most Occidentals against the eating of dogs is perhaps due principally to two reasons. First, we make a pet of the dog, and we do not like the idea of eating pets. This is no doubt the reason for the prejudice which most of us have against eating horse meat, though the best steaks of fine hotels are rumoured to be horse tenderloin. In the second place, we do not commonly eat carnivorous animals, and the dog is usually carnivorous.

There is also a complex of uncomplimentary ideas coupled with the dog which are typified in the phrases 'dog of an infidel' and 'dirty dog.' Yet in fact, the dog is superficially at least cleaner than the pig, and he is also used, paradoxically enough, as an example of unswerving loyalty. The Shang Chinese apparently had no prejudices against the dog, for we find a noble named the 'Dog Marquis,' who is an ally or a vassal of the Shangs. In later times we find the Chinese calling the barbarians by names which commonly include the character 'dog,' but whether this is a term of contempt or an epithet to denote fierceness is not altogether clear. As for the dog being carnivorous, this is not true of many modern Chinese dogs at all events. In Peking they are commonly fed on millet or other grain, being given no meat from one year's end to the next.

Whether the dog was used for hunting or for any purposes other than food in Shang times is hard to determine. The Tso Chuan tells us that in 605 B.C., the ruler of the state of Chin, wishing to rid himself of a troublesome minister, arranged an ambush for him in the court. But when the plot nearly fell through the ruler set a large and fierce dog,[6] which was by him in the court, upon the minister. This dog was evidently kept for its fierceness, and was no doubt used in hunting. We also find dogs depicted in hunting-scenes on bronzes, though not, I believe, as early as this date. This passage is the oldest reference I know to such use of dogs, though it does not follow that they were not so employed even in Shang times.

Whether sheep were domesticated in China in Neolithic times seems still to be something of a question, although bones which appear to indicate that they were have been found. In the Anyang ruins a number of sheep bones have been found, though they are not so numerous as those of cattle or pigs. Sheep are mentioned on the oracle bones as having been sacrificed with considerable frequency. The bones of goats have been excavated; whether these were domestic or wild is unknown, but I do not know of any instance of goats being enumerated among the spoils of the chase.

There are two characters meaning sheep, and two meaning cow. In each case the difference is that one form is the simple pictograph of the animal, the other shows the animal inside a building or corral. We might suppose that the latter forms stood for the domesticated and the former for wild species. But again this is made unlikely by the fact that neither sheep nor cattle are mentioned as being taken in hunting. The meaning of these variant forms is uncertain.

Pork was the chief staple meat of Neolithic men in north China. Swine were also raised extensively, it will be remembered, in prehistoric Europe. Neolithic men used the bones and tusks of the pig to make arrow-heads, carved pendants, and various other small objects. The importance of the pig in the diet of the men of Shang was second only to that of the ox. But it is interesting to note that whereas the pig raised by Neolithic men in north China was a northern type, *Sus scrofa*, the common Anyang pig was *Sus vittatut*, said to be a highly specialized breed of southern origin. Swine were sacrificed at Anyang in large numbers. Archæological evidence and the oracle inscriptions alike show that the wild boar as well as domestic swine were offered to the spirits.

Bones of the ox have been found in the remains of the black pottery Neolithic culture, both in Shantung and at Anyang. Whether it had been domesticated in Neolithic times is not certain; that it had is indicated by the statement of Dr. C. C. Young that the species was probably the same as that of the cattle of the Shangs. In Shang times cattle were principal among the domestic animals. They figure more frequently, and in greater numbers, on the oracle inscriptions than do any other sacrificial victims; their bones are the most numerous among those excavated.

We know very little about the methods of tending cattle used in those days. The most common form of the word meaning 'to herd cattle' is composed of an ox beside which is a hand holding a stick. Sometimes this stick is hooked at the end, like a shepherd's crook. Sometimes we find this character, with the crook, written with a sheep instead of an ox, in which case it presumably means 'to herd sheep.' One form of the character meaning 'to herd cattle' found in the bone inscriptions is very strange. It has the ox and the hand, but instead of the staff the hand is holding a brush. Near this brush are several dots; it has been suggested that these are drops of water, so that the whole character represents the washing and grooming of the ox. But this would certainly be unusual solicitude for the ordinary herdsman to show. Mr. Bishop has suggested to me that the dots in this character might represent flies, and the brush a flapper to frighten them away.

It has been suggested that more remote lands, farther from the settlements than the cultivated fields, were used as pasture. Since fences were doubtless rare or unknown, it was inevitable that these pasture-lands should become the subject of dispute between peoples bordering on them, each claiming the exclusive right to use them. In the reign of the king Wu Ting (1324-1266 B.C.) we find such disputes recorded on the oracle bones.

Messages were sent from outlying points saying: 'The T'u country has attacked two towns on our eastern borders; the X [this name has not yet been deciphered] country is also pasturing on the lands of our western borders.' Or again it is said that someone 'announces saying "The T'u country is pasturing on our lands, ten men." ' This apparently means that a herd of cattle in charge of ten men are encroaching on what is considered Shang territory. Whether these disputes over pasture-land were in themselves sufficient cause for war we do not know. But we do know that important and protracted wars were fought during this same period, and with precisely the states which were concerned in the grazing difficulties.

Identification of the water-buffalo among the Shang remains has been disputed, but the occurrence of the triangular horn-core and distinctive metacarpus place this beyond question, according to Dr. C. C. Young. The excavated bones of the water-buffalo are much fewer than those of the domestic ox. There is nothing in the bone inscriptions to tell us that the Shangs had this animal. Probably both varieties of oxen were designated by a single name; the modern Chinese call the water-buffalo simply 'water-ox.' We cannot tell whether this beast was used for food, for hauling purposes, or both.

Some years ago Laufer pointed out the curious fact that although the Chinese have had the cow and other milk-producing animals for thousands of years, and although they have been in constant contact with the Mongols and other milk-using peoples, they have never used milk or its products, and do not even know how to milk their animals. This curious avoidance of milk, he says, divides all Asia and Europe into two camps, an eastern and a western. The peoples of China, Korea, Japan and Indo-China, and all Malayans do not use dairy products, while all the Indo-Europeans, the Semites, Scythians, Turks, Mongols, Tibetans, etc., have used milk regularly from early times. The reason for this is not clear. Chinese sometimes say that they do not use dairy foods because it is cruel to deprive the calf of its mother's milk, but this is merely one of those 'good reasons' which can always be invented to explain actions which are based on long custom. Certainly the Chinese are not generally more kind to animals than are other peoples. Dr. Laufer makes the interesting observation that epic poetry is found among most of the peoples who use milk, but is not produced by any of those who abstain from it. He does not try to explain this.[7]

In recent years a few of the Chinese have begun to use milk, as a result of the example of foreigners in China. Ice-cream in particular has touched a responsive chord. But among many of them a deep aversion to milk and all its products still persists, as was shown by a recent incident. A Chinese who had lived many years on the borders of Mongol territory came to Peking. Speaking Mongol and knowing the customs of the people well, he found it amusing to pass himself off as a Mongol prince. All went well for a time, and he was wined and dined lavishly. But some of the Chinese were suspicious, and they decided to put him to the acid test. They invited him to a feast, but instead of the Chinese delicacies on which he had been gorging himself, they spread the table with milk, butter, and cheeses, all foods to delight the heart of a Mongol. The Chinese impostor fled in disgrace. No matter what might be at stake, he simply could not eat that food.

A number of Chinese authorities on the culture of the Shangs think that they were pastoral nomads, only recently having taken up agriculture when we find them at Anyang. Agriculture, they think, was still decidedly subordinate to stock-raising. With that verdict I find it impossible to agree. In the first place, this Shang culture is quite definitely a development out of the Neolithic cultures found in north China, and authorities on the north Chinese Neolithic are agreed that the men of that period, with their large numbers of pigs and their permanent dwelling-sites, depended primarily upon agriculture for sustenance. It is true that Andersson found one site which is an exception to this, in which the pig was rare and bones of cattle and wild animals predominated.[8] He has very plausibly deduced that in this one site we have evidence of a more or less nomadic, pastoral people, in whose diet an important place was filled by wild game. But it is to be noted, first, that this site was situated in the extreme west, at the very edge of the Tibetan plateau; and second, that it is considered to represent a stage corresponding to the earliest Neolithic which we know in China. This site, then, does not alter the fact that north China proper was inhabited for many centuries before Shang times by people who were, in so far as we can tell, thoroughly agricultural.

The second reason which prevents me from believing that the Shangs were primarily pastoral is the fact that the character, twice quoted in the previous chapter, which represents the end view of a building of elaborate construction, occurs on oracle bones which were inscribed not very long after the time when the Shang people are supposed to have first moved to Anyang. This character, showing the pounded earth platform and an elaborate sort of roof, is plain evidence of a knowledge of rather complicated buildings. If these people had been nomads they would have had no opportunity to acquire such knowledge, for we cannot suppose that they would have erected such buildings to use for a few days. On the other hand we have no reason whatever to suppose that there were other people more cultured than the Shangs, in this part of the world, who could have taught them to build.

The fact that the Chinese appear never to have used milk and milk products might also be urged as evidence against a completely pastoral period in their history, but this is perhaps debatable.

One circumstance with which those who believe in a pastoral stage in Chinese history must deal is the astonishing lack of support given to this theory by Chinese literature. The literatures of other pastoral peoples are full of pastoral similes,

After settling in Palestine the Hebrews became agricultural to a very large degree, yet the pastoral element in the Bible is so great and so familiar as scarcely to need illustration. The twenty-third psalm begins: 'The Lord is my shepherd—' Jesus is referred to as 'The Lamb of God.' Jesus Himself was no shepherd, but a carpenter, yet He preached the parable of the sheep and the goats, and used many pastoral figures. One could quote such instances almost indefinitely. In Chinese literature, however, we have a very different situation. In all the earliest Chinese literature I cannot recall a single pastoral metaphor or illustration, and I have gone through it with some care. Such figures of speech are certainly not common. On the other hand we find figures drawn from agriculture not infrequently. In the Great Announcement (written soon after the fall of Shang) we read: 'If, the father having broken up the ground, his son is unwilling to sow the seed, how much less will he be willing to reap the grain,'[9] and again: 'Heaven in destroying Yin is doing husbandman's work—how dare I but complete the business of my fields!'[10] Even building is a source of such illustrations, but not stock-raising.

The *Book of Poetry* is universally considered to be our best source of material relating to the common people in ancient China. The dates of its contents are not wholly agreed upon, but in any case they are not many centuries later than the beginning of Chou, or the end of Shang times. Had there been in Chinese life a tradition of the wild, free wanderings of the nomadic herdsman, we should find some faint echo of it here. But the fact is that references to cattle and to sheep in this book are very few indeed. They plainly indicate a situation in which domestic animals are raised in small numbers as an adjunct to farming, and as victims for the sacrifices. There is only one poem out of more than three hundred which speaks of either flocks or herds. This tells us of a flock of three hundred sheep and a herd of ninety cattle, and even they are definitely stated to be kept for sacrificial purposes.[11]

Even the most ardent protagonist of the theory that the Shangs were primarily pastoral admits that the oracle bones have very little to say about the raising of sheep and cattle. We find a tremendous number of instances of divination to determine whether the wheat crop, or the millet crop, or the yield of liquor for the year will be good, but even this authority cannot quote a single instance of such question about the increase of flocks or herds. He explains this, however, by saying that the increase of domestic animals is included by implication in divinations concerning 'the harvest of the year.' This is very possibly true. But it happens that the word meaning 'the harvest of the year' is a pictograph of a stalk of grain. When a stalk of grain can be used as the symbol for the entire produce of the year, this seems to indicate a state in which agriculture plays a definitely predominant rôle.

Our evidence is far from complete, but such as we have indicates that the ancestors of the bulk of the Chinese people never passed through a nomadic, pastoral stage at any time in their history. When we first pick up their record they are already an agricultural people, having as domestic animals the dog and the pig, and living in more or less permanent villages. We have no indication that there was a break in this economy, causing the mass of the people to take to a nomadic life with sheep or cattle. Rather, these animals seem to have been added as an adjunct to the agricultural life which was well established before their advent. Whether cattle and sheep were domesticated independently in north China, being captured from wild herds and tamed there, or whether domestic varieties of these animals were introduced, along with the technique of domestication, from elsewhere, is a question to which investigators have paid too little attention. It is to be hoped that we shall have more information on this point in the future.

In the second and third months, which apparently fell in the spring, the Shangs divined about the crops for the year. They also made special sacrifices to particular ancestors, asking them to grant an abundant harvest. The king himself went out from time to time to inspect the crops. Rain was of special importance. The climate of north China is very dry during autumn, winter, and most of the spring, and we find inscriptions which ask: 'Will there be rain enough for the millet crop?' or 'Will (the spirit) Ti decree rain sufficient for the year?' or simply 'We implore rain.' During the summer, however, there is a regular rainy season, during which violent cloudbursts may drown out the grain or even wash away the earth in which it grows. This is, perhaps, why they sometimes asked: 'Will it rain painfully?'

Wheat is mentioned in the bone inscriptions. This plant plays a prominent part in Chinese economy during the historical period, but it has not yet been found in Chinese Neolithic remains, according to Bishop. This has led to the supposition that it represents a cultural intrusion, probably from the West.

Millet has been found in Chinese Neolithic sites, and it is referred to very frequently on the oracle bones. This plant has been very important in the Chinese diet from Neolithic times down to the present. It is still the staple food of north China generally, the use of rice being chiefly limited to city-dwellers and the wealthy. While it is rather dangerous to place much reliance on slight variations in the form of ancient characters, these appear to indicate that both the spiked and panicled varieties of millet were cultivated by the Shangs. The character representing the latter includes the symbol for water in its composition, and we find it there to the present day. This is sometimes explained as due to the fact that alcoholic liquor was manufactured from this grain. This liquor was very important in ancient Chinese religion and in ceremonials generally. It was probably a kind of beer. We know very little about its manufacture or characteristics during Shang times.

The character for 'rice' occurs on the oracle bones, apparently as the name of a cultivated plant. Whether the Shang people grew rice is still a debatable question, however. Anyang is somewhat north of the zone in which rice is grown most commonly and most easily at the present day. At the same time rice is grown even in Manchuria, clear up to the Siberian frontier, though at least some of this is an upland rice cultivated without irrigation. That the Anyang climate was probably milder in Shang times has already been mentioned, and the fact that the water-buffalo was raised there seems to indicate that there was land suitable for rice culture. Swedish botanists have recently identified imprints found in Neolithic pottery from Yang Shao as being those of cultivated rice, which increases the probability that the successors of the Neolithic civilization in this area had rice also.[12]

Rice opens the whole question of irrigation. Farmers cultivating the Anyang site at present do not irrigate on the south bank of the river, which is somewhat higher, but they do irrigate on the north bank, where water is nearer to the surface. Wells are used, the water being hauled up in buckets by men or women, or raised by a water-wheel turned by a blindfolded donkey. On the whole of the oracle inscriptions there are only two places of which I know which definitely suggest irrigation. The character for 'field' is a rectangle divided by two lines crossing in the centre; these are said to represent either boundary lines or irrigation ditches, so that there is no real evidence here. But on one fragment of bone there occurs a character made up of a symbol meaning 'water' or 'running water' and this 'field' symbol. So much of the rest of the inscription is missing that the context cannot be discerned. The character by itself strongly suggests irrigation, and it corresponds to a later word having that meaning. Another fragmentary inscription, of which the context is again missing, contains the two words, in succession, 'water rice.' What may be the value of such fragmentary evidence, the reader must judge for himself.

Whether the ancient Chinese built dams is an interesting

question which seems to have received little attention. In the mythology we find stories of a minister who sought to stop the devastating floods, from which the Chinese seem always to have suffered, by means of dams. This brought him only the severest punishment from the emperor who, in this mythology, is supposed to have ruled over all of China even in remote times. His offence is said to have been that by building dams, he 'interfered with the free course of the natural forces.' His son, Yü, was appointed to continue the work; he followed the better plan of dredging the rivers deeper and giving them free course to the sea, and was so successful that he was appointed to the throne, and became the founder of the Hsia, the first hereditary dynasty, which preceded the Shang. This is the usual version of the story. But we sometimes find the man who dammed the rivers praised, as a benefactor of humanity, rather than condemned as a criminal. Much of this is, of course, pure myth, designed to explain the cutting of gorges through mountains, and similar natural phenomena. But it is possible that one or more disastrous experiences with dams may lie behind it too. For the rainfall in China is so seasonal, and rivers which are at times mere streams become such mighty torrents at others, that it would require a very strong dam to hold them. And such a structure, conceived as a benefit to mankind, could easily prove the cause of a great disaster, making a bad flood much worse when it broke and released its pent-up waters to add to the total. It is not to be wondered at if the people, seeing the waters rage and seethe and destroy, thought that they were angered, exacting a terrible vengeance because man had been so foolish as to try to imprison them.

Some textile plant was cultivated, in the belief of archæologists, even by Neolithic men in north China. Fibres of a sort of hemp are identified by the excavators among the Anyang materials, and this probably points to the cultivation of such a plant on a considerable scale. It is not to be supposed that the plants which have been mentioned exhaust the list of those which were cultivated by the Shang people. Plants and even seeds decay quickly under ordinary conditions, leaving little trace for archæology. On the oracle bones we could not expect to find mention of any save the most important staples and those which happened to figure in religious practices. Bishop thinks that 'leaf and root crops were pretty surely grown by the Neolithic Chinese, as by their modern descendants; for man must have brought plants of that type under cultivation far earlier than any of the cereals.'[13]

About the actual processes of agriculture in Shang times we know little. Whether the locss plains were ever covered with trees is a debated point; some believe that they were not, and therefore did not need clearing. Grass and other plants had to be eliminated, however, and it is said to have required three years to bring new land properly under cultivation. Nothing which the excavators are willing to describe as an agricultural implement has been found at Anyang, which leads to the belief that all of these were made of wood. The plough, pulled by an animal, is said not to have been used in very ancient China, but to have come in rather late in the Chou dynasty. In its stead a spade or spading fork was used.

Unlike many peoples, the Chinese have never considered field-work as being primarily women's work. The men have gone forth to labour in the fields, and the women have prepared their food and taken it to them. The commonest word meaning 'male' is a pictograph representing field-work. Silk culture, on the other hand, has been considered women's work from its earliest mention in literature. The character for silk is considered to be present on the oracle bones, but this is not wholly certain. A silk cocoon has been excavated in Neolithic remains, and showed clearly that it had been cut in half by men, in the opinion of some; others doubt this. The excavators at Anyang believe that they have discovered silk fibres, evidencing the use of silk thread, beyond all question. Tombs of a date only a a little later than Shang have yielded silkworms carved out of jade. And we find silk mentioned so frequently in early Chou literature, and occupying such a thoroughly entrenched position in Chinese culture, that it is difficult to conceive of it as having been a recent innovation. An inscription on a bronze vessel ascribed to the ninth or tenth century B.C. records the use of silk as a medium of exchange in a transaction involving the buying of five slaves.

A poem in the *Book of Poetry* describes silk culture.

> 'With the spring days the warmth begins,
> And the oriole utters its song.
> The young women take their deep baskets,
> And go along the small paths,
> Looking for the tender (leaves of the) mulberry trees. . . .
> In the silkworm month they strip the mulberry branches of their leaves,
> And take their axes and hatchets,
> To lop off those that are distant and high;
> Only stripping the young [?] trees of their leaves.
> In the seventh month, the shrike is heard;
> In the eighth month, they begin their spinning
> They make dark fabrics and yellow.
> Our red manufacture is very brilliant,
> It is for the lower robes of our young princes.'[14]

In the Shang economy wealth was produced or acquired by three principal means, namely, agriculture, herding, and hunting. We should probably add war, which, as a source of loot, may have been scarcely less important. There was unquestionably a certain amount of trade, but so far as the actual necessities of life are concerned communities must have been largely self-contained. This, in turn, must have made it more difficult to exercise absolute political control over a large territory than it would have been had there been more complete interdependence between communities. The rise of real monarchies in Europe came partially as a result of the increasing use of money, strengthening economic ties and facilitating economic control from a single centre. They had commodities which could be exchanged in Shang times. Horses and cattle, and grain to a lesser degree, lend themselves to such use. But any system based on such commodities cannot have the fluidity of a genuine monetary system.

So far as our evidence goes, the only money which the Shangs possessed was in the form of the shells of the cowry. Speaking strictly, we cannot prove that these shells were used in this manner in Shang times. But we find a certain amount of evidence leading to this conclusion in the oracle inscriptions, and we find them mentioned commonly in this connection in early Chou bronze inscriptions. One hundred and sixty-three of the smaller and more prized variety were found in a single Shang treasure pit. When we add to this the fact that these shells have been used as money in many parts of the world, the assumption that the Shangs used them in this manner seems thoroughly justified.

The cowry is a small marine mollusc, whose shell has been used for decorative and religious purposes and as a medium of exchange in many widely scattered places. Attempts have been made to explain all of these uses, in various places and by various peoples, from the one fact that one side of the shell bears some resemblance to the female organs of sex. This, it is said, has caused it to be prized as a charm for fertility, which, in turn, has caused it to be worn as an amulet and led to other decorative uses. These uses have caused it to become an article of value, which has had the ultimate result of causing it to be used as money. This one circumstance, then, that it has some resemblance to the female sexual organs, is supposed to account for the fact that it is found buried with the dead in Chinese Neolithic graves, that it is used as a decoration in Assam and in Sweden, and that it has been used as money in China and in Africa.

It seems quite unnecessary, however, to press this one explanation so far. That the sexual theory will hold in the case of its use in magic and religious connections may be true. But the fact is that the cowry is both durable and pretty enough to recommend itself for use as an ornament even to those ignorant of its more esoteric connections. And its use as money, in China at any rate, is quite explicable without resort to physiology. Three qualities are necessary in a medium of exchange. It must be at least relatively imperishable; the cowry is unusually durable for a shell. It must be easily transportable; cowries, especially when strung, are certainly that. It must be sufficiently rare and difficult to obtain so that an over-supply will not wipe out its value; in this respect, too, the cowry met the specifications in Shang times. Conchologists disagree as to the point from which the small cowries (*Cypræa moneta*) found at Anyang must have been imported, some holding that they lived in the Pacific south of the mouth of the Yangtse River, others that they were not found east of Singapore. But in any case, before reaching Anyang these shells had to be traded or carried over at least five hundred miles of territory peopled by fierce barbarians, across mighty rivers, and through forests full of ferocious beasts; this was certainly sufficient to insure against a too sudden flooding of the market.

In the inscriptions on bronze vessels cast during the early part of the Chou dynasty we see the gradual transition from the use of cowry shells to the use of metal as money. We also find records of military expeditions to 'punish' the barbarians on the sea coast; these records boast that they brought back much spoil of cowry shells. This, and improved communications, no doubt depressed the value of the cowry and hastened its abandonment as money. But the cowry had one quality, it should be noted, which even metal money has not always had in China. Really satisfactory money should have a standard, unmistakable value—a dollar should be a dollar. But a dollar is not a dollar if its value depends on its weight, which must be tried by scales each time it changes hands. Nor is it so if its value fluctuates with the purity of its metal, which must be judged as a part of each transaction. These uncertainties have often complicated the use of metal money in China and elsewhere. The cowry appears to have been free from these disadvantages. These little shells are very much alike and there is every indication that one of them had the same value as another. A string of cowries, containing a fixed number, was a string of cowries. It is true that imitation cowries, carved from bone, have been found even in Neolithic graves in China, and that metal money was cast in the shape of these shells in the later transition period. But these were imitations, not counterfeits, for they could have deceived no one.

As a medium of exchange the cowry could not have been very fluid, for its value was undoubtedly very great. Ancient cowries are commonly found pierced for stringing, and the unit in which cowries are measured in bronze inscriptions and on one of the oracle bones is the *p'êng* or 'double string.' The great Chinese archæologist, Wang Kuo-wei, believed that a *p'êng* consisted, at the most, of ten shells, and this conclusion seems acceptable. My notes record thirty-three inscriptions on bronzes of Chou date in which cowries are said to have been given, as reward for service or as a mark of esteem, to vassals by their feudal superiors. That cowries were used extensively for this purpose is shown by the fact that the character for 'reward' includes a pictograph of the cowry to this day. The numbers of cowries so given is significant. In eighteen cases, or more than half, the number of shells given is not mentioned. In these cases we may be sure it was small; these inscriptions were designed to record the glory of the maker for posterity, and nothing which could make him look important was left out. In the remaining sixteen cases we have one gift of five strings of cowries, nine gifts of ten strings, one gift of twenty, two of thirty, and two of fifty. The large gifts seem to be comparatively later, when communications were perhaps easier and cowries more plentiful than in the Shang period;

such statistics are dangerous, however, as the exact dating of bronzes is still very difficult.

We are justified in supposing that in at least some of the cases where the number of cowries given is not mentioned it was not more than one string. Yet all of the men so rewarded were important enough and wealthy enough to cast bronzes in commemoration of the gift. Five strings were given, with other gifts, it is true, to a military official important enough to be appointed by the king personally in a special ceremony in the ancestral temple. A gift of ten strings, and nothing else, was important enough to justify a ceremony of personal presentation by the king, again conducted in a temple.

If translated into ordinary commodities, then, a string of these cowry shells must have had a tremendous purchasing power. Whether in the early period it was ever broken up, and the individual shells used as money, I do not know. Even one of these shells must have equalled the value of a great many bushels of millet. These cowries must have been something like thousand-dollar bills in these days—wealth, good to have, exchangeable for very valuable luxury goods (such as fine bronzes), eminently suited for rewarding vassals, and useful in an emergency to bribe assistance in war or to buy off one's enemies. They were no doubt rendered as tribute to the Shang rulers by subject states. But they can hardly have been of much service to the individual who wished to go out shopping for articles of everyday use. Even if the supply of them had been large enough they could not have been used to pay soldiers. If a private soldier, buying a meal, must take ten bushels of grain as 'change' for his money, he could not carry it away in his pocket. The result was that ordinary payments had to be made in commodities, which were not easy to transport. The inevitable consequence was that much of the real power of government had to be left in the hands of local rulers, and this, in turn, meant that real control of a very large area from one centre was almost impossible.

There was transportation of commodities ever considerable distances—that we know. Bones of the whale which must have come from the Pacific have been excavated at Anyang, but they are few. Shells of *Lamprotula*, used for their mother-of-pearl, are found in great numbers; these are believed to have been imported from the Yangtse valley. The cowries themselves attest such transport. It is thought that ore for the casting of bronze came from some distance, and some of the manufactured articles found are believed to have been made elsewhere. No doubt many things came to Anyang as tribute from the surrounding territories. But this does not alter the fact that, in so far as our evidence shows, a great thriving trade carried on over long distances and facilitated by a fluid medium of exchange is unlikely.

CHAPTER VI

HANDICRAFTS

WE can form little just opinion of the handicrafts of the Shang people from the relics which remain to archæology. Even our own civilization, which flourishes in an age dominated by metals, would make a poor showing after being buried for three thousand years in damp soil which destroyed everything but stone, bone, metal, and earthenware. Our dwellings might persist better than those of Shang, but all wood-carving and the best of our furniture would perish. Our clothing, which plays so large a part in our life and thought, would be so much mouldered earth. Painting, music, literature, would leave scarcely a clue to their existence. Of writing there would remain only bronze plaques and corner-stones; from these archæologists might deduce that we wrote 'in set, abbreviated formulæ, more in fact of a technique to aid the memory than a true system of writing.'

We must examine the Shang relics scientifically, to be sure, but with the eye of scientific imagination. We must realize that most of the things excavated are things which were lost or thrown away, and the finest things are neither lost nor thrown away, save rarely. Until a few months ago we could only infer, from the carved bones preserved to us, that the Shang people were adept carvers of wood. Now we know, from the decayed but recognizable carvings found on the walls of tombs, that the beautiful and intricate patterns found on Shang bronzes were reproduced, with the same skill and delicacy, in wood. But there must be many other aspects of their craftsmanship which we cannot even infer.

That clothing was a matter to which the ancient Chinese

paid great attention and in which they took great pride we know from the literature of Chou times. In connection with finds even of Neolithic date, Andersson mentions 'about twenty globular buttons, in most cases cut out of marble. It strikes one that these buttons are very small (diameter only 4·5-11 mm.), and it seems probable that a people who used such small and neatly made buttons must have worn clothes made of fine material and of highly developed shape.'[1] Among the Shang finds there are small spiral-shaped 'buttons' with three points, made of mother-of-pearl, but it is doubtful that these were actually used to secure clothing because the points would have made them very troublesome and fragile. They are drilled for sewing or threading, and are probably ornaments to be worn on clothes.

Spinning whorls made of both stone and pottery have been found in Neolithic sites, and it has been pointed out that the same instrument, in virtually identical form, is used in China to-day. Various textile patterns have been found impressed on Neolithic pottery. Not only cloth but baskets and matting as well were woven both by the Neolithic people of north China and by the Shangs. One of the characters on the oracle bones shows that in Shang as in Chou times matting was spread on the floors of dwellings.

Both matting and cloth were used to wrap up bronze weapons and vessels buried in Shang tombs; pieces of them are often quite well preserved when the bronzes are excavated. The cloth is usually completely impregnated, and sometimes quite replaced, by the products of the corrosion of the bronze and other minerals. Under a microscope, however, one can see that in some cases the original cloth is still present. In any case, the form and weave of the textile is preserved; the threads are large and somewhat loosely woven, but the texture is smooth and even. Sewing was common, as is attested by bone needles in the Neolithic and bone and bronze needles in the Shang site. We have, of course, none of the actual clothing of Shang times, but characters on the oracle bones give us two pieces of important information concerning it. It was definitely tailored clothing, with sleeves, not merely pieces of cloth or skin thrown about the body. Furs as well as textiles were used to make such garments.

Although the men of Shang were expert in the casting of bronze this metal did not completely displace the stone utensils characteristic of the Neolithic cultures. This is probably because bronze was scarce, and had to be reserved for making articles of the greatest importance, such as weapons and ceremonial vessels. The most common stone utensil excavated on the Shang site is a type of rectangular or semicircular stone knife, of which great numbers have been found. Knives of this type are believed not to exist in Europe or the Near East, but they have been found in various places in north-eastern Asia, among the American Eskimos, and are even reported from South America. This is, then, another of the links which bind the Shangs, and Chinese culture, to an ancient Pacific culture area. Polished stone axes, a piece of a beautifully carved and inscribed stone vessel, stone dishes, mortars and pestles, and grindstones have been excavated at Anyang. Musical sounding stones, like those of later periods, have been found.

Stone weapons used by the Shangs include lance- and spear-heads and arrow-points. The latter pose something of a problem. The number of stone arrow-heads found at Anyang is negligible, while those made of bone and bronze are many. Why should they have preferred bone to stone for this purpose? Andersson points out that even in the Neolithic finds there are a great many arrow-heads of triangular shape, with a long narrow tang; this form, he says, is foreign to the stone material, and he concludes that it was borrowed from some people who already made arrow-heads of metal.[2]

I suggest that we must rather look for the solution of this problem to the bamboo shaft, which at once provides a reason for the shape of the Neolithic arrow-heads and for the fact that the Shang people preferred bone to stone. American-Indian arrow-heads are commonly made of stone. I know from having made them that it is not difficult to fashion arrow-heads if one has good flint, but it is very difficult to make a long, narrow neck of stone; it will almost inevitably break off in the process of manufacture. So far as I have observed, the Indians did not attempt this; they made a cleft in the shaft and inserted the arrow-head in it. In China, however, young bamboos provided the perfect shaft for arrows, light and perfectly straight; bamboo arrows are mentioned specifically in an early section of the *Document Classic* (the so-called *Book of History*).[3] But the bamboo, with its hollow centre, demanded that the arrow-head have a neck which could be inserted into the shaft. Every Shang arrow-head I have seen or seen pictured, whether made of stone, bone, or bronze, has such a neck; it was apparently wedged in the shaft by being wound with thread, and perhaps cemented. Yet the use of stone for this purpose was not abandoned completely; stone arrow-heads are mentioned as articles of tribute, both in the *Discourses of the States* and in the *Document Classic*.[4] But bone was better adapted than stone to making arrow-heads of this sort.

Ornaments carved from stone are found even in Chinese Neolithic remains. Stone bracelets of white marble, sometimes 'as wide as a loose cuff,' were found in a very early site. Stone rings having some resemblance to those found in the Shang site are among the Neolithic relics; the most interesting of these is a ring of 'flame-green jade,' 65 mm. in diameter. Many stone objects have been found in the Shang city which are like or identical in form with the ceremonial jades of the Chou period, many of which were worn as badges of rank.

The word 'jade' requires explanation. It is properly applied to stone of more than one colour and more than one variety of chemical composition. But it is used to translate the Chinese word *yü*, to which it is not always a complete equivalent. In actual practice the Chinese frequently apply the term *yü* to almost any variety of hard, fine-grained stone which takes a high polish. Beyond doubt much jade, in the proper sense of the word, has been found at Anyang, but it is possible that some of the stone which is so called is not jade in our sense. As for that variety of jade which is used to set finger-rings, a small piece of which may be worth hundreds of dollars, none of that has been found at Anyang, I believe.

The Shang people carved small figures representing pigs, birds, and men out of stone. That the manufacture of such decorative objects probably had a long history in China is indicated by the finding of a small figurine, representing an animal, and carved very skilfully out of marble, in Neolithic remains in Fêngtien Province. The finest Shang workmanship in stone was that which produced their sculptures, but since these really surpass handicraft and enter the category of art, discussion of them will be reserved to the next chapter.

Bone and shell were important materials for the Shang artisans. Bone arrow-heads have already been mentioned; they are the most numerous of the weapons fashioned from bone, though lance-heads were also made of it. Among the most numerous and characteristic bone utensils found are ladles, which are frequently decorated with elaborately carved designs. Bone hairpins, also numerous, are one of the most interesting types of articles found by the excavators. A great many varieties have come to light, but the most common is topped by the head of a cock. They are sometimes executed with the greatest care, and polished so highly that persons seeing them for the first time refuse to believe they are bone, or any other substance but jade. The exact use of these hairpins in Shang times we do not know, but in Chou times they were worn by both men and women. Men wore them to keep their ceremonial hats in position, so that they took on a more than casual importance.

The most arresting objects made of bone are large carved pieces, sometimes nearly a foot in length, covered with finely carved designs like those found on bronzes (see Plate VIII). Sometimes the design is inlaid with pieces of turquoise. Most of these seem to have been made purely as works of art, but on a few of them characters are inscribed. The inscription on the piece illustrated in Plate VIII, which also appears on another piece known to us, tells of a hunt in which the king was successful, after which he rewarded one of his attendants. Presumably this bone was made at the behest of the attendant to record this event; it was probably destined to be handed down in his family as an heirloom, recording the glory of this ancestor. This bone is interesting because if this is so it fills precisely the function which was filled by countless inscribed bronzes cast during the Chou period—a function like that of the inscribed loving-cup of the present.

The inscribed oracle bones also represent a handicraft which required no mean skill, but they will be treated elsewhere. Here we must mention, however, the practice of inlaying the inscribed character with either red or black pigment. It was not done frequently, and seems to have been limited to the reign of one king, Wu Ting. Its significance is unknown. Sometimes we find, on the same bone, the work of two diviners, where the characters carved by one have been inlaid with black, those of the other with red. The red pigment is believed to be cinnabar.

Whether the wall paintings found in the recently discovered tombs rise above the level of mere craftsmanship I am unable to say, as those pieces which I saw were mere fragments. Larger pieces were excavated intact, I understand, just after my latest visit to the Anyang site. The paint, which is said to be lacquer, is very well preserved indeed. The colours, red, black, and white, are still bright. Even from fragments it is apparent that the motifs used resemble those of the Shang bronzes, but are magnified a great many times.

The horns of cattle and the antlers of deer were used to make weapons and utensils. The tusks of boars and elephant ivory were carved into ornaments. Conch- and mussel-shells were used to make a variety of things, chiefly ornamental; the latter were also used, strangely enough, to make saws. Mother-of-pearl, like turquoise and boar's tusk ivory, was sometimes used as inlay.

One small object carved from bone, excavated from a Shang tomb in the spring of 1935, possesses an interest out of all proportion to its size. For it is a musical instrument, identified by Mr. Liang Ssŭ-yung as what is known as a *hsüan*, sometimes called a 'Chinese ocarina.' This instrument is said by Chinese tradition to have been invented about 2700 B.C. The Shang example is about two and a half inches high and more or less barrel-shaped. It is decorated with two so-called *t'ao-t'ieh*, or 'ogre masks,' such as are found on bronzes. There is a hole at the top to blow into, and five holes on the sides which may be stopped with the fingers to vary the pitch. Mr. Liang, who kindly demonstrated it to me, blew 'do, re, mi, fa,' and said that by blowing harder on one note it was possible to produce 'sol.' There are two remarkable things about this. In the first place, it shows that the Shang people must have known quite a little about music. Not all of the intervals were exact, though this might have been because the instrument was not completely clean. But the interval from 'do' to 'fa' was a perfect 'perfect fourth,' accurately tuned. The most interesting thing about this instrument is that the notes mentioned are the first five notes of the major scale, involving a half-step which is not present at all in the modern Chinese five-tone scale. They would seem, in fact, to indicate that an entirely different tonal system was in use at that time.

Study of the bone objects excavated, some of which are, happily, in an uncompleted state, tells us quite a little about the technique used. A blank was first sawed out of the bone; some of the sharp curves achieved in this sawing would do credit to a modern scroll saw. This was given a rough finish, no doubt, with a knife. Some of the marks left on roughly finished surfaces have the precisely parallel ridges which are left by a file, though I know of no such tool having been found. And some of the surfaces are polished to a high lustre. They used drills, slightly conical in shape, with great skill. Sometimes holes, started some distance apart, are drilled to meet exactly in the middle.

Naturally very little of Shang woodwork has survived being buried for three thousand years in damp soil. But the planks used in constructing the tomb chambers are still remarkably distinguishable to the eye, even though they are rotten. And we are able to infer in various ways that they must have used wood a good deal. The frames of their houses were made of it. Their bows, and the shafts of arrows, spears, lances, and battle-axes must have been made of it. Occasionally one sees what appear to be remnants of decayed wood still adhering to the tang of a dagger-axe. We know they had drums, and these were probably made with wood. Boats capable of navigating rivers, and chariots, both of which are mentioned in the oracle inscriptions, betoken a skill in carpentry distinctly beyond the rudimentary level.

Pieces of broken pottery are by far the most numerous of the objects found by the excavators at Anyang. Yet the unbroken Shang pots which have been found do not number more than ten. The reason is plain; they did not throw them away unless they were broken, and a pottery vessel is not an easy thing to lose. Not more than a hundred vessels have been reconstructed from broken pieces, but these are sufficient to give a very good idea of what Shang pottery was like.

It is rather surprising that the painted pottery of the late Neolithic period had vanished completely. It was a noble art—as fine, it has been said, as any art produced by Neolithic man anywhere. But it was a part of a cultural complex which had Western connections; the Shang culture, which had most of its ties in the East, knew it not. One lone painted potsherd has been found in the Shang remains, and that, a typical

PLATE IV

TYPICAL POTTERY OF THE SHANG PERIOD, EXCAVATED BY THE NATIONAL RESEARCH INSTITUTE AT ANYANG

THE TWO AT THE TOP ARE IN THE FORM KNOWN AS *LI*.

Official Photographs of the National Research Institute, reproduced by courtesy of Dr. Li Chi.

relic of the Yang Shao civilization, was probably already a curiosity in Shang times.

The Shang pottery is made of two materials, an ordinary clay and a white clay. From the white clay the finer type of Shang vessels were made. The point of origin of this white clay is not certainly known, but it has been suggested that it came from the region of *T'zŭ Chou*, some seventeen miles to the north of Anyang. *T'zŭ Chou* means 'porcelain district'; the town of this name was famous for its porcelain during the great porcelain days of the Sung dynasty, and still manufactures such wares. Whether the white pottery of the Shangs, which was not glazed, should be called 'porcelain' or not is a debated point.

The ordinary clay used for most of the pottery gave vessels of either grey or red colour, depending upon the baking. If the clay was oxidized thoroughly, it became red; if not, it remained grey. Some of the broken edges of red pieces show that the clay was red at the outside, where oxidation was complete, but still grey in the middle. The clay used for ordinary pots was of varying qualities of smoothness. Some vessels designed to be used for cooking had a great deal of sand mixed with their clay, intended, it is said, to aid in the conduction of heat from the outside of the vessel to the contents.

Much of the pottery was made by hand, without the use of the potter's wheel. No doubt the 'coiling' process was used, the vessel being smoothed off afterward either with the hand or by scraping with tools. In many cases, however, the potter's wheel was certainly used, and with no little skill.

The designs on the white pottery were carved in the wet clay. They often bear great resemblance to the designs found on bronzes. It is thought that vessels made of this white pottery were used, like bronzes, for ceremonial purposes. This is borne out by the fact that very fine specimens were buried in the great royal tombs. Designs on the other pottery were either impressed or incised in the wet clay. These patterns show a great deal of variety. Many of the patterns are made by pressing string or cord into the clay. One common pattern, consisting of small diamond-shaped impressions, is a good deal of a mystery. It could hardly have been made in any way save by stamping or printing, but if it was made in this way there should be joints where one impression leaves off and the other begins; so far no such joints have been found.

After being fashioned the Shang pottery was baked. According to Mr. Liang Ssŭ-yung it must have been baked in kilns, but none of these kilns has as yet been discovered.

Some of the pottery used by the Shangs has a glazed surface. Previous to this discovery it had not been supposed that glazed pottery was so old, and it was suggested by some that this was an 'accidental' glaze, some chemical constituent of the clay which was brought to the surface by the firing. The excavators point out, however, that the glaze does not occur with the distribution which we might expect if this were its origin; it is found on some parts of the pot and not on others, and there is an abrupt line of demarcation such as would be produced if the glaze were laid on purposely. The glaze is somewhat crude, indicating that the process was in its infancy. These glazed pots are brown in colour, with light grey 'freckles' in the glaze; they are commonly decorated with parallel wavy lines.

In size the Shang pots range from very small ones to pieces as much as three feet high and as much as eighteen inches wide. In form they have great variety; more than fifteen different types to which names can be assigned have been distinguished, and in addition to these there are still others. They were used for cooking, as eating utensils, for storage purposes, and no doubt as wash-basins. There is very little of inscription on the pottery, and all of the inscriptions which have been found were scratched in the clay after the pot had been completed and baked. Such scratched inscriptions are usually limited to one poorly executed character. This is, no doubt, in some cases the name of the owner of the vessel.

One fact in connection with the Shang pottery is well worth

noting. Almost every form that we find in Shang and later Chinese bronze ceremonial vessels is found in the Shang pottery. It has been suggested, and with great plausibility, that the bronzes were cast in forms already familiar through a long pottery tradition. One bronze vessel pictured in a work published by Umehara looks exactly like one of the crudest of Shang or even Neolithic pots.

CHAPTER VII

SCULPTURE AND BRONZE

UNTIL 1929, Chinese sculpture was supposed to date only from the Han period (206 B.C.-A.D. 220). But serious doubt was cast on this, in that year, by the finding at Anyang of a small fragment of a sculptured human figure. It was excavated in the ruins of the city. Careful digging in the neighbourhood of the find failed to produce any further pieces of this statue, or any other objects of the sort. For this reason, and because of the surprising nature of the discovery, some scholars considered it uncertain whether this fragment of sculpture should be assigned to the Shang period or not.

It is illustrated in Plate III. This piece is about ten inches high and eight inches wide. The individual is represented as sitting, the hands clutching the knees. Ornamentation resembling that found on Shang bronzes is engraved on the surfaces. A slot in the back of the figure has led to the suggestion that it functioned as a base for one of the pillars of a building. It has been pointed out that it is not unusual to find, among more or less primitive peoples, the burial of a human being as a sacrifice under a pillar, and it is suggested that this stone figure may be a substitution for such a rite.

Any doubt that this piece is Shang has been removed by the discovery of many beautiful pieces of sculptured marble in the great Shang tombs opened in the autumn of 1934 and the spring of 1935. At the same time, attention has been almost entirely diverted from the early find, for that fragment, while in the same general style, gave little suggestion of the perfection of technique to which the Shang people had developed the art of

PLATE V

A SCULPTURED SHANG *T'AO-T'IEH* OF WHITE MARBLE. HEIGHT, TEN AND ONE-HALF INCHES

THIS PIECE WAS PROBABLY USED TO DECORATE A BUILDING, FOR IT IS SLOTTED IN THE BACK SO THAT IT COULD HAVE BEEN ATTACHED TO A PILLAR. NOTE THE FINE TRACERY IN THE BACKGROUND. THIS PIECE IS SOMEWHAT CHIPPED AND ERODED, BUT THE SCULPTURES EXCAVATED FROM THE TOMB ARE FREQUENTLY PERFECT, WITHOUT BLEMISH.

In a Private Collection, reproduced by kind permission.

sculpture. A much better idea of this can be obtained from the piece of sculptured marble illustrated in Plate v. Particular attention should be paid to the traceries, in low relief, with which the background is decorated. This piece, which appeared on the Peiping antique market, has slots, apparently for attachment to the wooden parts of a building, like the human figure just mentioned. It is to be regretted that no illustrations of the excavated pieces can be included among the plates, but since they have been discovered so recently, photographs of them have not even been published in the reports of the National Research Institute, and they naturally wish to be the first to publish them.

These figures are in full round, not slotted like the pieces illustrated. Most of them are of white marble, though one fragment I have seen was black. The great tombs from which they were excavated have been looted, at least a thousand years ago and probably earlier; the pieces which remain are therefore those which these early excavators either missed, or did not think worth taking away. They are probably not the finest of the figures which were originally buried. Birds, tortoises, tiger-like crouching beasts, and animals difficult to identify are among those represented.

The largest of these sculptures which I have seen measured only a little over a yard in its greater dimension. But there is reason to believe that pieces of much greater size existed, but were carried away when the tomb was opened earlier. A head of an ox, excavated by the National Research Institute, is larger than life-size. It is fitted with a pin, to join it on to the body, which is missing; if this body was in proportion, it must have been huge. In a Peiping antique shop I have seen a piece of white marble, carved in the shape of a horn of a dragon, which is said to have been dug up by grave-robbers at Anyang, and which is completely in this same style. It has a tenon at its base, designed to fit into a mortise in the dragon's head. I believe that there is little doubt that it is a piece of a

Shang sculptured figure; since the horn itself is more than a foot in height, the size of the animal must have been very great.

The range of design in the Shang sculptures is in general that which is found on the bronzes. Some of the birds and animals represented on the latter are executed in stone, and the decorative motifs of the bronzes, the whorls and so forth, are carved on the surfaces of the statuary in low relief. As with the bronzes, there is a certain grotesqueness to the design; it rarely approaches the naturalistic. From this point of view it cannot be compared for beauty, to our eyes at least, with Greek sculpture. From the point of view of technique, on the other hand, it is difficult to see how this work could be surpassed. The design and the proportions, given the goal at which the sculptors aimed, are perfect. The finish leaves nothing to be desired, being as smooth as glass.

Perhaps the most perplexing of all the problems connected with this art is its complete disappearance. No sculpture has been reported from the excavations in the tombs of the rulers of Wei, the state which ruled the Anyang region in Chou times. In so far as we can tell, the art of sculpture vanished with the Shang rule. Whether it was in the hands of a few men who were killed or who fled we have no way of knowing. The very existence of such an art is not mentioned in the literature. Its only survival was in the carving of small decorative and ritual objects of jade or other fine-grained stone, using much the same motifs. Chinese sculpture, after the Shang period, seems to have become a miniature art.

If the Shangs excelled in their sculpture, they did so even more markedly in their casting of bronze. The best of the Shang bronze ritual vessels are almost undoubtedly the finest things of their sort in the world; in fact, they are probably the most exquisite (in the proper sense of that much abused word) objects which men have ever created from metal, regardless of time or place.

Occidental reactions to Chinese bronzes vary greatly. One authority on Chinese art has no liking for bronzes whatsoever; he says that as a decoration in his home he would as soon have an old stove. For many people Chinese bronzes are a taste which must be acquired, if it comes at all. The seeming grotesqueness of their design is likely to be repellent on first acquaintance. Only gradually does one come to realize that these animals and designs which seem grotesque to us had very definite meaning and function for the people who made the bronzes. As one sees more and the designs become familiar, he begins to appreciate the surpassing skill which was expended in combining these various motifs in delicately balanced designs which often cover every smallest spot of surface, yet managed to blend them so completely that there is no appearance of over-decoration. From appreciation some people pass to the stage of passion for these objects of ancient art, and this may become almost an obsession. Tales are told of foreigners in China who almost ruin themselves because they cannot forgo the opportunity to acquire 'just one more' fine piece.

It is natural that the finest Chinese bronzes should have been thought to be comparatively late. Fine bronzes of certain types have long been attributed to the Shang dynasty by Chinese connoisseurs. Foreign scholars have for the most part classed these statements with the tales of the unicorn, which appeared only in the reigns of wise emperors, and the archer who shot and killed nine of the ten suns which used to be in the sky. It is said that until a year or two ago no European or American museum would allow any bronze in its collections to be labelled as earlier than the Chou dynasty, which followed the Shang. Nevertheless, the new materials have proved that the laugh is this time on the foreigner. For it is not only true that numerous bronzes were cast in the Shang dynasty; it is also true that those bronzes were, in general, of the type which the Chinese have been calling Shang all these years. This is not to say that the Chinese may not have made many mistakes in their attributions, but they have at least not been guilty of the sweeping error of the foreign specialists.

That the Shang people had bronze was abundantly proved by the excavations at Anyang, even before the great discoveries of the year just past. Bronze objects found in the same undisturbed strata with the inscribed bones include weapons, tools, and ornaments. The weapons include arrow-heads, dagger-axes, and lance-heads. Among the bronze tools found are small knives, axes, adzes, needles, and awls. Small bronze ornaments are found in a shell pattern, and also shaped like the well-known design called *t'ao-t'ieh*, or 'ogre mask.'

Until the autumn of 1934 no complete bronze ceremonial vessel had been found by the excavators of the National Research Institute at Anyang. Because of this fact, there were those who said that such vessels had not been made in Shang times, and that the many fine vessels dug up by grave-robbers in the Anyang region were of later date. But those of us who specialized in the study of Shang culture knew that this was not true. Comparison of the decoration of these bronzes with some of the pictographic characters of the bone inscriptions, and with the decoration of bronze moulds, carved bone, and white pottery which had been excavated scientifically, proved that they were Shang.

The last shadow of doubt has been removed by the finding of dozens of Shang bronze vessels in the tombs which were excavated during the past twelve months. In size they range up to a rectangular cauldron twenty inches high and twenty inches long. Some of them are more interesting, in certain respects, than any of those secured by the grave-robbers.

Bronzes have been dug out of the ground in the Anyang region for some five hundred years, and Shang bronzes obtained in this way long ago are still in Chinese collections. But most of the work of the grave-robbers has been done in the last five or six years; in this period hundreds of bronzes have been taken out of the ground. They have gone into museums and private collections in China, Europe, America and, especially, Japan. Pictures of a great many of the vessels and rubbings of their inscriptions have been published, providing rich material for study.

Bronze was not merely used at Anyang; it was cast, and the metal from which it was made was smelted there. Pieces of malachite, from which the Shangs are believed to have refined copper, slag mixed with charcoal, pottery vessels apparently used in the refining process, and earthenware moulds have all been found in large numbers. It is thought that some kind of blast furnace, worked no doubt with a more or less primitive bellows, was employed. Deposits of usable ore are not known in that location at present, so that it may have been imported from some distance. They may have had some free copper to use in making bronze.

The formula usually given for bronze is eight or nine parts of copper to one part of tin. Three specimens of bronze excavated at Anyang have been subjected to microscopic examination by Sir H. C. H. Carpenter. He found them to consist of an average of about 83 per cent. copper and 17 per cent. tin. There may be very small amounts of other metals present, which were not detected in this examination.[1]

It is generally supposed that these Shang bronzes must have been cast by the *cire perdue* process. The essential procedure is as follows: An exact model of the vessel or other object to be cast is made in wax; all designs to appear on the finished bronze are carved or impressed on its surface. When its form is exactly that desired, it is coated with clay. The first of this clay is mixed with so much water that it is really liquid, and is put on with a brush, so that it will fill every tiniest aperture without any flaws. Coat after coat of this is brushed on and allowed to dry; then other clay is put round the outside until a sufficient thickness for the mould is attained. A few holes are left, so that the wax may run out and the bronze may be poured in. The whole mould is then heated; this bakes the clay and melts the wax, which runs out of the holes. This leaves a pottery mould, inside of which is a cavity which retains, to the smallest detail, the form of the wax model. All that remains is to pour in bronze (but so skilfully that it will run into every tiniest bit of tracery on the mould!), allow it to harden, break off the mould, and finish the vessel with tools.

It is in connection with this finishing that the superiority of the ancient Chinese craftsmen over many of their best rivals elsewhere appears. There must certainly have been little 'necks' of bronze, representing the holes through which the molten metal was poured, which had to be cut and smoothed off. But it is the opinion of connoisseurs that except for this the casting was so perfect, in the case of the finer pieces, at least, that no retouching was necessary. We think of the work of Benvenuto Cellini as superlatively fine, but those who have examined his castings say that they are full of spots where, the metal having failed to fill out the mould, metal 'plugs' have subsequently been inserted and finished off with tools. It is agreed that while a very few of the best living craftsmen in Europe or America, aided by all the resources of modern science and technology, may be able to equal the casting of the Shang bronze workers, they can do no better. Modern metal workers themselves candidly acknowledge this.

Some doubt as to whether a part, at least, of the Shang vessels were produced by the *cire perdue* process has been raised by the pieces of pottery moulds for bronze which have been found. In some cases these show perfectly smooth edges, and are even fitted with lugs so that they can be fitted together. Such moulds were obviously not produced in the manner described above. It has been said that these moulds were probably used for casting the wax models, and that may be the case. Yet there is other evidence which makes it seem that vessels were certainly sometimes cast directly from sectional moulds. The subject is one which should be investigated by experts in this field.

Let us examine in detail a particular bronze vessel of the type called *ku*. It is not of the finest quality. Dozens of such vessels have been unearthed at Anyang; it is probable that more than one of them belonged to every Shang family of any pretensions. I have seen the particular combination of decoration which is found on this *ku* repeated on several; no doubt vessels of this sort were turned out in considerable numbers, almost as a factory industry. Yet the casting of this vessel is very fine. Its delicate traceries look quite sharp and clear even through a magnifying-glass. Its corners are corners; if a projection was intended, even for the tiniest fraction of an inch, it projects. Most of the channels cast in its surface, making up the tracery, are one thirty-second of an inch or less in width. But these channels are not merely troughs, grooves of any sort. The walls of the groove go back straight, for about three sixty-fourths of an inch, until they reach the bottom. Then there is a square corner, and the bottom of the groove runs quite flat to the point where it meets the other wall, again in a square corner. In other words, a profile of these grooves would show, not a curve, but three sides of a rectangle. If one compares these vessels with some of the modern bronzes cast in China in the attempt to duplicate them the contrast is no less than pitiable.

It is probably too early to attempt a classification of Shang bronzes, but there are three general varieties discernible in those which are excavated and those which come on to the market. One variety, of which I have not seen many representatives, is comparatively crude. Whether it represents an earlier stage in the technique of casting or only a less costly type of bronze it is not possible to say at this time. Its decoration consists entirely of rather coarse lines, and it usually has little if any high relief.

A second variety is inlaid with black pigment, which is used to fill all the depressions. The nature of this pigment is unknown, as it has not yet been analysed. The effect of this filling of the depressions is to make the surface flat; only the pupils of the eyes of animals represented are sometimes in relief. Bronzes with this type of decoration are extremely handsome. Indeed, they are perhaps more handsome to-day than when they were used by the Shang people themselves, for the chemical action of the soil has turned the lines of bronze to a beautiful green or blue-green, which provides a finer contrast to the inlay than would the original colour of the bronze. Many Shang bronzes appear to be inlaid with red pigment, and I formerly supposed that they were. This seems, however, to be merely an accident of patination. The patina is in two layers, an outer red one and an inner green one; when the red patination is cleaned off the outside, but left in the depressions, it looks like a red inlay and is, in fact, very beautiful. It is this circumstance which is responsible for the clarity of the design in Plate VI.

The third variety of vessels which come from Anyang is that to which the largest number of specimens and the finest examples belong. In general, it is characterized by fine workmanship and a combination of large and bold design with quite delicate tracery filling in the background. It commonly has at least the eyes of animals represented in high relief, and may have a great deal of relief, standing out a quarter of an inch or more, from the general surface.

Most of the designs used on these Shang bronzes are conventionalized to a high degree, showing that the decorative art which they represent must have had a long history before these forms could be evolved. The animals most commonly represented are the dragon, cicada, ox or water-buffalo, sheep, a snake or worm, and birds. These animals are found in many forms, variations, and combinations.

The so-called *t'ao-t'ieh*, or 'ogre mask,' has presented one of the major problems of ancient Chinese art. The Chinese phrase literally means 'glutton,' and it has been suggested that this symbol was placed on so many bronzes as a warning against over-indulgence. This explanation seems completely inadequate.

PLATE VI

A BRONZE LIBATION CUP, *CHÜEH*, OF SHANG TYPE

THE SINGLE INSCRIBED CHARACTER BENEATH THE HANDLE IS ONLY HALF VISIBLE IN THE ILLUSTRATION. BELOW : AN ENLARGEMENT OF THE DECORATION, SHOWING A TYPICAL SHANG *T'AO-T'IEH* OR 'OGRE MASK.'

In a Private Collection, reproduced by kind permission.

As to its origin, Rostovtzeff says: 'It has the form of an animal mask, consisting of a pair of eyes, a pair of ears, two horns, and a crest. The animal certainly belongs to the family of felines. I have not the slightest doubt that what is meant is a horned lion-griffon, the most popular animal in the Persian art.'[2] The fact is, however, that the motifs found on Shang bronzes which are lumped together under the term *t'ao-t'ieh* are exceedingly various. Some have heads like those of dragons, others like oxen, others like sheep. Furthermore, there is only one mention of a creature named *t'ao-t'ieh* in all the thirteen Classics or in all of early Chinese literature, in so far as I am able to learn after a good deal of investigation. In this one case it refers to a man, not by any stretch of the imagination to anything like these beasts. By the next time it occurs in the literature, almost a thousand years after the Shang period, it is a conventional name for a decorative motif used on bronzes. The chances are that the Shang designers had never heard of a *t'ao-t'ieh*. But this need not prevent us from using it as a convenient term, if we remember that it means a type of motif and not a variety of animal.

A typical Shang *t'ao-t'ieh* is pictured in Plate VI. The peculiarity of the *t'ao-t'ieh* is that it represents the head of the animal as if it were split in two, and the severed halves laid out on either side, being joined in the middle on a line with the nose. The lower jaw is represented twice, once on each side. This makes possible a peculiar effect which is employed in a very large proportion of Shang bronzes, which is illustrated in Plate VI. If we take the two halves together they give a perfectly good *t'ao-t'ieh*, seen from the front, with two eyes, two ears, two horns, and the lower jaw represented twice. But let the reader cover the right-hand half of the picture with his hand. The left half is now a dragon, seen from the side. What was the ear before has now become the body of the dragon. In the upper left-hand corner we see what is the end of the ear of the *t'ao-t'ieh* or the tail of the dragon. But it is also the head and beak of a bird, and if we look at it from this point of view we can trace the body, feet, and claws of the bird. This same design is reproduced, with slight variations, on a number of Shang vessels. There are various other combinations of animals. Sometimes each horn of a *t'ao-t'ieh* is a small dragon, while the *t'ao-t'ieh* itself is a part of some much larger beast. This trick of combining several animals inextricably is a favourite device of the Shang designers.

We find a few, but not many, naturalistic animals on the Shang bronzes. Some of the birds are fairly realistic. The dragons on the bronze chariot fittings pictured in Plate XIV are conventionalized in a sense, but they suggest the freedom and grace of some such animal as the lizard. Charging elephants pictured on one Shang *ku* are quite realistic, their trunks having merely been lengthened to aid in the decorative effect.

Various other animals, chiefly conventionalized, are found on these bronzes; some of them the Chinese themselves do not attempt to name, being content to call them 'beasts.' Sometimes whole vessels are cast in the form of such animals. Vessels in the form of the owl have been found. More universally characteristic than any animal are the so-called 'thunder pattern' and 'cloud pattern.' Both of these consist of whorls, and opinions differ as to how they should be distinguished. According to one view the round whorl is the cloud pattern, while the square variety is the thunder pattern. These occur in ancient characters standing for rain and allied phenomena. It will be seen in the illustrations of Shang vessels that hardly one is without one or the other of these. Sometimes they constitute the sole decoration, except perhaps for a pair of eyes in high relief. These eyes, which are usually raised and which have a very prominent place in Shang decoration, probably have some religious or magical significance.

There is little doubt that every one of the designs found on these vessels was placed there because of some part which it played in the beliefs and practices of the time. Much of this symbolism is lost to us to-day. We know from the oracle bones, however, that the dragon had his place in the religion even of that early time. The wind, which was a deity, is pictured on the oracle inscriptions as a bird, and this may be the meaning of some of the birds found on bronzes.

A typical *ku* is decorated with *t'ao-t'ieh* of which the halves become dragons, cicadas, snakes or worms, and the thunder and cloud patterns. It would not be difficult to interpret every element in this design as figuring in religious or magical rites designed to secure good crops. The *t'ao-t'ieh* is perhaps intended to represent an ox, and cattle were important food animals and were used to sacrifice to the gods. We know how important rain was to the Shang people, from the fact that the bone inscriptions record many prayers for it; the meaning of the thunder and cloud symbols is obvious. We find a dragon deity on the oracle bones, and the dragon in later times has always been closely associated with clouds and often figures as the maker of rain. The dragon is said sometimes to take on the form of a water-snake. This leaves only the cicada; the noise made by this insect is heard continually during the summer in north China, making it a very apt symbol of the time when the crops are maturing. If we take all these things together it appears that such a vessel would have had special virtues as an adjunct of ceremonies designed to aid the securing of an abundant harvest. Whether this interpretation of these designs be the correct one it is impossible to say, but at least it gives some idea of what their significance may have been.

These vessels occur in a great number of shapes and styles. Here we can consider only the three which are most common: those known as the *ku*, the *chüeh*, and the *ting*. A typical Shang *ku* 觚 is illustrated in Plate IX. The ridges of metal running partially up the sides are usual, but not always present. This vessel was apparently used for men to drink from, and also had a part in religious ceremonies in which the worshippers no doubt drank with the deities. This is an extremely graceful shape. One *ku* which I measured held almost a pint of liquid when brimful. They must have made noble beakers.

The *chüeh* 爵 is said to have been used to drink from, but if so it must have been very inconvenient. As will be seen from the illustration in Plate VI, it had a small spout which would have made it necessary for the drinker rather to pour the liquor down his throat than to really drink. It was used for pouring libations to the gods, a function for which the spout is suited admirably. Several rather questionable statements are made about this vessel. It is said to have been an inverted helmet in origin, which had the legs and 'horns' added. The word *chüeh* is used as the name of a sort of bird; from this comes the story told by an ancient dictionary, which says that the vessel was made in birdlike form because the cry of this bird is '*chieh, chieh, tsu, tsu*'—'temperance, temperance, enough, enough.' These syllables were supposed to be called to the mind of the drinker by the goblet. This story has more of colour than of plausibility. There is some connection between the vessel and a bird, but what it is has not yet been satisfactorily explained. These vessels are commonly small. A Chinese work states their capacity to be one-third that of the *ku*; actually both of these vessels vary in size, but that ratio is not far from an average. The form of the *chüeh* is very graceful, though inferior and clumsy specimens are occasionally seen. The *chüeh* and the *ku* are the commonest Shang vessels found to-day.

After these the *ting* 鼎 is the form which most usually comes to light. I have seen a Shang *ting* hardly more than three inches high and not more than two inches in diameter, looking like a child's toy yet perfectly executed; some which have been found stand more than two feet high. The regulation *ting* has three solid legs, spaced evenly, supporting a bowl which may vary almost indefinitely in size and shape, surmounted by two handles or 'ears.' The name of this vessel is sometimes translated, not very lucidly, as 'tripod.' A Chou *ting* is illustrated in Plate XV. To be a truly typical *ting* a vessel should have a smooth bottom, either flat or rounded. Not a few of them, however, have bottoms which bulge as they approach each leg, thus showing that they are in reality *li* of which the legs have become almost but not quite solid. This is important because it shows the influence on bronze patterns of the *li* shape, which we have seen to be a development of the north-eastern area which moved westward. The *ting* is a vessel of various uses, but it seems probable that the finest of the Shang ones must have been used for sacrificial purposes or at least reserved for use at very important feasts.

Aside from ceremonial vessels the bronze objects which show Shang craftsmanship at its best are weapons. On the heads of dagger-axes, true battle-axes, and occasionally of lances we find patterns worthy of admiration. These are quite frequently inlaid with turquoise. Here the original weapons must have been more beautiful than the relics as we have them now. The greenish patina affords little contrast for the turquoise, but the original golden-brown of the bronze, gemmed with its mosaic of polished blue-green stone, must have been worthy of the trappings of a king. Such weapons may have been used more frequently on parade than on the battle-field. The same is probably true of such fine bronze chariot-fittings as those pictured in Plate XIV.

An impressive testimonial to the quality of the work of those who fashioned the Shang bronzes is the prices which they command at the present day. These prices are not merely due to antiquity, nor are they due to rarity. As a matter of fact, so many of them have flooded the market of recent years that prices have been cut to a fraction of their former level. Yet single pieces have sold recently for as much as sixty thousand dollars, U.S. currency. Such prices are not paid merely because these bronzes are authentic relics of the Shang dynasty; I have bought a double handful of perfectly authentic relics of the Shang dynasty, including some very attractive carved bone, for ten Mexican dollars. Such prices are paid for these bronzes because it is realized that they represent artistic craftsmanship at its highest and that, being among the finest productions of the human race, they have an unchanging intrinsic value. Japanese captains of industry are buying ancient Chinese bronzes as rapidly as they come on the market, paying the highest prices for them. A foreign diplomat recently suggested that they are doing this because they fear another inflation, and wish to put their money into things which, having permanent value, will not be affected by it.

The place of origin of the technique of bronze casting as we find it in China and of the designs found on Chinese bronzes are two questions which have been discussed exhaustively. They are related, but it will be more convenient for us to deal with the latter question, concerning decoration, first.

These motifs are among the finest decorative art produced by man; there is no difference of opinion about that. The Shang dragons, for instance, are sophisticated enough to fit into the most modernistic setting without any note of discord. Shang bronzes in general exhibit a degree of good taste, coupled with great strength of design, which is rarely to be met with in any art; they are definitely superior to the average of the bronzes of the later Chou period. Since by formula all good things in China are declared to have been imported from the West, this art has of course been said to be borrowed. Such statements have usually been made with extremely little basis of evidence. It has often been said that the Chinese got their various types of animal decoration from the Scythians, who lived in south Russia and western Asia. But those who make this claim admittedly do so on the basis of Scythian materials not older than the seventh century B.C.; the Shang materials antedate them by at least four centuries. Furthermore, the Scythian art has little resemblance to most of the early Chinese design. Of this Rostovtzeff says: 'Some features, of course, are common to the Chinese and the Scythian animal style: *the use of beaks and eyes as ornaments, the treatment of the extremities in a conventional way, the filling of the surface on the animals' bodies with figures of other animals*, the animal palmettes [italics mine]. However, it seems as if all these features, which are common to the Scythian and to the Chinese animal style, appeared in the Chinese art comparatively late.'[3] He dates them as being borrowed from the Scythians almost as late as the end of the Chou or the beginning of the Han dynasty. But we have seen that the characteristics described in the above italics are really typical of Shang bronzes which were being cast perhaps a round millennium before this date.

As a matter of fact the data which are given by those who seek to prove that the Chinese borrowed their designs from the Scythians do much to indicate the exact opposite. It is pointed out that many Chinese articles are found in Scythian remains of the sixth and fifth centuries B.C., showing that there was much contact with China. They point out similarities between Scythian and Chinese art at that period. Since we know these indicated characteristics to be ancient possessions of the Chinese, the conclusion that it was the Scythians who borrowed is hard to avoid. A typical Scythian standard top published by Rostovtzeff bears an eye which is beyond all doubt a Chinese conventionalized eye, represented in a manner which is peculiar and unmistakable. With the finding of more and more of naturalistic animals represented on Shang bronzes some European experts are now coming to the opinion that even the typical naturalistic Scythian animal style was borrowed from China. Time and further study alone can confirm this.

One trouble with Occidental opinions concerning the origin of Chinese bronze designs has been that Western students have often had little sound way of dating early Chinese bronzes. One European scholar of great reputation refers, for instance, to a certain well-known bronze as 'late Chou.' He does not mention, probably he does not know, that the bronze has an inscription. Yet that inscription is one hundred and fifty-one characters long. It contains the names of kings which help to date the bronze. The very form of the characters in that inscription is such that any person accustomed to reading bronze inscriptions, seeing no more than three words of it, knows at once that it is not 'late Chou.' The bronze in question is some five hundred years older than his statement would make it.

No close parallels to Shang bronze design have yet been proved to exist anywhere in the world. Exhaustive canvass of the motifs used to the west of China, made by those eager to prove that this art was imported, has yielded little or no results. Many have thought that there are resemblances between this art and designs found in the islands of the Pacific and in America, particularly among the Aztecs and Mayas. As to that I am unable to say. But there are, as I have been able to determine, certain specific similarities between the decorative art of the Shangs and of certain tribes of American Indians belonging to the group known to American anthropologists as the North-west Coast Indians. One of these resemblances is in the manner in which animal motifs are combined; another is the tendency to use isolated eyes as decorative motifs. More specifically, these North American Indians use the technique of representing an animal as if it were split and laid flat in two joined halves, just as we have seen was done in Shang design; these are the only two areas in the world in which this technique is used, according to my present information. This may be another indication of the Pacific affinities of Shang civilization.

The technique of making and casting bronze was almost certainly not invented in China. The bronze products of the Shangs were as fine as have ever been made anywhere; the development and perfecting of their processes must have required many centuries if not millennia. Yet in the remains of the black pottery culture at Anyang, directly under the Shang remains, not one trace of bronze has been found. If the bronze technique had been developed in China, it would certainly have diffused to some extent; at the very least we ought to find a few weapons captured from enemies, or arrowheads shot by them, in the black pottery remains. But we do not.

How long this technique had been in China before the beginning of our Great City Shang is a question which is difficult to answer. Many archæologists think that we must suppose a long period of development in China before this time. A contrary theory holds that bronze casting was brought into China as a completely developed technique by invaders from the West, who settled down as a predatory aristocracy living on the toil of the Neolithic aborigines, and that these invaders were the ancestors of the Chinese aristocracy of the historic period. It has already been pointed out that the use, by the aristocracy, of forms for their sacrificial vessels which we know to have long been typical of the pottery vessels of north-eastern China and no other region, makes this unlikely. Likewise the fact that the designs found upon these vessels are not known except in China militates against such a theory.

Those who hold that the culture of the Chinese Bronze Age was wholly intrusive, introduced by invaders, usually suppose that it entered by the northern steppe route, which comes down through Kansu Province. We have already seen that painted pottery, apparently an intrusion from the West, arrived first and lingered longest in Kansu. And it may well be that the bronze technique came to China through that region. The archæology of prehistoric Kansu is relatively well known, through the work of Andersson. He excavated a great many sites, both of villages and burial-grounds, covering periods ranging from the Neolithic down to sites of the Iron Age, which he has tentatively dated at from 600 to 100 B.C., half a millennium later than Shang times. In no one of these, not even the latest, was one single piece comparable to a Shang bronze found. There were bronzes, but they were uniformly small objects, such as buttons and small representations of animals; not one of them bore anything to compare with Shang bronze decoration.

The rudiments of the technique of making and casting bronze were almost undoubtedly learned by the Chinese from elsewhere. Its fundamentals were possibly, even probably, learned from the West. But it was raised, in the hands of the Shang people, to a degree of technical excellence which it has seldom attained anywhere in human history. It was cast in forms which are typically Chinese, and decorated with motifs which had their roots deep in the life and thought of the Chinese people. In this sense, then, the bronze casting of the Shangs cannot be called entirely a borrowed art.

Many of the Shang bronzes contain no inscriptions whatever. Those which are inscribed have one, two, or three characters, seldom more. These are very often characters which cannot be 'read,' that is to say, they do not occur as words in the oracle inscriptions or in the other Chinese literature we know. They are commonly supposed to be the names of clans, families, or individuals to whom the bronzes originally belonged; there can be little doubt that this is the correct explanation. Longer inscriptions no doubt occur, but they are rare. It used to be thought that every bronze containing such a name as 'Father Monday' or 'Father Thursday' was Shang, but we now know that this method of naming ancestors persisted well down into the Chou period. There are a few bronze inscriptions of some twenty or more characters, whose characters show a very close resemblance to those found on the oracle bones, and whose content seems to indicate that they are Shang. Scholars generally agree that these may be Shang, but that there are not more than ten inscriptions of such length which can be so dated. The *Discourses of the States* quotes a long inscription which is attributed to a Shang bronze, but there are both historical and grammatical reasons for doubting that this inscription could really have appeared on a Shang vessel.

Our discussion of bronzes has been limited, in this chapter, to objects coming from Anyang, for the reason that this site is the only one which can be certainly dated, at present, as of the Shang period. But there are many pieces of bronze, excavated scientifically and otherwise in widely scattered localities, which bear close resemblance to the Shang bronzes. In my experience, such pieces are usually of a quality inferior to that of the best which were produced at Anyang. Yet there is no reason to believe that the art of bronze casting, in Shang times, was or could have been limited to Anyang. The time will surely come when we shall be able to identify objects from many sites contemporary with the Great City Shang. But as yet we lack definite criteria for such identification.

CHAPTER VIII

SHANG SOCIETY

THE most obvious relation between human beings is that of kinship. Parents and children, brothers and sisters, even remote cousins are bound together by definite physical facts which have none of the provisional and arbitrary character which is present in the relations between friend and friend, ruler and follower, servant and master. The human infant is peculiarly helpless, and the child depends upon its parents for a number of years. All this has the effect of building up, in the family group, a similarity of tastes and habits, a feeling of thorough mutual acquaintance, and a loyalty which it is difficult for any other group to rival.

In China this family solidarity was augmented by the institution of ancestor-worship. One's ancestors were very powerful, able to send prosperity in all things if they liked, to punish even with death if it so pleased them. It was very necessary, then, to keep them in good humour. How could one do that? By sacrificing to them, of course. But their sacrifices were not a matter of the lifetime of one individual. They persisted as long, and only as long, as the family persisted. Anything which increased the power and prestige of the family as a whole was also a service to the ancestors, since it made more certain the continuation of their sacrifices. Conversely, any injury to the family was a direct injury to the ancestors. The motives, then, to family loyalty were very strong indeed. If one aided his family, even at the expense of his life, he would at least be sure of an honoured place at the sacrifices of his descendants. But if he played the traitor to his family his lot was a hard one.

Least of all, he would be despised by all men. Worse than this, he was an enemy of the spirits, and knew not when or how their terrible vengeance might descend. Worst of all, if his crime caused the extinction of his line, he might become the most unfortunate of beings—a hungry ghost, wandering about, solitary, unhonoured, without sacrifices.

It is not surprising that family solidarity and family loyalties have played, and still play, so large a part in Chinese affairs. This is one of the principal factors in Chinese history, and we shall have to go into it, later, in detail. As to the importance of the family in Shang times we have little information, and that little is gained largely by inference. It is an important fact that the rulers were all of one family, inheritance being a matter of blood relationship. While we think of this as being customary, it is by no means universal. Not only ancient and modern republics, but also various tribes of more or less primitive men have selected and still do select their rulers on the basis of other qualifications, without regard to relationship to a former ruler. From this one fact alone, then, we may be sure that the family was an institution of no little importance among the Shang people.

When the modern Chinese speaks of his 'family' he is ordinarily referring to a great many more people than is the Occidental who uses the same phrase. By 'my family' we usually mean not more than the people who live together in one household, that is, two parents and their children. The Chinese may mean all of the people having the same surname as his own—thousands or millions! At the least he will mean those living together in one household, and these will often be several tens of people belonging to several generations. What was the family organization of the Shangs we do not know, but we have good reason to suppose that it went beyond the mere group of a man and a woman and their children. For the kingship did not descend directly from father to son, but rather from elder brother to younger brother. Only, it would seem, if there were no younger brothers left did the throne pass on to a son.

This means that there must have been a recognition of very close relationship between the various sons of a king, even after they were grown to manhood and had wives and children of their own. There was almost undoubtedly a royal clan which exercised a general control of affairs and took a leading part in matters of administration and war.

Some interpreters have held that the family organization and even the sexual morality of the Shang people were very loose indeed. They go so far as to say that men of that time knew the identity of their mothers, but not of their fathers. While we have very little evidence on the question, one way or another, it is certainly not adequate to support this supposition. It is based chiefly on the fact that we may find a king offering sacrifices to his 'several fathers'; from this it is deduced that several men were married to one or more women in common, or perhaps did not bother to marry at all. But it is far more likely that the term 'father' was merely used to include paternal uncles, as we may find it so used in later Chinese. As to allegations of sexual promiscuity, these are made concerning many peoples who prove, on closer examination, to have a code which is very strict indeed.

Ancestor-worship is further evidence of the importance of the family in Shang times. Unfortunately the oracle bones give us little information about any but the royal family. But when we find ancestor-worship developed into such an elaborate institution in Shang times, and when we know that it was general a few centuries later, it is hard to believe that it was limited to the kings in the Shang period. At the least, the most important of the non-royal families must have sacrificed to the spirits of their forebears.

It is not possible to say definitely whether or not there was a definite aristocratic class, composed of a few of the most powerful clans, which exercised an autocratic sway over the rest of

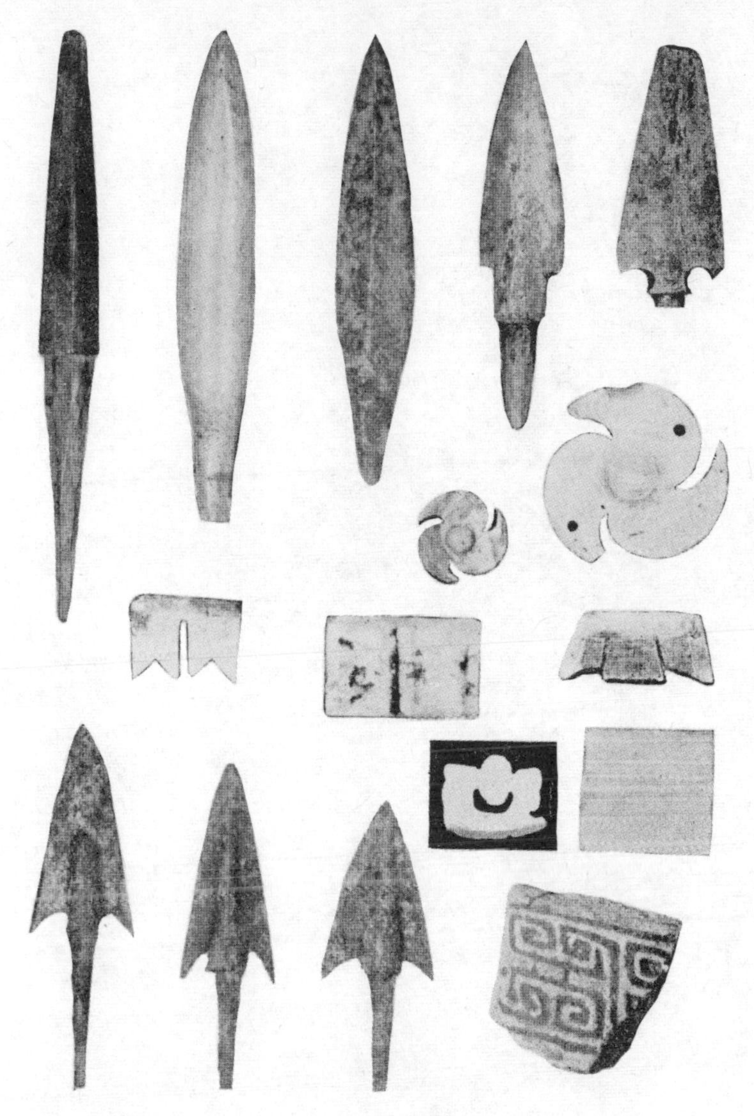

PLATE VII

EXAMPLES OF SHANG HANDICRAFT

THE ARROWHEADS IN THE UPPER ROW ARE CARVED FROM BONE; THOSE BELOW ARE BRONZE. THE POTSHERD IN THE LOWER RIGHT-HAND CORNER IS AN EXAMPLE OF THE 'WHITE POTTERY' MADE FROM PORCELAIN CLAY AND USED FOR CEREMONIAL PURPOSES. THE REMAINDER ARE SMALL DECORATIVE OBJECTS CARVED FROM MOTHER-OF-PEARL AND STONE.

In a Private Collection, reproduced by kind permission.

the people. It is quite possible that this was the case. Some believe that this ruling group were invaders, perhaps from the West, of different race from the Chinese and possessing a higher culture. Some of the reasons why this is improbable have already been discussed; we shall consider others when we come to examine the social organization of Chou times.

It is possible that officials, such as the diviners and priests, and envoys sent on diplomatic missions, were sometimes drawn from such an aristocracy. On the other hand, there is some reason for believing that they may originally have been rather humble servants of the royal household, whose positions gradually increased in power and dignity.

Various terms meaning 'servant' and 'slave' occur on the oracle bones. One of these is exceedingly interesting. It consists, simply and solely, of a picture of a human eye. This was a complete mystery until, very recently, a Chinese scholar published a brilliant piece of research unravelling its history. What made the puzzle even more baffling was the fact that the common meaning of this term, in later China, is 'minister,' as in 'Prime Minister.' The connection lies, first, in the fact that the picture of an eye was used as an abbreviation for 'head.' Thus we find that in drawing a horse or a tiger they sometimes drew merely the body of the animal, topping it with an eye to stand for the head. In counting the captives taken in battle the ancient Chinese spoke of 'so many head,' exactly as we speak of 'a hundred head of cattle.' But instead of writing head they abbreviated, and wrote the eye. This eye thus came to mean 'captive,' and then, because captives became slaves, 'slave.' But the further transition to 'minister' is interesting. The 'captive' became the slave or servant of his master. Gradually he or his descendants became loyal to the master and his family, and came to be looked upon as retainers or vassals who served of their own free will, and who were proud of their service. Finally we find it used of the chief followers of the king, that is, his ministers.

The history of this character suggests a whole cycle of social evolution, from a time when the strong dominate, plunder, and enslave the weak down to a period when titles and relationships, originally established by force, become the constitutional backbone of an orderly society based on mutual tolerance and mutual respect of rights and duties. Already in Shang times this character was sometimes used to mean an official of some sort, but we still find it also used in its more original sense of servant or even slave.

The female equivalent of this character was *ch'ieh*, the word now commonly used to mean 'concubine.' These, we may suppose, were female prisoners of war. They, like the men, were enslaved, and put to work at labour of various sorts. Even in early Chou times the *ch'ieh* is not always a concubine in the modern sense. She is a female slave, practically without rights or privileges, in some cases at least quite clearly a female serf. As such she may have had a husband, who was a male slave. Her master had sexual rights over her if he cared to exercise them, but probably he usually did not, except in the case of the most attractive women. These were taken into his household, put at lighter tasks, and actually came to fill the place of secondary wives. Gradually they and their children acquired rights and privileges, and the institution of concubinage developed.

One Chinese scholar says that all slaves were tattooed on the forehead, presumably to make it more difficult for them to escape. This is not certain. Just what was the status and treatment of servants and slaves in the Shang period we do not know, but they cannot all have been treated with excessive cruelty. For we know that they were often employed as troops in warfare, and they could hardly have been depended upon to fight if they had been smarting under rank mistreatment.

The position of women of the upper classes was probably good. Former queens were sacrificed to, independently as well as in company with their husbands. We find occasional records of divination on behalf of women. Polygamy was probably practised, but with moderation. The oracle bones tell us of one king with three wives, two with two, and twenty-six with only one. Perhaps these, like some later Chinese kings, preferred peace to a harem.

Altogether we have very little information concerning social organization in Shang times. On the other hand, we have a great deal of information, on this point, from a period a few centuries later. It is quite probable that conditions in the earlier period were essentially like those of the later; we might, then, present a picture of Shang society consisting of conjectures drawn from Chou conditions. But it has seemed better simply to present what few facts there are, and to allow the reader, when he comes to the Chou material, to make his own conjectures about the Shang period for himself.

CHAPTER IX

THE SHANG STATE

THE Great City Shang was, as we know, a capital, the seat of a king. But how large was the territory ruled from this centre? Kings have ruled territories as large as Europe and as small as a single city. Chinese history will tell us, if we will believe it, that the Shang king ruled all the world—all of the world, that is, which counted; the Chinese world, and even the barbarians beyond, though some of these were at times rebellious. But this is certainly not true.

In considering the question of the size of the Shang territories we must consider, first of all, what an exceedingly difficult thing it is for one man or a group of men to exercise real control over a large number of other men and a large area of the earth's surface. A ruler sits in his capital and issues an order. It goes to its destination and is executed, miles away, even though it may affect adversely the property and even the lives of many men whom the ruler has never seen. We accept this as a commonplace, but actually it is not far short of a miracle.

If we speak in the most general terms there are two varieties of influence, and only two, which can hold men together, obedient to the commands of a single government. One of these is force, the other psychology. There have been few, if any examples, in the history of man, of governments based on pure force which lasted more than a few decades. Experience has proved, time and again, that it is not difficult to set out with an army and cut a swathe of conquest and plunder across almost any amount of territory. The terrible name of the invader induces many states and cities to submit without a struggle; the conquered will join the triumphant armies, eager to share the further spoils. But once let the career of conquests reach a halting-place and the 'empire' thus built falls apart like a rotten fabric, unless an unusual intelligence has knit it together, in the wake of the hosts, with stronger and more permanent ties based upon ideas rather than on force.

It is possible, of course, for a small group of men to keep a considerable number of their fellows, and a small section of territory, in subjection by sheer force. But to do this the ruling group must possess weapons with which one member of the ruling group can withstand a number of the ruled, and these weapons must be not easily available to and not easily used by the subjected people. Probably the best example of this was the medieval European knight, with his armour. Encased in his steel suit, astride his charger, he could withstand almost any number of peasants or footmen. The people, on the contrary, could not easily turn his weapons against him. Armour was made to fit the individual, and to fight in it and use the arms of the knight required years of training.

In China we do not find such weapons. Chariots were, to be sure, a possession of the aristocracy, but chariots could be stopped by the simple expedient of digging a ditch. The most effective weapon was the reflex bow, a weapon almost twice as powerful as the ordinary European or English bow, able to pierce almost any armour in existence even later than Shang times. This bow was of complicated construction, but its materials were available generally and it could not have been kept as a rigid monopoly of one class or one locality. These things being so, it would not have been easy for the men of the city of Shang to dominate a wide territory by sheer force. Any garrisons which they might have posted at various points would have been of little use unless they had consisted of a number of soldiers equal at least to a large fraction of the subject population; this would obviously have been impracticable. In fact, then, they would have had to depend chiefly on psychological factors for their control.

Forms of psychological control are many. One of the most frequent and most reliable is religion. As we shall see, this played a great part in later Chinese history, and it no doubt had its place in the Shang system of government. The people subject to the Shangs were probably told, from time to time, how very powerful the ancestors of the Shangs were, how much they could help those who were loyal to them and how terrible it would be to find oneself among their enemies. But this could not have been permanently effective. For the moment the Shangs were defeated in battle by one of their enemies this would have indicated to some subject group that the power of the Shang ancestors was on the decline, and that the time might be a good one to test the prowess of their own ancestors.

A psychological force which is perhaps even stronger than religion is the hope of gain. The ruler may hold this out to his subjects in any of a number of forms. The most difficult but perhaps the soundest form which such gain may take is that of peaceful, well-regulated government, guaranteeing protection both from invasion and civil war, allowing the individual, in return for the payment of moderate taxes, to pursue his livelihood in security. This was what the Roman Empire gave, for centuries, and its success is unparalleled, unless by China. But we can hardly suppose that the Shangs had this to offer. It would have required an efficiency of administration, both civil and military, which we cannot suppose that they possessed.

Still another method of administration is by means of money, sent out by the central government as pay to officials and soldiers stationed in remote districts. But what knowledge we have of the economics of Shang times does not encourage us to suppose that money and commodities were so fluid as to provide an easy basis for this type of control.

It is none of these, however, which has been considered to be the method by which the Shangs held control of their large territories. Their kingdom is supposed, rather, to have been based on feudalism. Fundamentally this is a system by which government is, as it were, 'farmed out.' The king gives a specific piece of territory to a noble, as his fief. The noble governs the territory and collects taxes virtually as he pleases; in return for his fief he is expected to render specific services, usually military, to his lord, and perhaps to deliver stated amounts of goods at stated periods. If the Shangs used the feudal system it is hard to believe that they could have exercised very complete control over a very large territory for a very long time, because experience all over the world has shown that feudalism is a very insecure foundation for a state. The people who are the subjects of the vassal are his men, not those of the king, and the vassal is always tempted to fight with the king to see if he cannot reverse their positions. A great authority on feudalism in medieval Europe has said that every European vassal had such a war with his superior at least once in his lifetime. If we look at China, in the time after the Shang period, we can see that feudalism never succeeded in holding any great portion of China together for very long. It may have seemed to, at the very beginning of the Chou period, but this was due to unusual conditions following the flush of new conquests. This is another story, as we shall see later.

It is improbable that there was a feudal system in Shang times. The Chous, who conquered the Shangs, copied their institutions in many respects, as we know. And while the Chous did have a feudal system, they seem to have developed it themselves, starting from simple beginnings incident to their conquests. We do have, on the oracle bones, titles of rulers which later find their place in the feudal hierarchy, as one which is translated 'marquis.' But we know that in early Chou, and probably in Shang times, this was simply a name for a ruler, whether feudal or otherwise. There were many rulers contemporary with the Shangs, and some of them were subject to the Shang kings. But in so far as we have evidence it seems that these rulers were not feudatories, established over their territories by the Shang kings, but rather territorial or tribal rulers of long standing reduced by conquest to the place of vassals. This is a common situation. Rostovtzeff says of the conquests of Sargon I, in Mesopotamia: 'These conquests were not followed by the creation of one great empire, governed from one centre and including various nations. Sumer and Akkad were not strong enough to effect this. The conquering kings were content if their neighbours merely confessed themselves defeated, the sign of defeat being a yearly tribute. . . . The kingdom of Sumer and Akkad was always a union of petty kingdoms controlled by the kings of the ruling race, never a centralized kingdom ruled by a single king and his officials.'[1] This would seem in general to describe the situation in the Shang state.

If this was the case it meant that the petty states in nominal subjection to them must be kept in constant fear of the military prowess of the Shangs, else they would be likely to renounce their allegiance. And the territories controlled would become larger and smaller, according to the ability and energy of the ruling king. This seems actually to have happened.

Let us return to the question with which this chapter began—what was the extent of the Shang territories? A little more than a hundred miles to the west of Anyang is the divide of the T'ai Hang mountains. Beginning just north of the Yellow River, on a line with a point about fifty miles south of Anyang, they run in a slanting direction, north and a little to the east, to a point more than a hundred miles to the north of Anyang. In this extent they are broken only by a few trails. Behind this north-western 'back-drop' to Anyang lies the valley of the Fên River, good agricultural country and one of the three important districts in ancient China. This is now the southern half of Shansi province. That the Shangs controlled this area seems improbable. It is not easily accessible from Anyang. We know that some of their most important enemies lay to the west, and the Fên valley is a very likely location for some of them.

Some eighty miles south of Anyang flowed the mighty Yellow River. Even in later times it provided a considerable obstacle to military operations, and we may doubt that Shang control extended very effectively to the south of it. Tentative identifications of places to which the oracle bones tell us that the Shang kings travelled include several just north of the Yellow River, but none, I believe, south of it. This Yellow River is as migratory a stream as can be imagined. As late as 1852 it suddenly shifted its bed, and the mouth by which it empties into the Pacific, a distance of two hundred and fifty miles to the northward. Where it was in Shang times is not easy to say, but it may have passed only about ten miles to the east of Anyang, running north-eastward. Whether it was there or not, there are parallel rivers in this district which would have made Shang control to the east for a distance of even a hundred miles very difficult. On the north-east there are plains running almost into Manchuria, but the fact of Shang enemies on the north and north-west makes it very uncertain that they controlled all of this area. Considering natural barriers and the slight testimony of the oracle bones I arrive at a figure of something like forty thousand square miles as the largest area over which the Shangs could have exercised very effective control. Perhaps this is no more than a personal impression; it is given for what it is worth. The area may have been much smaller than this; Chinese scholars, even archæologists, generally think that it was much larger.

Was there more than one 'king' in this ancient Chinese world? According to the orthodox tradition, even yet held to by many thoroughly 'modern' scholars, there was not. A late book of ritual quotes Confucius as having said, 'In the heavens there are not two suns; on earth there are not two kings.'[2] The character which we usually translate 'king' is pronounced *wang*; its earliest form on the oracle bones is . This portrays a man standing boldly erect, arms outstretched, with his feet planted firmly on the ground; he is holding a piece of territory—let him take it who can. This character seems better fitted to represent a small local military chieftain than to be the symbol of the head of a highly organized government ruling a large country. And it evidently did have the narrower sense originally.

On the oracle bones there are only two places, I believe, where kings other than those of the Shang line may be mentioned by that title. It may be that the Shangs, like the later Chou rulers, liked to preserve the fiction that their *wang* was the only one in existence. But we may be sure that there were other chiefs living in the Chinese world of that time who considered themselves quite as royal as the Shang kings.

Of the relations of these states with each other we know little except their wars. It may be that war was their chief relationship. We do know, however, that the Chou people were in close cultural contact with the Shangs during the last years of the Shang rule, just before the Chou conquest. And we occasionally find mention, on the oracle bones, of the sending of envoys to other states.

There is some evidence, which we should perhaps not take too seriously, which seems to indicate that these envoys, and some of the other officials used by the Shang kings in their government, were not members of the royal clan, and perhaps not members of the higher aristocracy at all. Rather they appear to be servants of the king raised from more humble positions to fill high offices. This is not surprising, and not without parallel elsewhere. Members of the king's own family, or high nobles, could not safely be entrusted with too much power. There was always the chance that they might turn it to their own ends, and if they were disloyal they could not be punished at will and without consequence. But a servant was in a different case. He could not easily usurp the place of his master, even if he had the power. And if he was disobedient he could be executed on the spot, with complete impunity; he had no powerful clan to exact vengeance.

Two Chinese words meaning 'minister' or 'official' are especially important in this connection. One of them, originally meaning 'eye,' then 'captive,' 'servant,' retainer,' and 'minister' in turn, we have already discussed. The other is pronounced *shih*. Several words, slightly differing in form, have descended from the one ancestral root; their meanings include 'use, employ, order, send, business, affairs, clerk, recorder, diviner, historian, history.' This word appears on the oracle bones as a verb meaning 'to send,' as a noun meaning 'affairs,' and as an official title. Its most usual form is . This was first interpreted as a right hand holding a pen laid across a book; from this it was supposed that the word originally meant 'a writer.' This would be a very dignified origin for the later meanings of this character. But it has since been pointed out, on the basis of what we know of the bone characters generally, that there is no book in this word. Furthermore, we occasionally find two hands rather than one grasping this object; if the object is a pen this is strange. I believe that nowhere in Chinese is a pen represented as being held in two hands. There is abundant evidence to show us what the held object is. The whole thing is a cup-shaped tally-holder, used for keeping score in an archery contest; the hand holding it is that of the score-keeper.

The bow and arrow was the chief offensive weapon of China until very recently. Archery contests were held, before the imperial court, as late as the present century, and we know that archery contests were very important in ancient times. They kept the score by means of wood or bamboo tallies, which were put into or taken out of a cup according to fixed rules. Naturally there had to be a servant specially appointed to keep this score, and he was the original *shih*. We find the score-keeper called by this name even in later Chou times. The servants designated for this service had to be intelligent, and their status was no doubt raised by the appointment. As writing developed there were other records to be kept, and the *shih* naturally took this duty upon himself. As these records developed into history, the *shih* became a historian. As learning developed, he became a scholar.

Gradually, by a process whose outlines we shall trace later, the scholar rose to a place of power and influence. He was given lands, a fief, in lieu of salary for his services. These things occurred, so far as we can tell, later than the Shang period, so that the earlier *shih* is the spiritual and professional rather than the physical ancestor of his powerful equivalent in later times. Gradually there developed the situation whereby, in later Chinese government, virtually all power rested in the hands of the scholars. But the position of these proud mandarins evolved, if we may trust our evidence, from the humble office of the score-keeper in the archery contest.

CHAPTER X

WAR

OCCIDENTALS commonly refer to the Chinese as a fundamentally pacific or even pacifistic people, and look upon their recent civil wars as an anomaly. The Chinese, who know their history better, know that it has had at least its due share of wars, as fierce and as destructive as any contemporary wars of other peoples. But although their past has been dotted with these conflicts the Chinese believe that there was a time, some thousands of years ago, when there was no war, when the benevolent rule of sages combined with the as yet uncorrupted goodness of men's hearts to produce a time of 'great peace.'

Scientific historians, Chinese and Western, possessing the new materials, know that this, too, is but a dream. As far back as we can trace Chinese civilization, that far can we trace war. Even where our record stops, the red trail of destruction seems to continue, pointing back to an earlier time of which we know nothing, yet indicating that then, too, there was the killing of man by man.

If we are to locate the traditional Chinese time of 'great peace' it must be far back in the Neolithic stage. Experts agree that in the earlier of the Neolithic sites known to us there is little evidence of warfare. But here we find a curious fact, contradicting the usual opinion that the Chinese are and have been pacifistic. Arrowheads were comparatively rare in Neolithic sites to the west, in Kansu, but in the east, in Honan and Shantung, the later 'cradle of Chinese culture,' they were comparatively plentiful. Not until we come to the 'black pottery culture' do we find walled towns in the Neolithic remains. But in this era we find that at Ch'êng Tzŭ Yai, in Shantung, there was a rectangular city surrounded by pounded earth walls which still, after the erosion of much more than three thousand years, stand ten feet high and more than thirty feet thick at the base; the total extent of these walls is well over a mile. A similar wall, of as yet undetermined dimensions, was found in the 'black pottery' Neolithic culture stratum at Anyang; arrow-heads accumulated against the base show that it was used as a defensive fortification. We have already seen that the black pottery people are in many respects the direct cultural ancestors of the Shangs, and thus of Chinese culture. Thus it appears that at an early date the inhabitants of the eastern, more 'Chinese' part of the north Chinese area were more warlike than were the inhabitants of the western area who were more likely to be influenced by peoples living farther to the west.

The bow was the chief offensive arm of Chinese warfare down to the advent of fire-arms from the West. Archery was still practised by the Manchu bannermen down to the end of the late dynasty. Periodic examinations were held in which candidates for military office shot at a target in the presence of the emperor. The candidate was mounted, and had to ride past the target at full speed, discharging three arrows as he rode. Many men who took part in those contests are still living in Peking, and the bows which were used in them are still to be purchased in 'curio' shops.

These bows are not to be dismissed lightly. Their power is very great, sometimes reaching a pull of one hundred and sixty pounds, which is far greater than that of the 'long-bow' of the English yeoman. This is what is known as the reflex or 'Tartar' bow. Its form is not that of a simple bow, but rather the complex shape which we call a 'cupid's bow.' It is made of flexible wood combined with horn and sinew. How early such bows were made we do not know, but the *Book of Poetry* says:

> 'Well fashioned is the horn bow,
> And swift is its recoil.'[1]

And elsewhere:

> 'How they draw their bows of horn!
> How their arrows whiz forth!'[2]

In both of these passages Legge translates 'bow adorned with horn,' but the meaning seems rather to be that of a bow of which horn is an integral part. The character which we find on the oracle bones for 'to shoot with bow and arrow' is ; all the forms known to me show this same, to us, peculiar shape, so that there is no question that the common bow of the Shangs was of this type. This being so, it seems probable that we must carry the horn and sinew construction back to that period, for it would not be easy to make such a bow of wood alone.

The pellet bow, using small missiles of stone or other material, was used by the Shangs, as is shown by the oracle inscriptions. This weapon functions much like the ordinary 'sling-shot' made by boys nowadays, with a forked stick and heavy rubber bands. Pellets of clay and stone, found in large numbers in Neolithic sites, may have been used in this weapon.

The reason for supposing that arrows were made of bamboo has already been discussed in connection with their manufacture. The representations of arrows on the Shang bone inscriptions make it clear that the shaft was feathered at the rear end.

Archery has always been important in Chinese culture as a practical skill and as an accomplishment of the gentleman. Archery and charioteering were two of the 'six arts' in which every aristocrat was tutored. Confucius himself considered it important enough to be worthy of discussion, as several passages in the *Analects* show. He said: 'In archery it is not going through the leather (of the target) which is the principal thing, because people's strength is not equal. This was the old way.'[3] One of his disciples said of him: 'The Master angled, but he did not use a net. He shot with the bow, but not at birds perching.'[4] Bronze inscriptions show that in early Chou times even the sons of kings, together with other young aristocrats, studied archery in schools established for the purpose. Kings themselves participated in archery contests as a form of recreation; these matches were followed by feasts and drinking bouts. The *I Li*, the oldest book of ritual preserved to us, gives the ceremonial to be observed in connection with the great formal archery contests which were participated in by high nobles and even by the king. These seem to have filled a place like that of the tournament in medieval Europe. The etiquette to be followed is prescribed even down to such details as the proper manner in which to pick up the bow and the arrows on various occasions.

Our direct evidence for these archery contests goes back no further than the early days of the Chou period, immediately after the Shang. But we have very good indirect evidence that such contests were held among the aristocrats of the Shang capital also. The reader will remember the word on the oracle bones which means 'official,' which has later come to mean 'historian,' and so forth, which originally meant 'one who holds the tally-cup,' that is, the score-keeper for the archery contest. Since this word came to be used for very important servants or even ministers of the king, we cannot but suppose that archery contests, much like those of later times, were held by the Shangs.

If these meetings were festive occasions, they had a grim background. The nobles themselves went to war, in Chou times and probably earlier, and the skill which meant no more than a cup of wine and a bit of chaffing at home meant life or death on the battle-field. The power of the ancient bow as a weapon may be gathered from the fact that in 575 B.C., two warriors, trying their skill before a battle, set up coats of armour made of leather possibly reinforced with wood, and succeeded in shooting a single arrow through seven thicknesses of armour. Another sort of evidence of the importance of the bow in warfare is the fact that rulers, rewarding military commanders for victories over their enemies, commonly presented them with a bow and arrows, lacquered with cinnabar or otherwise richly finished. A great number of bronze inscriptions tell us of these gifts, and they are also mentioned in the extant literature.

Among the weapons, beside arrow-heads, which have been excavated by the National Research Institute and by grave-robbers, the most numerous is the *kê*. The central weapon of the three illustrated in Plate XII is of this type. Since this peculiar weapon is pointed like a dagger but used as an axe, we may call it a 'dagger-axe.' The bronze heads of these weapons average about nine inches long. A wooden shaft was set at right angles to the blade, while the tang passed through the shaft. These weapons occur in various styles; some of them must have been fastened to the shaft with cord or wire, while others may have been secured by one or more rivets. Some of the dagger-axes which appear on the Peking market, the spoil of grave robbers but presumably from Anyang, are not of this type, but instead have a hole in the metal of the head in which the handle can be inserted, just as in our common woodman's axe (see the piece on the left in Plate XII). Regular battle-axes, sometimes with blades as much as seven inches broad, appear with both of these haftings. Such weapons must necessarily have been intended for close range fighting.

Some of the weapons of this type are so beautifully decorated as to cause us to doubt that they were intended to be used in actual combat. Sometimes we find an elaborate design on the very blade of the battle-axe itself. More often the decoration is limited to the part of the head opposite the blade; here we very frequently find a design or characters inlaid with many pieces of turquoise. If they were not designed for use in battle, the only alternative is that these weapons were made for purely ceremonial use. That there were such weapons is proved by the occasional appearance of dagger-axes in which the head is chiefly of bronze, but the actual blade is thin polished jade, so frail that any attempt to use the piece as a weapon must immediately ruin it. And some of the beautifully decorated *kê* made entirely of bronze are so thin as to be quite impractical. Nevertheless it is not the case, as has sometimes been stated, that none of the bronze weapons were intended for actual use. Some of them are quite plain, and there is no reason why even those intended for use should not have borne a certain amount of decoration. Often we find what appears to be the family name of the possessor of the weapon inscribed or inlaid upon it; certainly this is altogether appropriate on a weapon intended for actual use.

Heads of spears and lances have been found, in the Anyang excavations, made of stone, bone, and bronze. One type of lance, called *mao*, is of special interest. Its head is much like an ordinary spear head, but its handle, we are told, was sometimes as long as sixteen or even twenty feet. This weapon was commonly used by one of the soldiers riding in a chariot, and it is referred to in the literature as a weapon of defence. We can easily imagine that if a line of chariots, either holding its ground or retreating, projected a number of these lances like so many spikes of a picket fence, it would damp considerably the ardour of an attacking force, which might well hesitate to impale itself.

Prior to the sensational discoveries of May 1935, it was possible to say very little that was definite about the use of defensive armour in the Shang period. It seems to be the case that ancient Chinese armour was made for the most part out of leather, sometimes reinforced with wood. Such armour could be extremely resistant. Laufer describes 'an armour, in the form of a vest, made from extremely hard, heavy, tanned moose-skin of two thicknesses, the two layers being tightly pressed together,' made by Alaskan Indians. 'It is proof,' he says, 'against musket balls fired at a reasonable distance.'[5] How early plates of bone or of wood were sewed into the leather, to increase its invulnerability, is a debated point. We have seen that the *Tso Chuan* says that in 575 B.C. two officers set up coats of armour and shot at them with the bow, piercing seven plates or thicknesses at once.[6] The word used here to mean 'plate' includes the symbol for wood as an integral part, which makes it necessary to consider whether we must not date wooden slat armour from a period earlier than has been supposed. Andersson has even found in Chinese Neolithic remains bone splints which he thinks may well indicate the existence of bone slat armour at that early period.[7]

Wood and leather rot in the damp Chinese climate, so that it would be difficult to establish, by excavation, the date at which armour made of these substances was first used in China. Armour of some sort is mentioned constantly, as a commonplace, in the *Tso Chuan*, beginning with its very first year, 722 B.C. The *I Li*, earliest of the books of ritual, lists the helmet and armour among the instruments of war to be buried with every member of the aristocratic class.[8] In one document of the Shu Ching, called *The Harangue at Pî*, helmets and armour are mentioned;[9] this book probably comes from the Western Chou period, before 770 B.C., but it is not possible to date it exactly.

But none of this sheds much light on the question of armour in the Shang period. It was raised in an acute form by the appearance on the Peiping antique market, in 1934, of three bronze helmets, the spoil of grave-robbers and said unquestionably to emanate from Anyang. It was claimed that they were Shang, and their patination made this quite possible. They were shaped like a medieval casque, fitting well down over the back of the neck. One of them fitted perfectly the head of a rickshaw coolie on whom it was tried. Unfortunately their surfaces did not bear decoration, from which it might have been possible to date them. On the top of each was a short bronze tube, into which a plume or other decoration might have been fitted. This was interesting in connection with the character , which occurs several times on the oracle bones, showing a warrior holding a dagger-axe and wearing some sort of head-dress topped by a forked plume or similar decoration. Two of these helmets were acquired by the Nelson Gallery of Art, Kansas City, and I understand are now on exhibition there. At the time they turned up, when I examined them, it was my opinion that they were 'possibly Shang.' Metal armour at such a period was unheard of, of course, and at least one Occidental authority had gone so far as to say that metal was never used in Chinese armour until late Chou times at the earliest. But as opposed to this there existed an early Chou bronze inscription which seemed clearly to mention metal armour. This was the state of affairs in April 1935.

In May the excavators of the National Research Institute found more than seventy bronze helmets in one of the great Shang tombs at Anyang. That they were unquestionably Shang was shown not only by their location, but also by the fact that the surfaces of some were decorated with the typical designs found on Shang bronzes. Most of them were crushed, but two were almost perfect. The shape was essentially like that of the two helmets acquired by the Nelson Gallery. These helmets were excavated just after my most recent visit to Anyang so that I did not see them myself. I am indebted for their description to Mr. Liang Ssŭ-yung.

This find puts an entirely new complexion on the whole question of ancient Chinese armour. While it was limited to helmets, it would seem that once the principle of using metal for protection in battle was understood the making of breastplates and so forth could have followed without difficulty. Probably one of the principal reasons why more metal armour has not been found is the comparative scarcity of metal. It is significant that while the number of helmets found buried in this one tomb is great, it was probably the tomb of a king.

The shield has not been identified, I believe, on the oracle bones. It is mentioned, however, in the passage in the *I Li* mentioned above, in early bronze inscriptions, and frequently throughout the early literature. It is pictured in inscriptions on bronzes which probably date from the Shang period. As has been said, however, it is very difficult as yet to distinguish with certainty between Shang and early Chou bronzes, and I prefer not to use material drawn from inscriptions on bronzes which are supposedly Shang, but which have not been excavated scientifically.

In the fully historical period of Chinese antiquity, beginning with the eighth century B.C., the chariot occupied the entire centre of the stage in connection with war. The importance of states was measured by the number of war chariots they could muster—we read of 'a state of a hundred chariots' and 'states of a thousand chariots.' The chariot, drawn by horses, was used by the Shangs as early as the reign of Wu Ting (traditional date, 1324-1266 B.C.); this is proved by an inscription on one of the oracle bones which can be definitely dated in his reign. They probably had the chariot before this time. It does not appear that the chariot played so great a part in warfare, in the Shang period, as it did later. This is merely deduction from the fact that chariots are mentioned comparatively infrequently in the inscriptions; in all of the published material, well over ten thousand pieces, the character for 'chariot' appears only some nine times. It is not to be assumed from this that chariots were very rare, for there is little reason why they should be mentioned. But where in Chou times they speak of raising so many hundred chariots for a military expedition, leaving the footmen accompanying each chariot to be implied, the oracle inscriptions speak only of raising so many thousand men.

More than four hundred pieces of bronze chariot-fittings were excavated by the National Research Institute at Anyang in a single pit which was used, it has been suggested, for a great 'chariot sacrifice.' Remarkably enough, no horses were buried together with the chariots. Mr. Liang Ssŭ-yung believes that the chariots were taken apart before being buried. A large number of horse skeletons have also been excavated at Anyang; in a single pit there were thirty-eight of them, probably buried as a sacrifice. These horses wore bridles, beautifully studded with a great many decorated bronze 'buttons'; these are still in place, tracing the lines of the straps composing the bridle. In their mouths are snaffle bits, very modern in appearance.

That the Shangs drove at least two horses in a team we can tell from the pictograph for 'chariot.' In Chou literature the teams referred to consist of four horses, but in a Chou tomb twelve chariots were found with seventy-two horses, which would mean six horses to each chariot. It has been suggested that the four-horse chariot was introduced into China by Western people, rather than invented in China. But we have very good evidence that the Chinese chariot was first driven with two horses, and that the team was gradually enlarged to four on Chinese soil. On the Shang bones and in bronze inscriptions the pictograph for 'chariot' shows a pole projecting from the body which is crossed by a beam to which are attached two fork-shaped yokes, for two horses. The character retained this form even after four horses were regularly driven. The reason for this is that the other two horses were not yoked like the centre pair, but attached by loose traces, apparently to the chariot directly. The two loosely hitched outside horses were called 'the two third horses,' a name which seems strange enough until one realizes its history. This term comes, I suggest, from the fact that at the time when only two horses were used to pull the chariot it was sometimes necessary to add a third horse to help to pull it out of mud, or over especially difficult terrain. There was no place to yoke this horse, so it had to be put on loose traces. One can see extra draft animals, usually donkeys, added on loose traces to help to pull carts in Peking at the present time, every day in the year. Later, two of these animals were added, one on each side, and finally the regular team came to consist of four horses hitched in this manner. But each of the extra horses was still called a 'third horse.' This term, which is thoroughly Chinese in the character and not of foreign derivation, would never have been used unless the transition from two to four horses had taken place within the sphere of Chinese culture. As we have seen, the horse was known in north-eastern China as early as late Neolithic times. Vehicles were first drawn by two horses, and later the four-horse team was evolved in China by a process parallel to that which took place in Europe, rather than borrowed from it, as has been held previously. After all, this development is a simple and a logical one, which could easily have happened more than once.

It is not possible at this time to say at what point in this development the Shangs stood. They may have driven only two horses; this was apparently done at times even in the Chou period. The Shangs may have used four or even six horses on occasion. We cannot tell. A hunting scene on a bronze cast long after the end of the Shang period shows two horses controlled by four reins. The Chous used an ingenious system of six reins to drive four horses.

From the pictographs on the oracle bones we can learn a good deal about the Shang chariot. It must have had much resemblance, in its general structure, to the familiar chariots of the Greeks and Romans. It was two-wheeled, and the wheels were not solid disks but genuine wheels with spokes. A crude scratching of a chariot on an excavated piece of Shang pottery shows seventeen spokes in one wheel and nineteen in the other. Excavated wheels of Chou chariots show eighteen spokes. Some of the Shang chariots, with their bronze fittings, must have been truly magnificent. Such fittings as those shown in Plate XIV are done with a finish, extending to the smallest detail, which is not surpassed by the appointments of the finest custom-built automobile.

Getting these chariots about over the country must have constituted a good deal of a problem at times. There is no record of paved roads, and in war they could not even keep to the roads at all times. The *Discourses of the States* tells us that even as late as the sixth century B.C., officials travelling were accompanied by an extra chariot to carry them in case of a breakdown. The *Tso Chuan*, in telling of a great battle between the states of Chin and Ch'u, in 597 B.C., gives this story: '(In the flight) a chariot belonging to Chin sank in a rut, and could not proceed. A man of Ch'u told the occupant to take out the frame for weapons. After this it advanced a little, and then the horses wanted to turn. The same man advised his enemy to take out the large flagstaff and lay it crosswise. When this was done the carriage was able to get out of the hole. Its occupant turned around and said to the enemy who had assisted him, "We have not had so much experience as the men of your great state in the art of fleeing!" '[10]

The ordinary Chou chariot carried three men, the driver, a spearman or lancer, and an archer. But there were also chariots which functioned as 'flagships' as it were, carrying the commander of the army or of a unit of it, and a drum and flag by which the signals to advance or retreat were given. These commanding chariots, carrying perhaps a duke or even a king, were naturally focal points of a battle. They directed the fighting, and much of the fighting had as its purpose the disabling of these key chariots and the capture of the rulers who rode in them. In the description of a battle the names of the occupants of the commanding chariots are ordinarily stated first, just as the names of champions on either side are given in descriptions of medieval European battles. The following brief description from the *Tso Chuan* of a battle which took place in 589 B.C., gives a picture of the part played by the commanding chariot:

'Both the armies were drawn up in array at Kan. Ping Hsia acted as charioteer to the Marquis of Ch'i, while Fêng Ch'ou-fu acted as spearman on the right. On the side of the State of Chin, Hsieh Chang drove the chariot of K'ê, Chêng Ch'iu-huan being his spearman on the right. The Marquis of Ch'i said: "Let me exterminate those and I will then take my breakfast." Having said this he galloped forward, not waiting to have his horses clad in armour. K'ê (of Chin) was wounded by an arrow, until the blood ran to his shoes, but he never let the sound of the drum cease. (But finally) he said: "I am in pain." Hsieh Chang said: "At the first encounter an arrow pierced my hand, going up to the wrist. I broke it off and continued my driving, till the left wheel is stained a deep vermilion. How could I dare to speak of my pain? Do you, Sir, bear yours." Huan said, "From the first encounter, whenever we have come to difficult ground, I have got down and pushed the chariot along. You, Sir, have not known of it because of your distress." Hsieh Chang said: "The eyes and ears of the army are on our flag and drum. It will advance or retire as this chariot does. While there is one man left to direct this chariot we may achieve success. Why should you for your pain cause the failure of our ruler's great enterprise? When one dons his armour and takes his weapons, it is to go in the way of death; you are not in pain to death—strive to combat it." With this, he held the reins with his left hand, and with his right took the drumstick and beat the drum. The horses dashed on, unable to stop, and the army followed. The army of Ch'i was defeated decisively.'[11]

While we do not know how chariots were employed in battle in Shang times there is some reason for supposing that the number of chariots was smaller in proportion to the number of soldiers than was the case later. If this is so they were probably used chiefly to transport commanders and to direct the fighting. In so far as one can tell from the accounts the chariot itself was never a very formidable engine of war. It is true that there is some intimation that charges were led by a group of them. But the bow and arrow can be discharged from the ground as well as from a chariot, and with surer aim. The spear or lance carried by the chariot was no doubt formidable, but it could, after all, menace only one man at a time. The frequency with which important nobles were wounded and even killed in battle shows that chariots afforded no certain protection to their occupants. Even in Chou times their chief use was probably in the fact that they gave to the commanders a mobile point of vantage from which to direct operations. They did also constitute a force which could be moved quickly to any point in the field at which a special emergency might arise.

Soldiers are usually referred to on the oracle bones simply as so many 'men.' Typical inscriptions are: 'It is asked, if three thousand men are raised and ordered to attack the country of X, will the expedition receive assistance?' or 'It is asked, shall we not raise five thousand men?' Occasionally, however, we have such questions as: 'It is asked, shall the many *ch'ên* not be ordered to attack the country of X?' This word *ch'ên* is the one which, as we have already seen, is really a pictograph of an eye, but came to mean captive, then slave or servant, then officer. It is difficult to say whether, in this place, it means slave or officer. We sometimes have still another word used in just such divinations; this word has been translated as 'servant,' but the translation is not certainly correct.

If we may judge from the early Chou situation, most of the members of the aristocracy were military officers when the need arose, and kept themselves constantly drilled in the arts of war. Foot-soldiers, on the other hand, were largely drawn from the tillers of the soil, drafted for the occasion. The *Book of Poetry* is full of the laments of such men, taken from their families and sent away on campaigns which dragged out long beyond all expectation—while their families were in want, if not starving.

The armies of the Shang period were not very large, but

neither can they be considered extremely small for ancient times. The raising of three thousand men is mentioned frequently. Five thousand occurs less often. There is no mention, so far as I know, of raising less than a thousand men for a military expedition.

Just how these campaigns were organized and carried out we do not know. In preparation for them there was much divining, asking the spirits about every aspect of the matter. If their enemies raided them they told the spirits about it, and asked what to do. If an enemy was approaching they asked the spirits whether to go forth and meet him in battle; the alternative, one supposes, was to allow him to approach their fortifications before joining the issue. In asking about setting forth to battle they often added the question: 'Will we receive aid?' meaning, apparently, the aid of the spirits. They also asked about sending out letters to vassals or allies, directing their co-operation in the campaign.

Deliberate campaigns of size seem to have been launched in the spring, just as is the case in China to-day. But there were sporadic engagements necessitated by encroachments on their borders and surprise raids by their enemies. The oracle bones preserve for us records of many announcements, coming in from the borders, telling of this or that foray or trespass by enemy or neighbouring states. Frequently they tell of the capture of a few men, often between ten and twenty, in such an attack. These unfortunates were doubtless carried off to a fate of either slavery or sacrifice. One of the words used to mean 'a surprise attack' is a pictograph of a drum; this is used because the warning was given, when such an attack was discovered, by beating an alarm drum. There were night attacks. We have one piece of bone which was used for several nights in immediate succession to ask always the same question: 'This night will the camp be free from misfortunes, peaceful?'

There is one story concerning a descendant of the Shangs which must be mentioned in any discussion of their warfare. It concerns Duke Hsiang of Sung. Sung was the state in which descendants of the Shang kings continued to rule, as vassals of the Chou house, after the latter had conquered Shang. The incident, which is given as having occurred in 638 B.C., is as follows:

'An army of Ch'u invaded Sung. . . . The Duke of Sung was going to fight, but his Minister of War remonstrated strongly with him, saying, "Heaven has long abandoned the House of Shang. Your Grace may wish to raise it again, but such an attempt would be unpardonable." The Duke, however, would not listen to him, and in the eleventh month, on the day Chi Ssŭ, the first day of the moon, he fought with the army of Ch'u by the Hung River. The men of Sung were all drawn up in battle array before the forces of Ch'u had finished crossing the river, and the Minister of War said to the Duke: "They are many and we are few. Pray let us attack them before they have all crossed over." The Duke replied: "It may not be done." After they had crossed over, but not yet formed their ranks, the Minister again asked leave to attack, but the Duke replied: "Not yet." Only after the enemy was fully prepared was the attack begun.

'The army of Sung suffered a disastrous defeat. The Duke himself was injured in the thigh, and his guards of the palace gates were all killed. The people of the state all blamed the Duke, but he said: "The superior man does not inflict a second wound, or take the grey-haired prisoner. When the ancients had their armies in the field they would not attack an enemy when he was in a defile. Though I am but the unworthy remnant of a fallen dynasty, I would not sound my drums to attack an unprepared enemy." '[12]

Are we to suppose, then, that in Shang times war was conducted on lines so chivalrous? Perhaps—but considering what the oracle bones tell us of surprise attacks and nocturnal raids I doubt it.

We know from the oracle bones that the chief enemies of

the Shangs were located in the north and west. The Chous, who finally conquered them, came from the west. When the Chou people succeeded to control of the Shang territory they had their chief difficulties, on the other hand, with tribes living in the south and the east. From this it has been supposed that the southern and eastern people were vassals or at least allies of the Shangs, for the same reason becoming bitter enemies of the Chous who conquered the Shangs. This is a possible explanation, but it is not the only one. The Shang capital and its environs could be reached by land from the north and west, and wars were to be expected in consequence. To the east and the south there were large rivers, which probably made the temptation to send raiding parties much less attractive to either side. It is quite possible that the Shangs and their southern and eastern neighbours kept the peace, most of the time, merely because they could not do otherwise without considerable difficulty. There is one bone inscription, however, which speaks of a raid from the south. Chinese literature preserves a tradition that the last king of the Shangs carried on a successful war with the tribes to the east, on the sea coast. The oracle bones have some inscriptions which may confirm this. If this is true it is possible that this same success so weakened his resources that it made the conquest by the Chous a much easier matter than it would otherwise have been.

CHAPTER XI

WRITING

CHINA has been much misunderstood and much misrepresented in the West. But no aspect of her culture has been less appreciated or more maligned than her system of writing. This is chiefly because it is radically different from the systems of writing to which we are accustomed.

Our own alphabet is believed to have begun with picture-writing. But at an early period the system was changed so that the symbols stood, not for objects or ideas, but for the sounds of the words used for those things. Thus a picture of a bee, for instance, might have been used to stand for the letter 'b,' or the sound which it represents. This is a change which took place in many languages. This same principle is used to some extent in Chinese, but this language has never made the change to become completely phonetic, or alphabetic. For this reason some linguists have supposed that Chinese is still the crude type of picture-writing that other languages were before they developed phonetic writing. One writer says: 'The Chinese system of writing, though it is still practised in the twentieth century, is in reality a semi-primitive system.'[1]

To say that such statements are absurd is to treat them mildly. Chinese is one of the most complete, complex, and sophisticated systems of writing known. Its development has not, it is true, followed the same lines followed in the development of most other languages. Man has not followed the same lines of evolution as those followed by the pigeon. But we do not consider the pigeon a better animal than man, merely because it can fly and we cannot. The pigeon has specialized on wings, man has specialized on developing his hands and his brain. We have specialized on the representation of sounds; the Chinese have specialized on making their writing so suggestive to the eye that it immediately calls up ideas and vivid pictures, without any interposition of sounds. Some linguists have supposed that the Chinese did not write phonetically because they were not intelligent enough to work out a completely phonetic system. Nothing could be farther from the truth. Even in Shang times the phonetic principle was known and used to some extent in Chinese writing. But the history of the language shows that when this principle threatened to usurp too large a place in the system it was deliberately rejected in favour of the ideographic one, not once but many times.

The origins of writing must always remain a mystery. We cannot, in the nature of the case, find documents telling us how the first man first happened to make the first crude start toward setting down his thoughts. But we do know that writing in many places grew out of the drawing of pictures, and we may be quite sure this was the case in China. Early man had a surprising amount of urge toward artistic expression, as European cave-drawings and American rock-carvings show. In China we find this expressed, in the early Neolithic period, by designs impressed in pottery and by a single sculptured animal found in a cave-deposit; in the later Neolithic we have beautifully painted pottery on which a few pictures of animals and a man occur. The Shang people, as we have seen, possessed a high degree of artistic taste and skill which was demonstrated in their pottery, their paintings, their carving on wood and bone, and above all, in their sculpture and bronzes.

The Shang people had a highly developed artistic sense, their writing is the earliest Chinese we know, and that writing contains many words which are obviously pictures of the objects they represent. But the writing of Shang times is not picture-writing, it is not crude, and it is not primitive. In fact, *every important principle of the formation of modern Chinese characters was already in use, to a greater or less degree, in the Chinese of the oracle bones, more than three thousand years ago.* This has been one of the most surprising revelations of the recent discoveries.

While the statement in italics is true, it can be misunderstood in two ways. In the first place, it is not to be supposed that Chinese writing has not changed, and changed profoundly, from Shang times to the present. Nothing could be farther from the truth. To take the one matter of size of vocabulary, the oracle bones are estimated to contain a maximum of two thousand five hundred different characters, while the Chinese vocabulary of to-day is estimated at around seventy thousand characters. Grammar and style have evolved to a point undreamed of in Shang times. The form of the characters themselves has so altered that the most learned Chinese scholar is usually unable to recognize the most familiar character on the oracle bones unless he has made a special study of archaic Chinese.

Secondly, it is not to be supposed that a lack of originality among the later Chinese is responsible for the fact that new characters formed since that time have been built on principles already in use in Shang times. This is so merely because the foundation principles of the language had been worked out, as completely as is possible, by that time. Unless it had branched out along an entirely new and divergent path, Chinese would logically have had to develop along the various lines which had already been begun. It was as unlikely that the Chinese would abandon those principles as it is unlikely that we shall abandon the Latin alphabet. We may modify details of the system, and alter the letters beyond recognition, but the system itself approaches perfection for our purposes. Such an approach to perfection for the purposes of Chinese had already been made by the writing system of the Shang period.

It is useless, then, to try to trace the beginnings of Chinese writing in the Shang materials. Archæologists are still searching for primitive Chinese, and it may be that they will find it. The chief fear is that it was written on perishable materials. At present we can only guess as to the early stages of this progress from pictures to literature, and the reader is competent to do his guessing for himself. One thing, however, we can say, and that is that religion must have played a considerable part in the development of Chinese writing. The Chinese had, and have, the idea that deities and the dead cannot, under most circumstances, be spoken to directly, that is, they do not ordinarily understand human speech. Various peoples pray, verbally, to their gods, but the Chinese write to them. The message is written on inflammable material and burned, and the smoke going to the heavens carries the message.

The *Discourses of the States*, an ancient work, tells us that on one occasion the spirits of two former rulers of the small state of Pao presented themselves, in the form of two dragons, at the court of one of the Hsia kings (Hsia is the name of the dynasty supposed to have preceded the Shangs). This king seems to have been a churlish fellow where ghosts were concerned, for he immediately wanted to put them to death. He divined, however, and was told that this would be unwise. It was finally decided that the best thing to do would be to secure some of the dragons' spittle and store it away. A cloth was spread to receive it, but it was still necessary to ask the dragons to spit. Being spirits, they could not be spoken to. But they could read, and as soon as a letter was written and shown to them they spat and disappeared.

Whenever a noble set out from his capital on any business, and when he returned, he made a full announcement of the matter to his ancestors in the ancestral temple. Some of these announcements are plainly stated to have been written; it is probable that all of them were. An interesting ceremony, of which we have no specific evidence for the Shang period, is that whereby treaties between states or rulers were solemnized. A sacrifice occupied the central place in this ritual; the blood of the sacrificed animal was used to seal the compact. It was smeared on the lips of each of the contracting parties and on each of three written copies of the treaty. A copy was taken by each of the parties concerned, and the third copy was buried with the victim (burial was one form of sacrifice), filed, as it were, with the spirits. They were expected to act as guarantors. 'Whoever shall violate this covenant,' we read in one such treaty, 'may the bright spirits destroy him, causing his armies to be defeated and his state to be lost to him utterly!'

There is abundant evidence that this custom of writing to the spirits was used in Shang times. We find many times on the oracle bones a character composed of a mouth and a book, which means 'to tell in writing,' and it is used in connection with communications directed to the spirits. To make this plain they sometimes add the character 'spirit' as a part of the word.

We know that the Shangs considered their ancestors and deities of supreme importance, and were very anxious that they should understand the needs and difficulties of their worshippers and help and advise them. Advice could be got from the spirits, as we know, by divination, which did not necessarily involve writing. But if the ancestors were to be told what their descendants wanted it was necessary to write to them. Here, then, was a powerful motive to the development and perfecting of a writing system. The Chinese of to-day bears many clear indications of the part played by religion in its development. An important word meaning 'to honour' or 'honourable' was originally a verb meaning 'to present wine to the spirits'; this term is frequently used in polite conversation at the present day. The character for 'blood' which is used, for instance, in modern medical books, shows a dish of blood set out, probably, for sacrificial purposes. The common word for liquor was originally a verb meaning 'to pour a libation.'

We might simply list the various principles on which the Chinese have formed their characters, but such lists have little interest unless they are well illustrated. Chinese writing has been represented as a mysterious, incomprehensible sort of system whose principles, even, could be grasped by the Occidental mind only after years of dry and unrewarding toil. It is proposed to allow the reader to judge of this for himself, and at the same time to give some idea of the principles of the language, by analysing a sentence of Chinese, word by word, and letting the reader read it for himself. It is proposed that the reader shall read the sentence which, in modern characters, is as follows:

臣	見	來	鳥	自	東	林	集	于	室
(The) servant	saw	come	birds	from	(the) eastern	grove	(and) collect	on	(the) house.

The translation is, of course, literal; a complete translation would be: 'The servant saw birds come from the eastern grove and collect on the house.' The characters given above are in the form used to-day, but in every other respect this is an example of Shang dynasty Chinese. All of these words occur on the oracle bones, and the grammar is that of the bone inscriptions. This sentence itself does not occur on the bones, however. It was constructed to show as many as possible of the principles on which Chinese characters are based. Let us examine the characters one by one.

The first is now pronounced *ch'ên*. It was originally a single human eye, written thus . This pictograph of an eye came to be used, it will be recalled, to represent a head, as a matter of economy. When captives were taken in war they were called so many 'heads,' as we speak of 'a hundred head of cattle.' But this eye came to be used here also instead of the word for 'head,' so that we have the word for 'captive' written with this eye; when used in this sense the eye is usually turned to stand on its corner, thus . Since captives were often enslaved this word developed to mean, successively, 'slave,' 'servant,' 'retainer,' and finally 'minister of state,' in the sense that the ministers are the servants of the king. Even in Shang times this word had developed to be an official title, but it continued to be used to mean 'servant.' The modern form, , resembles closely the second ancient form, where the eye stands on its side.

The second character also contains an eye. It is pronounced *chien*. Its form on the oracle bones is . The portion of the character below the eye is the body of a man; he is facing to the left, with his arms extended in front of him. This, then, is a pictograph of a man whose head is 'all eye'; it came to be specialized as meaning 'to see.' In the modern form the eye has again been tilted to a vertical position, and the man's body has dwindled to what looks like two legs, giving the form 見.

In translating our sentence this word was rendered as 'saw,' although actually there is no sign of the past tense. In modern Chinese the tense is often unexpressed if it is sufficiently clear from the context; if not, a word is added to show the tense, as we say 'did see.' The Chinese of the oracle bones did not, so far as we know, have these auxiliary words to show tense. One specified 'to-day,' 'formerly,' 'to-morrow,' and so forth, to show whether an action was present, past, or future. But we must remember that the oracle bones were not the only Chinese writing which there was at that time, and that, on the bone inscriptions, we cannot expect to find the most complicated of expressions. The formulæ used in connection with divination were highly technical, brief, concise to the last degree, just like our weather reports or stock market quotations. If a king asked the spirits: 'Will I receive a good harvest?' all that had to be written was: 'I receive harvest?' It is obvious that the tense is future; the king is not asking whether he is receiving, or has received, a harvest. But we cannot suppose that all of the writing of the Shangs was as brief and technical as this.

The third character demonstrates the principle of 'phonetic loan.' It is pronounced *lai*. It is a drawing,  , of a variety of growing grain; the roots, leaves, and drooping ears are plain. We find it as a part of other characters having to do with grain. But the present meaning of this character is 'to come.' It happened that when they wanted to write the word 'to come,' there was no character for it. But there was a character for this kind of grain, and its name, when spoken, was very much like or perhaps identical with the sound of the verb 'come.' This character was 'borrowed,' therefore, to stand for this verb, much as we might draw a picture of a saw to stand for the past tense of the verb 'to see.' Finally, this character was used so much in its borrowed sense that it lost the meaning of 'grain' altogether, another character taking the place it originally filled. Had this principle been used widely and without opposition Chinese might have become completely phonetic and even alphabetic. The modern form of the character *lai*, 來, differs very little from that used in Shang times.

The fourth character, pronounced *niao*, is a perfect example of the masterly way in which the Shang scribes often reduced their pictographs to the simplest possible forms, yet sacrificed nothing of vivid pictorial suggestiveness. This character, which means 'bird,' is nothing more nor less than a picture. We sometimes, but rarely, find it in a complicated form like  . But they early reduced it to the form  . Here we have an unmistakable bird, but written with four strokes of the pen or stylus, much more quickly than we can write 'bird.' This form is not only economical; delicately carved on a smooth piece of tortoise-shell it is, I believe, among the most beautiful symbols to be found in any writing anywhere. The modern forms of this character cannot compare with the ancient from an artistic point of view. 隹 is more like the abbreviated form, but the form most used at present to mean 'bird' in a general sense is 鳥.

In the translation this character was rendered as 'birds,' although the text contains no sign of the plural. But since they are said to 'collect' it is obvious that more than one bird is meant. If there were doubt as to the number any of various auxiliaries might be used to show that it was plural.

The fifth character, *tzŭ*, occurs on the oracle bones as . It is apparently a nose, and commonly means 'self'; a Chinese to-day, when speaking of himself, points to his nose. It is also commonly used as a preposition meaning 'from,' and this is its usual sense on the Shang bones. In the process of its conversion to an easily written modern form, 自, this character has changed considerably.

The sixth character, *tung*, appears on the bones in the form . This is composed of a tree, (roots as well as branches appear in this pictograph), with the sun behind it. This depicts the sun as it is just rising behind a tree, and this stands for the quarter of the sunrise, the east. The modern form is 東.

This character means 'east,' but in our sentence it is rendered as 'eastern.' This is because Chinese does not inflect its characters to distinguish them as nouns, adjectives, verbs, and so forth. This is a great convenience, and leads to confusion much less often than one might suppose. Auxiliary words can be used to make the parts of speech clear if they are needed.

The seventh character, *lin*, is composed of two trees, , and means 'grove' or 'forest.' The modern form is 林.

This character demonstrates the principle of simple addition of elements to form a new character. In the word meaning 'east,' it was necessary that the sun be depicted behind the tree; if it had been above or beside the tree the meaning would have been much less clear, if not lost entirely. But here the two trees could be one above the other, if that were more convenient; what is important is simply that the idea of 'more than one tree,' representing a grove or forest, be made clear. In this case we have simple duplication of the element. Frequently we have two different elements combined in this way. Thus the sun and the moon written together stand for one of the principal characteristics which they have in common, that is, 'brightness,' 'clarity.' But this meaning does not derive from the relative positions in which they appear in the character. Position is very important, however, in the next character.

The eighth character is pronounced *chi*. From its form on the bones, , the reader will at once recognize that it depicts a bird perching on a tree. But how does this convey the idea of 'collect'? Here we have an example of the far search which the student of Chinese etymology must sometimes make if he would find the original forms of the characters, which reveal the principles on which they were made. The original form of this character seems to have disappeared completely from all archaic inscriptions; oracle bones and bronzes, in so far as I am aware, know it not. But we find it preserved by one ancient dictionary, written shortly after the beginning of the Christian era. And this form is  , three birds perching on a tree. Here then, we have our clue. The habit of birds to 'flock together' is proverbial with us; the Chinese employed it to express the idea 'to collect,' 'to gather.' But to put three birds on the tree every time one wrote this common word took too much time; they abbreviated to the one bird, more than three thousand years ago. The modern form, 集, is a faithful reproduction, in the modern technique of writing, of the abbreviated form.

The ninth character is pronounced *yü*. It occurs in the bone inscriptions in a number of slightly different forms; a typical one is  . This word is a preposition meaning 'at.' A theory as to its origin was propounded nearly two thousand years ago, but it is not satisfactory. We have a number of pronouns, prepositions, and other words of this sort, which show that there was a long development of the art of writing before the earliest documents we have were produced. But as to the details of that development and the origins of many of these words we can only conjecture. The modern form of this preposition, 于, differs scarcely at all from the ancient form given above.

The tenth and last character in this sentence is pronounced *shih*; it means 'house' or 'building.' The Shang form was  . Here we have illustrated a new and important principle for the formation of characters. The dome-shaped outer line represents a house and, strictly speaking, it should be sufficient to convey that idea. But the Shang people had several words for various kinds of houses and buildings, and they wished it to be quite clear which word was meant. The sound of the word intended here was like the sound of the character which is drawn inside the house. What they did was to take the pictograph meaning 'house' and a character having a sound identical with or very similar to the ancient equivalent of *shih*, and combine them into a character which indicates 'a word meaning house and pronounced *shih*.' The modern form is composed of the modern equivalents of these two elements, 室 .

This principle is used a great deal in forming Chinese characters. One famous European scholar has gone so far as to assert that ninety per cent. of all Chinese characters are formed on this principle. I have carefully analysed, from this point of view, a number of specimen passages of Chinese taken from various periods, ancient and modern, and from various types of literature. The criterion used in the analysis was a dictionary composed by this same scholar. But the result showed that in Chinese as it is actually written decidedly less than one-half of the characters employed contain any phonetic element whatever.

We have now analysed each of the characters contained in our sentence. Altogether, in modern form, they read:

臣 見 來 鳥 自 東 林 集 于 室

It is suggested that the reader identify as many as he can, and try reading the sentence. The translation was given on page 163. If the reader succeeds, after merely reading over this brief discussion, in remembering the meaning of as many characters as it is hoped that he will, he may understand why the task of learning Chinese is not quite so difficult and not quite so dry as it is sometimes said to be. It is not to be supposed, of course, that all Chinese is as simple as this. The language has its difficulties, like any other. And those difficulties can be surmounted, like those of any other.

But we wander from our subject, which is not Chinese in

general but the Chinese writing of the Shang period. The similarity, in the case of the characters analysed, between the Shang forms and the modern forms is noteworthy. Not many systems of writing used more than three thousand years ago have survived and are in use to-day with so little fundamental alteration. The principles which we have seen illustrated in these characters are those upon which Chinese characters generally are constructed. Only one basic principle was not represented in our sentence. That is the principle of what we may call 'diagrammatic characters.' This is found, for instance, in the character meaning 'up, above, to ascend,' which we find in the bone inscriptions as , simply a horizontal line with a short horizontal line above it. In the character meaning 'below,' the short line is below the other.

While the Shang oracle bones do not give us the crude, original stages of the development of Chinese writing, they do give us a tremendous amount of information about that development. They give us forms of Chinese writing older than any known previously. Even more important, it is possible to trace the development of individual characters during the period represented by the bone inscriptions themselves, and that development was sometimes very great indeed. Characters which started as thoroughly pictorial became conventionalized almost beyond recognition. Some went through several changes of form in this brief time. It is evident that there were no dictionaries or 'copy-books' in those days. The scribes who carved the bone inscriptions followed a tradition, but they were free to make changes to suit themselves. The important thing was to express the idea; if that was done clearly, the form taken by that expression might vary considerably. We find, as has been mentioned, a word which means 'to tend animals,' which is commonly written as an ox beside which is a hand holding a staff. But we sometimes find, instead of the staff, a sort of brush with several small dots around it. One explanation makes the dots drops of water, so that the whole character

PLATE VIII

A CARVED BONE TROPHY, APPARENTLY OF THE SHANG PERIOD

THESE RUBBINGS SHOW ITS TWO FACES, ONE DECORATED AND THE OTHER INSCRIBED. THE INSCRIPTION RECORDS A ROYAL HUNTING EXPEDITION AFTER WHICH THE KING GAVE REWARDS WHICH ARE HERE COMMEMORATED. LENGTH, ELEVEN INCHES.

Reproduced by courtesy of Professor Shang Ch'êng-Tso.

depicts the washing of an ox. According to another the dots are flies, and the brush a flapper to scare them away. Such differences are sometimes found in the writing of the same period or even in the writing of the same man. Larger differences occur when we compare successive periods. At one time in the Shang period a definite fashion developed for writing in the style, long since abandoned, which had been used a century earlier.

The inscriptions on the oracle bones are not merely our sole remaining documents which were actually written during the Shang dynasty. They are also the only literature which has come down to us from that time. We have a number of books written just after the end of the Shang period which have been copied and re-copied, and have come down to the present time in what is substantially their original form. It used to be thought that a few of these dated from Shang times, but the research of the last few years has shown that this is not the case. A few poems do actually give us some of the ideas of the Shang people, since they were written by their descendants after the Chou conquest. As to the other books supposed to be Shang we can only conclude that they are forgeries of a later date. This is proved by their ideas, their language, and their style.

On the other hand, it is not true that the oracle bones were the only literature existing during Shang times. We know this for several reasons. In the first place we find in later Chinese literature dynastic lists of the Shang kings which agree to an astonishing degree with the information gleaned by archæology from the oracle inscriptions. And the books of early Chou times show an easy familiarity with the names and history of Shang kings which can only mean that the later writers knew Shang books which have since perished. Also we find in early Chou books a very high appreciation of the value of history. But the Chou people, who conquered the Shangs, were very largely barbarians, as we shall see. They had little or no tradition of a literature or a history of their own. Such an appreciation of history is most plausibly explained as having been taken over from the Shangs, who did keep historical records.

It may be said that this history could have been kept verbally, as oral tradition is handed down among many primitive peoples. It is true that the great works of Chinese literature have been memorized and recited orally by Chinese scholars even down to the present day. And if we look at peoples without writing, who transmit their literature in this fashion, we may suppose that this memorizing is a survival of a time when the Chinese could not write. But there is much evidence, into which we shall not go here, to indicate that the memorizing of books was a late rather than an early thing in China. Some two centuries before the Christian era the first Emperor of the Ch'in dynasty attempted to destroy most of the ancient books, and all but succeeded. A few years later there was a feverish activity to recover copies of these books, and at about the same time they became the centre of a phase of Confucianism which might almost be called a cult of books. As a result these ancient works were looked upon with especial veneration and were memorized, some of them for the first time.

But in Shang times there were written books, many of them. We know this from the occurrence on the oracle bones of the word 'book,' written . This character is still in daily use. The vertical lines are strips of wood or bamboo on which the characters were written in vertical columns. The horizontal lines joined by a loop represent a piece of cord with which the strips were tied together and kept in proper order. When not in use the whole 'volume' could be rolled up and laid away. Actual Chinese books of this variety, some two thousand years old, are still in existence, but we have none as old as Shang times.

It is sometimes said that the ancient Chinese must have written very little, because it is supposed that their method of writing was very slow and difficult. It has been thought that the use of the writing brush, dipped in ink, dates only from the Ch'in dynasty (221-207 B.C.), while before that time characters were scratched or carved on wood or bamboo. The new discoveries have given the death-blow to such theories. The writing-brush is clearly depicted on the bone inscriptions. Three pieces of bone and one piece of pottery have been excavated which bear characters which are not carved but written with ink and a brush. In fact, even the designs of the late Neolithic pottery are thought to have been painted with a brush.

Even before these discoveries, however, the use of the brush for writing was clearly evidenced in ancient literature. An early book of ritual tells us that for every funeral of even a very minor member of the aristocracy a silken banner was prepared, on which his name and other information was written. To write on a silken banner without using a brush and some type of ink or paint is almost impossible. Whether the men of Shang wrote books on rolls of silk as well as on their strips of wood we do not know, but this too was done at an early date.

It is sad to think of the literature which has undoubtedly perished at Anyang. If we had here the dry climate of Egypt there is no question that many a roll of bamboo tablets would have been recovered, each with its story to tell. For these people did not merely possess writing—they used it. If nothing else, the development of the language proves that. The simple needs of the oracle inscriptions do not call for the highly developed medium of expression which we find in them, nor would they ever have called it into being. Nor can we suppose that the knowledge of writing was limited to a few men, or to this one city. Even in Shang times the sending of letters from one place to another seems not to have been uncommon. In the conduct of war, for instance, reliance was not placed in verbal commands. Written orders were sent, to assure that there would be no mistake in carrying out the projected campaign.

CHAPTER XII

THE GODS OF SHANG

THOSE who generalize have labelled the Chinese as 'ancestor-worshippers.' While this cannot be taken without qualification, it strikes closer to the mark than do many such statements. It is true, of course, that China has the 'three religions' of Confucianism, Taoism, and Buddhism, but it is also true that the cult of ancestors has found a considerable place for itself in connection with each of these. Many have held that ancestor-worship is a comparatively late development in Chinese religion, which was originally concerned with nature powers such as mountains and streams, or was perhaps a pure monotheism. Recent discoveries fail utterly to support this contention. The farther back we go in our investigation of Chinese religion, the greater is the part played by ancestors.

Foreigners commenting on Chinese ancestor-worship sometimes go too far in either of two directions. On the one hand, they may depict it as a weird, mysterious, 'Oriental' practice which Occidentals can never understand. Again they tell us that it is nothing more than a form of paying respect to the dead, exactly as we hold funerals and put flowers and tombstones on our graves. The latter may be true for a few Chinese at the present day, but it is in no sense true of the attitude of the ancient Chinese nor of that of the great majority of the people to-day.

If we think of it as a mere putting of food instead of flowers on the grave, or before a tablet representing the ancestor in a temple, we shall quite fail to understand the vital motivation of ancestor-worship—the greatest force which has held the

Chinese people to traditional ways. The ancestor was no powerless corpse lying supine in the grave waiting for his descendant to pay respect to him or not, according to the descendant's whim. On the contrary, the ancestor's real power began when he died. For then he was transformed into a spirit, of powers undefined but vast. He was more or less vaguely dependent on his descendants for food, in the form of sacrifices, but he could very well see that these were forthcoming, or make his descendants wish that they had been.

The activities of these spirit ancestors are not altogether unlike those of the Greek gods. They were not, it seems, either omnipotent or omniscient, yet in practice they were very nearly so. Success in hunting, agriculture, war and other activities was theirs to give or to withhold. Famine, defeat, sickness and death were the penalties which they could and did hurl at any who had the temerity to displease them.

But we must not suppose that the attitude of the ancient Chinese toward their dead was wholly one of awe and fear. Nor can we accept the interpretation of sacrifice which would make it a simple 'bargain' with the spirits, to deliver so much in sacrifices in return for the delivery of so much in prosperity and other blessings. To be sure there was this aspect of the matter, just as there are those who contribute money to the religious enterprises of Christendom for the same reason. But there was also not a little of real devotion to the departed, and real grief at their death. Among the evidence for this is the Shang word meaning 'death,'  , a pictograph of a mourner kneeling with bowed head beside a corpse.

More than three hundred Shang tombs have been scientifically excavated at Anyang, in a single tremendous cemetery lying about a mile to the north of the Huan River, on the south bank of which the capital city was located. From these we can gain a good deal of information about burial customs. One curious fact is that more than forty of the skeletons were found lying face downward, extended prone. This burial position has been said to be unique in the world. Mr. Bishop tells me, however, that it is used at the present day by the sweeper caste in India, with the idea of keeping the ghost from walking.

No coffins have been found in these tombs, nor have they appeared, in fact, in any excavated Chinese burials until late Chou times. This does not necessarily mean that the coffin was never used, but its absence is certainly remarkable. There is some indication that the corpse was wrapped in matting before burial. We know that bronze objects buried with the dead were often wrapped first with matting and then with cloth, and it would not be remarkable if the dead were treated in the same way.

Objects buried with the dead varied according to the importance of the individual. In very small graves a single bronze dagger-axe, perhaps accompanied by pottery vessels, was sometimes buried. Other individuals, no doubt of high rank, were surrounded in the grave by an almost incredible profusion of beautiful bronze vessels. The great tombs, which were almost undoubtedly royal, have been looted of most of their contents, but from what remains we can tell that they must have been filled with such a wealth of objects as to make them veritable subterranean treasure-houses. White pottery vessels of almost incredible workmanship, large marble sculptures executed with tremendous labour and perfect technique, bronze sacrificial vessels as much as twenty inches in height, bronze helmets by the score and weapons by the hundred accompanied the Shang rulers to the grave.

In later times, articles buried with the dead in China have been such as were not of use to the living—objects crudely made, vessels deliberately fashioned with holes in their bottoms, and the like. It has been stated as a principle that objects buried in Chinese graves were always so. Recent excavation in Shang and early Chou tombs does not support this. The Shang people buried with their honoured dead objects in such quantity and of such quality as must have in some measure impoverished the living, especially when we consider that bronze was almost certainly scarce. They did not, of course, consider these things wasted. The help of the ancestors on the battlefield was considered far more valuable than the possession of a few extra weapons.

The Shangs did not bury their kings with such lavish expenditure of labour as the Egyptians put into their pyramids. At the same time, the construction of one of their royal tombs was no mean task. The beginning was the digging of a pit, in the case of the largest tomb forty-three feet deep and sixty-five feet square—large enough to contain a good-sized four-story building. Two of the five large tombs known were in the shape of a cross, rather than square. In the middle of each of the four sides a broad sloping stairway was constructed. The excavators have done their work carefully and one can still see the places in the earthen treads which were worn down by the feet of the labourers who built the tombs and carried their furniture down them, more than three thousand years ago. At the bottom of this pit a wooden tomb chamber was constructed, about ten feet high and a little smaller than the bottom of the pit itself. The walls of this chamber were decorated, in places with almost incredibly fine carving, in others with polychrome painted designs. Then the funeral was held, the body and other objects were put in place, and the whole excavation, every inch of the way to the surface, was filled with pounded earth. This last process alone must have required the labour of a small army of men for a long period. As will be discussed later, the funeral was probably accompanied by the sacrifice of many human beings. It was, altogether, a ceremony not unfitting the passing of a king, and the inauguration of a royal ancestral deity.

Once dead, one became a spirit. The Shangs had two words to designate such beings. One is , which resembles a man with a large head of rather fearful aspect; this word we might legitimately translate 'ghost.' We find it also as part of a word meaning 'to fear' or 'to respect.' This is written , a ghost holding a rod symbolizing his power to chastise those who displease him. The other word might properly be translated as 'spirit'; its form, , is something of an enigma. It may represent the spiritual forces streaming down from the heavens to men below. Whether or not this be the correct interpretation, we know that the spirits did live in the upper air, for they are spoken of in the oracle bones as descending, sending down blessings, and so forth.

If we may judge from the oracle bones the Shang people called upon their ancestors for aid, and sacrificed to them, more than all their other deities put together. But if we ask to what ancestors they sacrificed, we must limit our discussion to the royal family. There is little doubt that the high officials carried on worship of their ancestors, and it may be that this practice went all the way down to the common people. But the oracle bones, being produced almost if not quite exclusively for the king and his family, tell us little or nothing of the religion of anyone else. Forty-two male ancestors and brothers of male ancestors, belonging to twenty-six generations, are named on these bones as having been sacrificed to. The earlier of these are perhaps only mythical, but the later generations tally with Chinese history to a high degree of accuracy. Sacrifices were made by the kings to elder brothers who had died as well as to father, grandfather, and earlier ancestors. Ancestors who had never attained the throne were sacrificed to with the same ceremonies given to those who had reigned as king.

Different tendencies in sacrificing were followed in different periods. The king known as Wu Ting, supposed to have reigned from 1324 to 1266 B.C., took a great interest in his ancestors and in religious ritual. He sacrificed a very great deal to his ancestors of quite remote generations. Later kings preferred to expend their offerings, most of the time, in the service of more immediate ancestors. Wu Ting seems also to have taken a good deal of interest in his genealogy, and perhaps to have given new sacrificial names to some of his further ancestors.

Special names for the dead and for deities are known in various parts of the world. Not only is it considered disrespectful to call such beings by their personal names, but it is also thought that a magical power is associated with such names. Their being spoken might harm or anger the possessors. The Jews did not speak the real name of God. In ancient Egypt a mere mortal might compel a god to do his bidding, if he knew the god's secret name. So it is that in China the personal name of an emperor was taboo, and it was a criminal offence even to write a common word, such as 'black,' if it happened to be the name of an emperor of the ruling dynasty. Many an unfortunate Chinese has lost his life because he happened to write such a word, intentionally or unintentionally. This type of legally enforced taboo is later than the Shang dynasty, but even at that time the personal names of ancestors were not used in divining or in sacrificing to them.

Except for very remote ancestors, they were called by the name of a day of the week (the Shang 'week' had ten days). This is said to have been either the day on which they were born or on which they had died. To the name of the day there was added the relationship in which the ancestor stood to the descendant who was divining or sacrificing. Thus we find mention of 'Father Monday,' 'Mother Thursday,' 'Grandfather Tuesday,' and 'Elder Brother Saturday' in their Shang dynasty equivalents.

Former queens as well as kings were sacrificed to. We find three queens associated with the same Wu Ting mentioned above, and two queens mentioned with two other kings. But female ancestors were sacrificed to separately, also. Sometimes we find them supervising the most important matters, such as the harvest, but in general they occupy a subordinate position. There is a curious exception to this. When the Shangs divined about sacrificing to a king or queen, they did it on the day of the week used in his or her ceremonial name. But when a king and a queen were sacrificed to together, two such days were usually involved, and in this case not the man's but the woman's day was used.

The giving of children to women was the special business of female ancestors, if we may trust the very little evidence which comes down to us. We find one case in which a woman, petitioning for a son, even sacrifices a human being to one of the former queens.

Ancestors were not the only deities with whom the Shang people had relations, and to whom they offered sacrifices. Among the other powers mentioned we find the feminine element not lacking. The 'Dragon Woman' is a mysterious figure of whom we know little more than the name. The 'Eastern Mother' and the 'Western Mother' appear more frequently, but we hardly know more about them. We find sacrifices to East, West, and South, but not to the North—why, nobody knows. There is a 'Ruler of the (Four?) Quarters' who is mentioned not infrequently, whom it is thought well to feed with cattle and pigs.

Mountains and rivers are quite important in our later records of Chinese religion, but there is no mention of mountains as deities in these early materials, so far as I know. There is one reference to sacrificing to a river. History tells us that shortly before 1190 B.C. there was a drought so severe that the Huan River, beside the city of Shang, ceased to flow. One of the oracle bones records 'a burnt offering of four cattle to the source of the Huan River.'

The earth was sacrificed to. As we shall see in discussing the religious customs of Chou times, the earth was symbolized at a later period by a small mound. Such a mound was found in every village, as a local deity, and it made something of a centre of village life. This mound is represented by a word made up of 'earth' and 'spirit.' In Shang times it is the 'earth' symbol alone which we find referred to as a deity, yet the meaning is probably the same. Sometimes it is specified as 'the earth of the region.' In any case it is a sort of agricultural deity, probably as old as any Chinese religious idea we know. In later times we find mention of a 'Queen Earth,' reminding us of the Occidental 'Mother Earth' conception, but it is impossible to say whether the earlier deity was considered to be masculine or feminine.

No discussion of the nature powers which figure in Shang religion would be complete without mention of the wind. Sacrifices to propitiate the wind, made at Anyang, were peculiarly appropriate. The modern visitor to that region, blinded by a pitiless and incessant hail of dust and sand, with all of his exposed skin turned literally to the colour of the soil, and fairly blown off his feet, wishes fervently that he possessed a charm effective to quiet that energetic demon.

In addition to these fairly common denizens of the supernatural we find occasional reference to other and very puzzling individuals. Sometimes one hesitates even to venture a translation of their names. A 'Snake Spirit(?)' is one of these. Then there is the statement which we find added to questions on various topics, such as the declaration of war—'Below and Above agree,' or 'Below and Above do not agree.' What does it mean? We don't know. Perhaps it has reference to the spirits of the earth and of the heavens. Perhaps we have read the words wrongly, and it does not mean 'Below and Above' at all. Then there is 'King Wind,' perhaps the same as the wind without the title. And we have the 'Wind, the envoy of Ti,' or just the 'Envoy of Ti.'

This Ti is an important but puzzling deity. It is impossible to understand ancient Chinese religion unless we understand him, partially at least. He is referred to either as Ti or as Shang

Ti. The Shang simply means 'upper' or 'superior,' and Shang Ti is sometimes translated as 'the Ruler Above.' The term Shang Ti has been generally adopted by Protestant missionaries to translate the name of the Christian God; for more than three thousand years it has stood for one of the chief deities, or perhaps the chief deity, of the Chinese.

While the deity may be called either Ti or Shang Ti, Ti by itself has another meaning. Even in the Shang dynasty we find it used as a part of the name of certain kings. And for the last two thousand years and more Ti has been the official title of Chinese rulers; in this sense it is usually translated 'emperor.'

Many explanations, of great variety, have been given for the origin of the word Ti. We shall not try to go into all of them here. But there is one of these theories which, whether it be correct or not, is at least the most plausible one that offers. It was first propounded by Mr. James M. Menzies, a Canadian scholar who is one of the very few foreigners who have made real contributions to the study of the oracle bones.

According to this theory Ti was originally the name of a sacrifice. This statement is based on the fact that in Shang dynasty Chinese the word Ti is almost (sometimes quite) identical with another word, pronounced *liao*. This word *liao* is a pictograph of a bundle of wood, burning, ready to have an animal placed on it as a burnt offering; it means 'to present a burnt offering.' Since these words are so nearly alike in form, we have on the oracle bones such sentences as '*liao* (present as a burnt offering) five bulls to Ti,' with *liao* and Ti written identically. It is thought, then, that Ti was at first merely the name of a way of sacrificing to the ancestors or other deities, but that gradually men confused the sacrifice itself with the deity sacrificed to, and came to think of it as a separate deity.

This process whereby the human mind takes sacrificial techniques and thinks of them as deities can be illustrated elsewhere than in China. The Aryans of India first worshipped

PLATE IX

A RITUAL DRINKING-VESSEL, *KU*, OF SHANG TYPE. HEIGHT ABOUT TWELVE INCHES

Reproduced by courtesy of Mr. P. C. Huang.

gods who lived in the heavens. They sacrificed to these gods, pouring clarified butter into a sacrificial fire known as Agni. This sacrifice was accompanied by the recitation of a sacred formula, or Brahman. The entire ceremony caused the gods to grant to their worshippers the things which they desired. And for this the gods were praised. But later it was pointed out that after all there was no reason to praise the gods, for it was not they, but the sacrificial procedure which produced the blessings. In fact, it was the fire, Agni, which wafted the sacrifices to the heavens and forced the gods to give their worshippers what they wished. And so Agni came to be a high god. But finally it was said that all of these statements were wrong. It was really the sacred words, the Brahman, which were recited with the sacrifice, which gave it its effect, while all the other parts of the ceremony were merely incidental. And so Brahman came to be the highest deity, the original creator of the world.

With this in mind it is not hard to believe that the Chinese may have taken the name of a sacrifice and turned it into a god, Ti. But if we ask how this god was conceived by the men of the Shang dynasty we have a question not easy to answer. Since some of the Shang kings are called by such names as 'Ti I' and 'Ti Hsin,' it is said that 'Shang Ti' may be merely the 'Highest Ti,' that is, the first ancestor of the Shang kings. This is possible but not proved. Some say that Ti is a collective name for all of the royal ancestors. It may have been so in origin, but there is reason for doubting that it had this meaning when the oracle bones were written.

If we ask what Ti did for the Shang people we are on firmer ground. He was especially concerned with the making of war. When they divined about whether or not to make an attack on an enemy they frequently asked, 'Does Ti agree?' They apparently hesitated to go into battle unless they could feel sure that he was fighting with them. He was asked about the crops for the year. Ti had a good deal of control over rain.

On the oracle bones we read 'Will Ti decree rain sufficient for the year?' And he had the habit of sending down general good luck or misfortune, on occasion, as pleased him best. All these things, and others, he did. But in almost none of his activities did he have a monopoly. Ancestors and other deities had, at times, almost all the powers wielded by Ti.

Christian missionaries have long sought to show that the original religion of the Chinese was monotheism. For some time the task has been given up as hopeless. Now, as a result of the new discoveries, an attempt is again being made to show that the men of the Shang dynasty were originally monotheistic, worshipping Ti only. Whether this be true or not, it is quite certain that in the period we know they were by no means monotheistic. Their ancestors were god-like, if not gods, and wielded about the same power as that of Ti, in about the same manner in which he wielded his. In fact, there is some possibility that they are right who say that Ti himself was originally a deified ancestor, the progenitor of the Shang kings, and thus that every important god of the Shangs was an ancestor.

CHAPTER XIII

THE COUNSEL OF THE GODS

HOWEVER remote Chinese ancestor-worship may seem from our experience, it is not difficult for us to imagine the circumstances under which such a practice developed. Most of us have known one or more men or women, of age and experience, who have come to be indispensable to a group of people around them. Perhaps it is a grandfather or grandmother, to whom a whole family brings its troubles. It may be the leader of a political movement, or the guiding genius of a business. When such a person dies, he leaves behind a number of people who feel themselves 'at a loss,' without direction. This is a universal human experience; it happens to-day in New York, Paris, and London as it happened over three thousand years ago in China.

Even to-day, some people go to 'mediums' to get into touch with the dead, so that they may continue to receive the advice cut off by death. This too was done in ancient as in modern times, in all parts of the world. Just how the ancient Chinese came to work out their peculiar technique for communicating with the departed we do not know. It is probable that they had more than one method, even in Shang times; we know that the Chinese had 'mediums' and various methods of such conversation with the dead only a short time after the end of the Shang dynasty. But for us it is very fortunate that the Shang people had one method which employed writing on bone, because bone is one of the few materials able to survive, in the climate of north China, and preserve its record for our information.

Divination by means of cracks in bone produced by heat is

not limited to the Chinese, but it is doubtful that any other people has worked out such a refined technique for the purpose. It is interesting to note that this type of divination is carried on, in a crude form, by the Mongols at the present day. Mr. F. A. Larson, writing in 1930, says: 'Lamas have many ways in which they read the future. The most common is the use of the breast-bone of the sheep. The bone is cleaned and dried; then it is placed in a fire and burned well through. The fire produces different cracks and lines in the bone. From these lines the priest calculates an answer to whatever question may have been asked—whether it is safe to start on a journey, if a certain date is auspicious for a wedding, if a certain well will be a good place by which to pitch the yurta, and so on.'[1]

We have already seen that in the Neolithic black pottery culture divination was carried on by a method very similar to that of the Shang people. The Neolithic divination bones we know are scapulæ, chiefly of the ox. The Shangs divined with the shell, usually the under-shell or plastron, of the tortoise and the bones of the ox, usually the scapulæ or leg bones. But were these the bones of just any ox, whose meat had been used for roast beef? Or were they the bones of a bullock which had been specially prepared for communication with the gods by being sacrificed, and thus endowed with special spiritual powers? We cannot say. But as to the tortoise we have a little more information.

Tortoises figure prominently in Chinese mythology. Even to-day when one visits Chinese temples, and examines the stone tablets set up by various emperors and others in their court-yards, he frequently finds them resting on the backs of gigantic stone tortoises. Tortoises were regarded with considerable awe and veneration in ancient China, as an amusing story in the book of Chuang Tzŭ shows. Chuang Tzŭ was a Taoist philosopher of about the fourth century B.C., a mystic and a recluse. The prince of Ch'u, having heard that he was a wise man, sent two high officials to ask him to take charge of the administration of the state of Ch'u. They found him on the bank of a stream and made their proposal. Chuang Tzŭ went on fishing without turning his head. But he said, 'I have heard that in Ch'u there is a sacred tortoise which has been dead now some three thousand years. The prince keeps this tortoise carefully enclosed in a chest on the altar of his ancestral temple. Now would this tortoise rather be dead and venerated, or alive and wagging its tail in the mud?' The two officials had to admit that it would prefer to be wagging its tail in the mud.

'Begone!' cried Chuang Tzŭ. 'I too will wag my tail in the mud.'[2]

In ancient times the tortoise was an object of considerable value. In the *Book of Changes*, a work of about the end of the Shang period, we read of one worth ten *p'êng* or strings of cowries or shell money.[3] This is quite a large sum; the king, in rewarding his retainers for notable services, often gave less but seldom more than this amount. The tortoise which was worth so much is described as one which 'cannot be opposed'; its oracles, one supposes, were so unfailingly correct that they could not be questioned. We find large tortoises mentioned among the objects of tribute sent to the king.

That the tortoise shell was not considered merely a dead and passive piece of bone, used as a mere tool in divination, is indicated even by the oracle bones themselves, which say, 'It is asked, does the tortoise decree . . . ?'

The tortoises used seem all to be of one species, which has hitherto been unknown to science. It has been named, from the Anyang region, *Testudo Anyangensis*. Whether the species is extinct or still living is not yet known. Many of the tortoise-shells found have been quite large, more than a foot in length. It appears that the tortoises were sacrificed before being used for divination, and in this way brought into special relationship with the spirits. It is possible that the shell was still further consecrated by being smeared with the blood of a sacrificed bull.

Before being used the bones and shell, the latter in particular, went through a considerable process of preparation. All rough projections on the edge of the tortoise-shell were sawed off, and the whole circumference was filed and polished until it was regular, smooth, and rounded. The surface of the tortoise-shell, and of many of the bones, was polished to a sheen which still, after being buried in the ground for three thousand years, gleams like polished metal. The leg bones used were split so as to make small flat slips of bone. Finally, a number of pits, about three-quarters of an inch long and shaped like a football but narrower, were cut in the back of the bone. It was estimated in advance how many times the piece of bone or shell could be used for divination, and that number of pits was cut. On a large tortoise-shell there may be as many as seventy-two.

We have no record of the ceremonies which surrounded the actual divination. They were probably conducted in the ancestral temple, and when the question at stake was an important one, such as whether or not to launch an expedition of war, they must have been impressive. The divining was done, as a rule, by one of a small group of official diviners. In the time of Wu Ting, for instance, there were nine of these men whom we know by name. The king seems to have done his own divining at some times and under some circumstances; the latest kings of the dynasty, in particular, seem to have preferred to conduct this important matter themselves.

Essentially the process of using the bone or shell for divination was one in which the application of heat produced a T-shaped crack, of variable size and shape. From these variations the oracle was read. Figure 2 is a diagram showing how these cracks were produced. The oval-shaped pit of which the two ends are A and A′ did not extend quite through to the surface of the bone, but it left the bone very thin in the middle of the oval. Any application of heat, then, would produce a crack from A to A′ and beyond more readily than elsewhere, and it was this crack which formed the head of the T. The heat was not applied in the centre, but to one side or the other. It has been suggested that a piece of burning charcoal was placed on the bone for this purpose, but this could hardly have given enough heat; probably a red-hot bronze point was pressed down at the proper place. In Figure 2 the black disk at B represents the charred spot produced by this application of heat. Wherever the point was applied, it produced two cracks, which intersected at the centre of the pit, at C. One crack was from A to A′, running through C; the other was from C through the point of the application of heat, in this case B, and beyond.

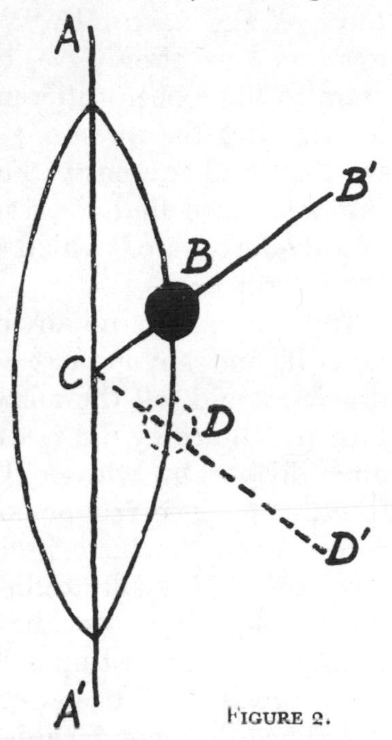

FIGURE 2.

We do not know how the answer to the question was read from these cracks. So far, studies of the bones in the attempt to reveal this have failed. But no such studies have been carried out on a very extensive scale, I believe, and they may yet succeed. We have descriptions of the method of interpreting these cracks, written many centuries later, but they are too elaborate. One of them tells us that there are no less than twelve hundred indications to be read from these two lines. There was certainly no such refinement of the matter in Shang times, as we know from the fact that the very terms used in the elaborate later formulæ were unknown to the Shangs.

Fundamentally there were two answers, 'yes' and 'no,' or 'fortunate' and 'unfortunate.' If it was asked, for instance, 'Shall I send out an army to oppose the attacking force of the enemy?' the answer was either affirmative or negative; it was not necessary to wait for the enemy to scale the walls while the diviner used calculus to plot the result. That there were only two basic answers is shown by the frequent occurrence of divination in pairs. Thus we find the question, 'Will it rain to-day?' and next to it, 'Will it not rain to-day?' Although the answers were of only two types, affirmative and negative, there seem to have been different degrees of the affirmative type, at least. After the question, 'Will there be a good wheat crop?' we may find the entry 'Fortunate,' indicating that there will. But again we find, on rare occasions, 'Greatly fortunate' or 'Vastly fortunate,' which one would suppose to indicate still better crops.

It is unusual to find any indication of the answer. The diviner himself, and anyone else who might be concerned with these oracles, could tell the answer from the formation of the cracks directly. But they did not throw these bones away immediately after divination, without keeping any account of whether the forecasts were correct or not. In a few cases we have the results recorded on the bone itself, as, 'Will it rain to-night?' and a later entry, 'It really didn't rain.' A later Chinese volume on divination tells us that the chief diviner kept a record of all his prophecies, and cast up at the end of the year to see how much of the time he had been right and how often mistaken. Whether the Shang diviners did this we do not know, but the excavators report that they have found the divination bones used during one year stored away together. In any case the record of the Shang diviners must have been satisfactory, for they seem to have held office for a long time. Two of them that we know of served under two successive kings.

Did these diviners themselves have any active part in producing the answer given by the bone or shell? Could they manipulate the oracle? I believe they could. If we consider that there were only two fundamental answers given, 'yes' or 'no,' and that the whole reply was read from a T-shaped crack, it is probable that the direction taken by the crack running out to the side, either horizontal or sloping upward or downward, was a deciding factor. If so the diviner could certainly influence the result. Let us look again at Figure 2. We have seen that when the heat is applied at B, the crack will run from C through B. But suppose instead that the heat is applied at the point indicated by the dotted circle at D. Examination of a number of these cracks shows that the smaller crack will then run from C through D out toward D′. The diviner of much experience could probably use this fact to get the result he wished.

The manipulation of oracles is a common practice, in various parts of the world, and we have historical cases of it in ancient China. In 632 B.C. the Marquis of the state of Chin, falling ill, called in his diviner and told him to find out the cause. This same ruler had previously taken the state of the Earl of Ts'ao away from him. A retainer of the deposed Earl went to the diviner and bribed him to tell the Marquis that his illness was all due to his conduct toward the Earl of Ts'ao. This the diviner did, giving his ruler quite a moral lecture. 'It is by propriety that righteousness is carried out,' he declared. 'It is by good faith that propriety is maintained; it is by equal justice that depravity is corrected. If your lordship lets these three things go, in what position will you be placed?' The Marquis was pleased, and restored the Earl of Ts'ao.[4]

On the other hand, we must not suppose that it was necessarily proof of duplicity for a diviner to take a hand in determining the answer of the oracle. On another occasion an able statesman was asked by one of the feudal lords to divine about the political events of the near future. The statesman accepted the command and in due time delivered the answers to the ruler. Thereafter, events moved exactly as he had predicted, and someone praised his skill as a diviner. Whereupon he disclaimed all ability at divination, but hoped that he had enough judgment to be able to predict what was obviously going to happen. These events were somewhat later than the Shang dynasty. But if the diviners even of the Shang period could influence the oracles, this fact has great significance for the history of Chinese politics. For these diviners were educated men, and they were the forerunners of the scholar-statesmen who have dominated Chinese government almost to the present day. If they sometimes made the oracle answer as they wished, we need not suppose that they were always rascals. They may merely have been giving the king sound advice in a form in which he was fairly sure to take it.

Once advice was obtained by divination, was it always acted upon? For the Shang period we have little way of knowing. The addition of such remarks as 'It really did rain' on the bone seems to indicate some suspicion that the oracle was not always infallible. Certainly in later periods they very frequently divined to see if they could get the answer they wanted, and if not they went ahead and did what they had intended to do all the time—much as most of us use human advice. Once King Ling of Ch'u (540-529 B.C.) divined asking whether he would conquer the world. The reply was unfavourable. He dashed the tortoise-shell away from him, looked up to heaven and cried, 'What? This little thing you will not give me? Very well, then, I will take it for myself!'

In using a particular piece of bone or a tortoise-shell for divining there seem to have been no set rules as to subjects. Sometimes we find a large tortoise-shell all used for divining about the same thing; at other times there is a great variety of topics. Sometimes they used the same piece four times in a single day; after this it might be a month or six weeks before it was used again. We may find on the same piece of tortoise-shell divinations spread over nine months. When the king went travelling a tortoise-shell was taken along and used at various points on the journey to indicate what should be done next, much as some people use a tourist's guide in these days.

What is most important and most fortunate for us is that, in whatever manner they got the answers to their questions and whether they followed the advice or not, they carved the questions on the bone after divination. This practice appears to have died out after Shang times; bone was still used to consult the oracle, but the answers were written in a book, which was much quicker and vastly easier. Even in Shang times not all of the questions were written on the bone. Only about one-tenth of the divination bones and shells excavated are inscribed. It is not the case, however, that they wrote the questions in one period only, for we have inscriptions which we can date in every period of later Shang times. Even on inscribed tortoise-shells the number of questions written may be no more than half the number divined about, as shown by the cracks. Why they wrote down any of the questions, and how they selected those which were to be written, is a mystery. It cannot be that they wrote down the most important ones. One can hardly conceive of a less momentous question than 'Will it rain to-night?' yet we find this question, carved with the expenditure of no little labour, time and again. Was it mere pride of crafts-manship which caused them to do it, forming the characters as beautifully as they could? All that we can be sure of is that they did not do it in order to assist the archæologists of the twentieth century—but the archæologists owe them a great debt of gratitude.

If we seek to enumerate, or even to classify, the various subjects on which the Shangs sought the advice of their gods, we have no easy task. In the first place they probably limited themselves to asking questions of the first importance, such as whether to make war or conclude peace. But it was only a step from this to asking whether the time was auspicious for setting out on a journey or going to hunt in a particular locality. And if one is planning a hunting party for the morrow, it is surely worth while to find out in advance whether it will rain, or whether high winds and dust will spoil the visibility and ruin one's aim so that hunting will be impracticable. All of these things are, after all, matters of some consequence; knowledge in advance may make it possible to alter one's plans for the better. But they must have drifted gradually into a state where they asked about virtually everything. On the last day of every ten-day 'week' they divined to find out whether the next week would be lucky or unlucky. Even here we may suppose that in a week foredoomed to be unfortunate they refrained from important activities as much as possible. But when it is asked whether a sick man will recover or die, it cannot help the situation much to learn that he is going to die, unless indeed one plans to help him do it quickly!

Several Chinese scholars have proposed classifications of the various subjects concerning which the Shangs divined. One of the best of these contains twelve items, as follows:

(1) Sacrifices. This is a subject to which we shall have to recur. The oracle was asked to what spirits sacrifice should be offered, when it should be made, what kind of animals or other things should be sacrificed, what colour and how many they should be, and so on.

(2) Announcements made to the spirits. It is not quite clear whether they first asked whether such and such an announcement should be made and then, if the answer was favourable, made the announcement, or whether the divination itself served as the announcement. In any case they told the spirits about all sorts of affairs, from the fact that their enemies had made a raid and carried off a number of captives to the fact that someone had fallen ill. Apparently the spirits, thus informed of the difficulties of their worshippers, were expected to do something to remedy them.

(3) This heading has to do with a subject, divined about a good deal, which even the scholar who made this classification does not pretend thoroughly to understand; it may have something to do with state or diplomatic banquets. This is only one of a number of places in which investigation has as yet failed to reveal the secrets of the oracle bones.

(4) Journeys and halting. It was customary to ask whether the circumstances were favourable before setting out on a journey, and to question as to the advisability of spending the night or a longer time at any point on the road.

(5) Hunting and fishing. They asked not only whether it was fortunate to go hunting and fishing, but also where to go. Since the oracle could answer only 'yes' or 'no,' it was necessary to ask about one place after another until one was indicated as fortunate. We often find that the diviner later set down, on the bone, a record of what animals and how many were bagged; this was no doubt to prove that he had indicated a good place.

(6) War. When to send an army, and how many men to send, when to meet the enemy in battle and when to remain on the defensive—such questions come under this heading.

(7) Crops. The prospects for each kind of grain, and for the year's output of liquors, were inquired about in detail. In addition they asked about the general agricultural outlook for the year.

(8) Rain, snow, wind, and fog.

(9) Good weather. They were especially anxious to know when the weather would clear up after a storm.

(10) Illness and recovery.

(11) The (ten-day) week, that is, whether it would be a lucky or an unlucky period.

(12) Miscellaneous subjects.

This catalogue does very well as a suggestion of the matters concerning which the Shang people consulted their gods. But it does not, of course, begin to exhaust the subject. There are a great many questions which one would have a hard time placing in this list, not because there is no heading which they fit, but because they fit more than one. Thus when it is asked, 'If the king hunts to-day in Shuai, will he not encounter heavy rain?' we might list this both under questions about hunting and those about the weather. If it is 'Tzu Yü is ill; should his retainer Fu announce this to the spirit of Father I?' we may call it divination about an announcement to a spirit, or about an illness.

The twelfth or 'miscellaneous' class in this list must be indeed a large one, to include all matters not mentioned in the other eleven. Some of these are quite important. They include what we might call 'diplomatic' questions, having to do with relations between the Shangs and other peoples, perhaps their vassals. This whole subject is little understood, but in those days as in these one of the questions to be considered, when planning to make war, was what other states to assist, and what states one could count upon as allies. Here as elsewhere they asked for advice. The ancestors were also expected to answer more intimate questions of state, such as whether the queen would have a son.

Dreams are mentioned rather often on the oracle bones. The kings dreamed about ghosts, sometimes about 'many ghosts'; these and other dreams needed explanation, and they went to the diviner to find out whether they were of good or evil omen. The Shang people were constantly seeking the assistance of their gods; at the end of many questions we find 'Will I receive aid?' or 'Will the king receive aid?' Sometimes they ask specifically, 'Will the spirit of Grandfather I not aid the king?' But the spirits might hurt as well as help, and we find oracles which remind us of medieval tests to determine whether someone seriously ill was being bewitched. 'Is the spirit of Grandmother Chi harming the son of Hao?' 'Is the spirit of Grandfather Hsin injuring me?'

Since their writing was pictographic, many of the words used by the Shangs are literally picturesque. None is more so than one of the words they use to mean 'evil.' We find it used constantly; in hunting, in war, in the week to come, will there be, they ask, 'no evil'? The word is , a snake striking at the foot of an unsuspecting man about to step on him. No better symbol could portray the hidden danger which lurked everywhere, against which one must forewarn himself by every possible means—by borrowing, if possible, the far-seeing eyes of the gods themselves.

CHAPTER XIV

SACRIFICE

THE custom of making sacrifices probably began as a simple act of providing food for the dead. There is little obvious difference between a man who has just died and a man still living; it is natural to suppose that the needs of the one are essentially the same as those of the other. Even at the present day it is the custom, in China, to lay out food for the dead, near the corpse, shortly after death.

It was observed that the food provided did not dis appear; it was not eaten, at least not in a physical sense. But the man who died did not disappear physically, either. Something, some unseen essence, went out of him, and left him dead. His friends and relatives saw him, moving and talking, in dreams; waking, and realizing that he was dead, they supposed that it was this essence, his ghost, who had come to them in the night. A man who is dead does not breathe; since his breath and the essence of his personality leave him at the same time it is natural to suppose that the breath is the essential man. That is, of course, why we call this essence by the word 'spirit,' derived from the Latin *spiritus*, 'breath.' The Chinese have the same idea. But if the dead man is an invisible essence, leaving his physical form behind, then it is logical to suppose that he can partake of the essence of food, while leaving the physical substance unaltered.

This idea, that the spirit can use sacrificed food without destroying it, is common to many peoples, and is a very convenient one. It allows the food to be used twice, once to feed the spirits and again to feed the worshippers or the priests.

And it has the added advantage of allowing the human beings, in eating, to dine with the gods and to partake of viands which have been endowed with special virtues by coming into contact with the spirits. This idea lies at the root, historically, of the communion service in Christian churches, though it has been overlaid and obscured by many later alterations.

Not all of the food sacrificed by the ancient Chinese was subsequently eaten by the worshippers. Liquor was sometimes spilled on to the ground, animals were sometimes buried and sometimes burned. Sacrifice by burning has enjoyed great favour in many parts of the world, and for a very evident reason. This process converts most of the sacrificed food into smoke and savours. These are very much like the breath which is supposed to be the stuff that ghosts are made of. And they are wafted toward the heavens, where many peoples, including the Chinese, have supposed their gods and their dead to dwell.

Sacrifices of food were made to persons and things other than the spirits of men. But it is safe to suppose that this was done because these things, such as wind and earth, were conceived to possess the qualities and the appetites of human spirits. Thus we may be fairly sure that anything which we find offered, in sacrifice, to the spirits is something which men themselves conceive as suitable to eat or possess. It may be, however, that they do not dare to eat or possess it themselves; we cannot say that every people practising human sacrifice has necessarily practised cannibalism.

The ancient Chinese considered their sacrifices to be an actual feeding of the dead. There is a great deal of evidence for this; a story which comes from a period slightly later than Shang times makes it especially clear. There was a high official who had an especial liking for water-chestnuts; in this he showed good judgment. This delicacy, now to be obtained chiefly in Chinese restaurants, was common to both Europe and China in prehistoric times. This official was so extremely fond of them that he left explicit orders that they were to be sacrificed to him during the year following his death; in this period sacrifices were especially frequent, apparently with the idea that the newly disembodied spirit was to be weaned gradually away from too much dependence on the things of the flesh. After this period, he said, the things sacrificed could be those regularly prescribed, but during the first year he insisted on his water-chestnuts. The story has a sad sequel. His son was a strait-laced scholar who declared that his duty to maintain the regular observances came above his filial duty to carry out his father's wishes, and the sacrificing of water chestnuts was not done.

The overwhelming majority of the objects which the men of Shang sacrificed to their gods were animals. From this it has been argued that the Shang people were unquestionably pastoral. But this does not hold at all. Many religions show a marked preference for the sacrifice of animals even though they may be scarce, the populace at large being almost entirely agricultural and its diet chiefly vegetarian. There are several reasons for this. One of them is the fact that there is a drama about the slaughter of an animal, whose life goes out in a twinkling, whose blood gushes forth, which no amount of ceremony can put into the offering of grains or vegetables. Sometimes the life itself is conceived as being offered to the gods.

Another reason is the tremendous conservatism found in religious ceremonials everywhere. There is some indication that even later than the Shang period rulers may occasionally have gone out to hunt and fish personally to secure victims for sacrifice. Thus they maintained a custom coming down from a remote period when hunting and fishing were of primary importance in the lives of the people. In the ritual of one sacrifice we read that 'the king must personally shoot an arrow into the bull for the sacrifice.' Such shooting of a domestic animal with an arrow has no use whatsoever; it is clearly a survival, in the ritual, from a much earlier day, and not from a pastoral but from a hunting period. We find traditions maintained in this way in religions everywhere, and it is quite beside the point to say that the people of Shang were pastoral because their sacrifices consisted chiefly of animals. Will the archæologists of the future say that we were still employing crucifixion in the twentieth century because the bishop's mitre is still surmounted by a cross?

The animals regularly sacrificed by the Shangs included cattle, sheep, pigs, and dogs. The excavations indicate that wild boars and perhaps other wild animals were sacrificed. The oracle bones show a very few instances of the sacrifice of some bird, perhaps the pheasant or the chicken, and of horses. Mention has already been made of the finding of thirty-eight horses, wearing beautifully decorated bridles, buried together in one large pit, apparently as a sacrifice.

Animals of both sexes and various colours were used for sacrificial purposes. The number was ordinarily small, from one to ten. A typical sacrifice might include two pigs, three sheep, and five oxen, though a combination like fifty dogs, fifty sheep, and fifty pigs is not altogether rare. A single sacrifice involving as many as three hundred cattle is rare, but we find it recorded. Another great offering to three former kings included 'one hundred cups of liquor, one hundred sheep, and three hundred (cattle).'

Liquor is apparently the only product of the soil which the Shang people offered to their gods. Intoxicating liquors have been coupled with religion by peoples almost everywhere, and for a very obvious reason. The power which alcohol has to infuse life and 'spirits' into the dullest of men, to cause them to become at least temporarily cheerful in almost any circumstances, and to throw them into a state resembling the trance of the mystic, must always appear in the nature of a miracle even to the most sophisticated.

In addition to animals and wine the Shangs sacrificed some variety of semi-precious stone; this is usually read as 'jade' and it was probably something of the sort. A single inscription indicates that they may have sacrificed shell money. If so, this is the earliest known forerunner of the now common custom of sending money to the spirits. Everywhere one goes in modern China one sees shops with strings of small, peculiarly shaped oblong paper boxes, coloured like silver and gold; these are 'ingots' of these metals, waiting to be purchased and burned for the benefit of the dead by some pious descendant.

The most important sacrifices of later China have been conducted in the open air. Our records of Shang sacrifices mention only temples as the place of sacrifices. These are called by various names, the most important of which is 宗. This is composed of a house within which is the symbol, it will be recalled, for 'spirit.' It is, then, 'the house of the spirits.' To this day this word means 'ancestral temple,' and it has come to have a great variety of other meanings; among these is 'all the people of one surname,' that is, all of the people linked together by the fact that they are descended from, and presumably worship, one ancestor. Whether all sacrifices were made in one temple, which is called by various names, or whether these stand for different buildings, we cannot tell. Among these names are 'South House,' 'House of Sacrifice,' and 'Great House.' A graphic designation sometimes used for the temple of sacrifice is 'The House of Blood.' The spirits were thought especially to drink the blood of the sacrificial victim; a later noble, fearing the extinction of his house, declares that his ancestors will no longer 'eat blood.'

Of the times of the year when the Shangs offered sacrifices of various sorts we know little. It is safe to assume that they presented special sacrifices in the spring, to assure a good crop from the newly planted seeds, at the same time when we find them divining anxiously about this. There is one reference to what may be a 'spring liquor sacrifice'; if this is the correct reading, the liquor was probably an offering of the first that was made. The ancient Chinese drank newly fermented liquor, without ageing. It is altogether probable that they had some sort of autumn thanksgiving ceremony, after the harvest. It would probably be possible to work out a cycle of the Shang sacrifices, from the oracle bone material now available, but it would be a considerable piece of statistical labour which has not yet been done. The Shangs called a year a 'sacrifice'; this probably refers to a regular cycle of sacrifices gone through once each year.

The number of different names used by the Shangs for their various methods of sacrificing is quite bewildering. As early as 1914 one scholar had identified eighteen different names, and it is probable that to-day at least an equal number could be added. Yet we are unable to say whether each of these is a different kind of sacrifice, or if some of them are just variant names for the same rite. The difficulty is not lessened by the fact that a great many of these words have no equivalents in later Chinese, even during the ancient period. No other people, in this part of the world at least, had such a religious vocabulary.

If we cannot be sure that a number of these terms do stand for sacrifices, we obviously cannot hope to describe the sacrifices for which they stand in great detail. A few of them are, however, graphic enough; is obviously a bird of some sort, being held, head downward, by two human hands and being presented to the spirits. is apparently the head of some animal, again held by two hands, being placed on an altar. We have a similar character showing the presentation of pieces of jade. Another sacrifice of the same class is represented by a picture of a jar of liquor standing on some sort of table or altar. These sacrifices all belong to what we might call the simple presentation class, wherein the thing given to the gods is simply lifted up before them or laid on a table or altar.

A different type of sacrifice is that in which liquor was poured out, in a libation, and allowed to spill upon the floor or ground. This is the way in which liquor was usually presented, and this type of sacrifice has persisted to a much later time.

Perhaps the commonest, and certainly the most dramatic method of sacrifice was by fire. Whether the fire was intended only to roast the animal, or to consume it utterly, we cannot say. It is possible that only certain parts of the animal were placed in the fire. Two other common methods of making the presentation were by burying the animal, and by throwing it into water. A certain amount of mystery surrounds these types of offerings.

A later book of ritual tells us that 'the emperor, in sacrificing to streams, throws the victim into the water, and buries it in the ground when sacrificing to the earth.'[1] But on the Shang oracle bones we find that the Huan River and the earth are sacrificed to with burnt offerings, while offerings thrown into water and buried in the ground are made to the ancestors of men. The buried offerings made to the ancestors might be explained easily if the ancestors were believed to live under the earth in a lower world like that of the Greeks. But as we have seen, there is good evidence to show that they were thought to live in the heavens. However, the excavators have found more than forty instances of honourable burial in Shang times, in which the body faces downward. This might be considered to be some evidence of a belief that the spirit abode was under the earth. As we shall see, there were two opinions as to the location of the dwelling-place of the dead in later China, and it is barely possible that this division of opinion goes back to Shang times.

We know very little about the actual ceremonies of the sacrifice. It was prepared for by divination, asking about every detail. We have seen that with few exceptions the Shang people called each of their ancestors after one of the days of their ten-day week, and that that day was ordinarily the one on which offerings were made to him. Ten days, or one week, in advance, they divined, asking whether the sacrifice should be made. Later, ordinarily the very day before the sacrifice, they divined again asking what victims to use, how many, their colour, etc. They also divined as to whether the king should personally go to inspect the sacrificial animals. Only perfect animals, we may suppose, could be used.

We do not know who were the individuals who conducted the sacrifice itself. There were probably special priests who had charge of this, just as there were special diviners who had charge of communication with the spirits, though it is quite possible they were the same persons. On the oracle bones we have a word, composed of a man kneeling beside a spirit and raising his arms in supplication, which later means 'priest.' But whether it had that meaning in Shang times is not clear.

Of the purposes of sacrifice we have already spoken. Apart from what was probably a genuine desire to provide for the comfort of their ancestors, they sacrificed from a desire to cause their gods to be well disposed toward them, to aid them in their various undertakings, and to give them special help in time of danger. But there is another type of offering which was made, together with a specific request for a specific return. With especial frequency we find such sacrifices made for the sake of inducing the spirit named to grant a good crop. We often find it used as a prayer for rain.

Was there human sacrifice in the Shang period? Up to the time of the archæological discoveries of the past twelve months it was the opinion of most of the Chinese experts in this field that there was not. Some of them may even yet hold to this opinion. But even before the finding of this new evidence there was overwhelming proof, in my opinion, in the oracle inscriptions alone, not only that there was human sacrifice but also that it was practised commonly and on a large scale.

There is a word on the oracle bones which sometimes means 'attack,' as in war, and sometimes stands for the sacrifice of human beings. It is 伐, clearly a man across whose neck is the blade of a dagger-axe; he is quite evidently in the act of being killed, probably decapitated. It is pronounced *fa*. When we read of a sacrifice to an ancestral king, including several cattle and sheep, and see '*fa* ten men,' we naturally suppose that this means what it appears to say. But some of the Chinese experts disagree. They say, what we must certainly admit, that our evidence shows that the men of Shang were by no means untutored barbarians. They would therefore, these experts conclude, have been incapable of large scale and repeated human sacrifice. Instead, they point out, this word *fa* is explained by late books of ritual to mean 'a sacrificial dance, accompanied by music,' and that is what they interpret it to mean on the oracle bones.

The fact is that this dance is probably the harmless survival, at a later date, of what was originally a rite of human sacrifice. We find such survivals everywhere. One group of North-west Coast American Indians has a ceremonial in which a slave used to be killed as a sacrifice. Later this aspect of the ceremony disappeared, but the ritual survived and the slave was merely bitten by one of those taking part, in symbolic token of the former sacrifice. This is undoubtedly what happened in the Chinese ritual, where the whole thing was turned, at a later period, into a dance. But when we find, as we do in one inscription on the oracle bones, '*fa* ten oxen,' we can hardly suppose that the oxen danced.

Further evidence that *fa* meant 'to sacrifice a human being' is provided by two inscribed weapons which passed through the Peiping antique market. One of them, illustrated in Plate x, I first saw and photographed in the shop of a Peiping dealer;

it has since been acquired by the Nelson Gallery of Art, in Kansas City. From its supposed place of origin, patination, decoration, and inscriptions, it is undoubtedly Shang. The inscriptions on the other weapon are virtually identical. The axe illustrated is seven and a quarter inches broad and nine and three-eighth inches high, large enough and heavy enough to decapitate a human being. The three-legged vessel represented on one side of the head is a *hsien*, 'steamer'; this pictograph is used in the bone inscriptions as a verb meaning 'to sacrifice.' The pictograph on the other side is a highly pictorial version of *fa*; the human victim, the axe with its blade across his neck, and the hand of the executioner grasping the axe are all clearly discernible.

It is a mistake to suppose that human sacrifice cannot be carried on save by 'barbarians,' devoid of all culture. The story of Abraham and Isaac will be remembered. As a matter of fact, if one believes in sacrifice, then human sacrifice is its logical conclusion. For if one be truly devoted to his gods, then nothing is too good for them, and if one be a human being, he naturally considers human beings the finest of living creatures. Plutarch records that the Greeks sacrificed human beings at one time during the life of Themistocles, and on other occasions; he mentions similar action by the Romans in the time of Marcellus. The Aztecs, when they were conquered by the Spaniards, were a highly civilized people. Their capital was a city of seventy-five thousand, their architecture was one to boast of, they possessed a considerable literature. Yet they made human sacrifices on a large scale and in a peculiarly revolting manner, plucking the living heart out of the breast of the victim. The inhabitants of the proud city of Carthage were sufficiently civilized to dispute supremacy with Rome herself. Yet they sacrificed their own children. They were placed in the arms of a brazen image of Moloch, inside which a furnace raged. It was ingeniously contrived so that they slowly slipped, one by one, into the flames, while the crowd of wor-

PLATE X

A CEREMONIAL BRONZE AXE, PROBABLY USED FOR DECAPITATING HUMAN SACRIFICIAL VICTIMS AT ANYANG

BREADTH, SEVEN AND ONE-QUARTER INCHES; HEIGHT, NINE AND THREE-EIGHTHS INCHES. FOR DESCRIPTION AND EXPLANATION OF THE INSCRIPTIONS, SEE PAGE 206. NOW IN THE WILLIAM ROCKHILL NELSON GALLERY OF ART, KANSAS CITY.

Reproduced by kind permission.

shippers applauded. If we find, then, that the men of Shang sacrificed their enemies, and that by decapitation, which is still practised in Europe, we cannot out of hand declare them beyond the pale of civilization.

In the centuries following the end of the Shang dynasty, concerning which we have connected history, human sacrifice was less common, no doubt, than in the earlier period. But it occurred and can hardly be said to have been rare. In 892 B.C. the king caused the feudal lords to boil the Duke of Ch'i to death in what was undoubtedly called a sacrifice. In 641 the Duke of Sung, wishing to consolidate his power, called a meeting of a number of the feudal lords. The Viscount of Tsêng came, but was late. He was made an example, and sacrificed at the Altar of the Land. The Duke of Sung did this, we are told, 'to awe and draw to him the wild tribes of the east.'[2]

The *Tso Chuan*, a very ancient history, tells us that in the year 532 B.C. 'in the seventh month, P'ing Tzŭ invaded Chü and took Kêng. He sacrificed his captives, for the first time offering human beings at the Po Shê altar.'[3] The next year, we read in the same work: 'In the eleventh month the Viscount of Ch'u extinguished the state of Ts'ai and sacrificed Yin, eldest son of the marquis, on mount Kang. Shên Wu-yü said: "This is inauspicious. The five animals used as victims cannot be employed one for another; how much less can a ruler of a State be employed as a victim! The king will have occasion to repent of this." '[4] At this time, and much earlier, a definite conscience against human sacrifice was developing, but the practice persisted.

The same history makes mention three times, in the years 627, 588, and 537 B.C., of the practice of consecrating drums by smearing them with the blood of a sacrificed human being, usually a captive of war.[5] In the three cases mentioned the sacrifice was only considered, but not carried out. Does this mean that it was never actually done? Quite the reverse. From the nature of the accounts it is perfectly plain that such sacrifices were so frequent as to call for no mention, while the uncommon fact of a change of plans caused these instances to appear in history.

Still another type of human sacrifice was not uncommon. The reader will remember that in one of the tales of *Sindbad the Sailor* that adventurer found himself in an Oriental country, married to an agreeable wife, only to have her die and find that he must be buried alive with her. Such burial of husband with wife is rare, but for wives and servants to be buried with their lord has been common in many lands, including China.

In 621 B.C. Duke Mu of the state of Ch'in died, leaving orders that three of the most able men in the state were to be buried with him, as attendants in his tomb. An ode in the *Book of Poetry* tells of this incident, dealing with each of the three in turn. Of the last it says:

> 'Who followed Duke Mu to the grave?
> Tzŭ-ch'ê Chên-hu.
> And this Chên-hu
> Could withstand a hundred men.
> But when he came to the grave,
> He looked terrified and trembled.'[6]

A later account says that still others were buried with this duke—in all, one hundred and seventy persons.

We find other instances of this practice in 594, 589, and 581 B.C. A little later, in the time of Confucius, we read that 'Ch'ên Tzŭ-ch'ê having died in Wei, his wife and his major-domo planned to bury some human attendants with him in his tomb. They had already decided upon the victims when Ch'ên Tzŭ-kang (younger brother of the dead man and a disciple of Confucius) arrived. He was told of the plan. '"Our master," they said, "when he was ill (being away from home) had no one to attend him in this lower world. We request you, therefore, to provide some attendants for his spirit, by burying some servants in his tomb." Tzŭ-kang replied: "To bury living persons with the dead is contrary to proper usage. However, if the nature of his disease makes it necessary that he have attendants in the grave, who could fill that place so well as his wife and his major-domo? If the burying of attendants may be avoided, I desire to avoid it; if not, then I wish that you two shall act in that capacity." It was decided not to use attendants.'[7]

Despite the opposition to this custom, which by this time was very strong, it is said that when the First Emperor of Ch'in died, in 210 B.C., his entire harem was immolated with him.

To this day there survives in China a custom which is strongly reminiscent of human sacrifice. It is mentioned frequently in Chinese novels and still occurs, I am told, from time to time. A bandit, who has committed many crimes, and has murdered, perhaps, a military or police officer, is finally apprehended and put through the regular trial. After he has been condemned to death he is executed in a special manner. A tablet is erected to the spirit of the murdered man, and the criminal is made to kneel in front of it. Announcement is then made to the spirit that this criminal is to be sacrificed to him, giving satisfaction and revenge for his crime. The man is then killed in front of the tablet.

These things being so, if we find from the oracle bones that there was human sacrifice in the Shang dynasty, it cannot be said that this is anything unique in Chinese history. On the other hand, there is no question that the Shangs sacrificed human beings with a casualness, and in numbers, which are unparalleled in later times. In subsequent periods we do not find sacrifices involving a few cups of wine, five cows, three sheep, and ten men indiscriminately. Nor do we find, as in the Shang sacrifices, human victims numbering as many as a hundred or even three hundred slaughtered at once—this not in one inscription, but in several. It has been said, and probably correctly, that this was the chief method by which the Shangs disposed of their prisoners of war. They had slaves, but they had apparently not worked out a system for taking care of great numbers of slaves.

If the evidence of the inscriptions be doubted (and there are those who do doubt it) let us see what archæology has to say about human sacrifice. First, as to Neolithic China. Andersson, describing a cave excavated in Fêngtien Province, in the extreme north-east of China, writes: 'Some animal bones were . . . found in the cave deposit, but these were entirely subordinate in number when compared with the startling abundance of human skeletal remains which form by far the larger part of the collection . . . more than forty individuals of different sexes and ages, from small babies to very aged persons . . . it was exceedingly rare to find two bones still attached to each other in normal articulation. Not only this, but the skeletal elements, such as leg bones and skulls, were found to be in a very broken state, the skulls in fact being mostly reduced to pitiful fragments. . . . I have considered the possibility of the cave being a place where some religious ceremonies, including the sacrifice of man, had taken place.'[8]

In the excavation of the site of the Shang capital human bones were found at various places in such condition that they were obviously not those of persons carefully buried. Some of them were crushed and broken, and had evidently been treated quite carelessly.

In the spring season of 1934 the excavators discovered a huge subterranean tomb on the site at Hou Kang, already mentioned, about two miles south-east of the city proper. The central cavity digged for it was twenty-two feet square and more than thirty feet deep. On the south, starting from a point sixty-five feet from the tomb, is a causeway seven feet wide, sloping to the bottom, down which the corpse and other articles could be conveyed. On the north, starting from about thirty feet away, a flight of steps six feet wide leads down to the tomb. Altogether it occupies, from north to south, a distance of nearly one hundred and twenty feet. A chariot and many other articles were probably buried here; it was quite evidently the tomb of some very important personage, perhaps a king. The whole of the central cavity, twenty-two feet square and thirty feet deep, was filled in with pounded earth, like that of the house foundations. To pound this earth was a tremendous labour. It was intended to protect the dead; actually it betrayed the location of the tomb, which was robbed, in all probability within a few centuries after it was made. The robbers were very thorough; they dug a huge pit, leaving untouched only a crust of about two feet in width, around the edge. In this two-foot crust of pounded earth the excavators found more than thirty human skulls, placed in the earth and crushed as it was pounded. There is nothing more of the skeletons, only the skulls. The excavators consider that, including those which must originally have been in the centre, the heads of not less than a hundred human beings were buried here. And there is good evidence that these were the heads of human victims specially sacrificed at the funeral, rather than merely heads taken in war and hoarded for this purpose. For some of the cervical vertebræ are still associated with them; these would have dropped off, due to decomposition, if the victims had not been very recently killed.

The exact date of this tomb is still uncertain. It was so thoroughly looted that almost no artifacts were left to make dating possible. The form of the tomb, with two approaches rather than four, resembles that of the tombs of Chou date, excavated at Hsün Hsien, rather than of the great Shang tombs excavated north of the Huan River. And some believe that this is a tomb of the Chou period. On the other hand, while we know that human sacrifice was practised in Chou times, it does not seem to have been carried out on so large a scale. In the eighty-six tombs, large and small, which were excavated at Hsün Hsien, only one case of what looks very much like human sacrifice was found. In one tomb, above the main burial, a skeleton was found of a man buried face downward, with his hands tied behind his back. But in view of the scarcity of this evidence it is doubtful whether we can assign the Hou Kang tomb, with its numerous victims, to Chou date.

No such doubt attaches to the great number of human sacrificial remains found in the Shang grave-field north of the Huan River. In a corner of one of the great tombs three skeletons were found, crushed into the pounded earth. From the elaborate head-dresses inlaid with turquoise, associated with them, it is believed that these were women, possibly royal concubines buried with their lord.

The great problem in connection with human sacrifice in the Shang period has been how they disposed of the bodies of the great number of human victims which the oracle bones lead us to believe were sacrificed. We read of ten, a hundred, three hundred men being sacrificed at one time, and yet until the autumn of 1934, not a single skeleton of an indubitable Shang sacrificial victim had been found. This was almost enough to make one believe in the theory that these people were not really sacrificed at all, but merely put through some symbolic ritual. But now we know. In the spring of 1935 alone almost a thousand headless skeletons of Shang sacrificial victims were excavated. Including those found in the autumn of 1934, more than a thousand have been recovered up to this time.

All these decapitated victims have been found in the general area of the Shang cemetery north of the Huan River, but they are buried in special pits. Human sacrificial victims are usually named, in the oracle bone inscriptions, in multiples of ten, and this corresponds with the fact that in every case these skeletons are buried in pits which contain ten individuals. The bodies are buried in rectangular pits; sometimes the wrists are crossed behind the back, as if they had been tied. The skulls are buried separately, in square pits near by. Ten skulls are buried in a pit, standing vertically in regular rows, all looking toward the north. I have seen many of these skulls and skeletons in the process of being excavated.

The objects found with the skeletons are interesting. They include such things as small bronze knives and axe-heads, and grinding-stones, always ten to a pit, apparently one for each man. It would appear that in preparation for the ritual of sacrifice each victim was given an outfit including specified objects, and possibly clothed in a ceremonial garb, and that these were buried with him after he was slain.

One phase of the human sacrifices of the Shangs is exceedingly strange. The victims are spoken of sometimes as so many men, sometimes as so many 'captives,' but most often as so many 'Ch'iang.' This word is written ; the lower part is a man, the upper, the horns of a sheep. It means, as old books tell us, 'western barbarians who raise sheep.' There is a group of people living in western China to-day who are known by this name, but whether they are descendants of the 'Ch'iang' mentioned in the oracle bones would be very hard to determine.

When there is mention of the sacrifice of a large number of men, a hundred or three hundred, it is always these 'Ch'iang' who are named as victims. For this reason it was at first thought that this word, on the oracle bones, did not have its later meaning, but was merely another form of the word for 'sheep.' More thorough study has disproved this, and shown that it cannot possibly mean 'sheep,' but rather has its usual meaning of 'men who herd sheep.' For we find, in the same sacrifice, mention of 'so many Ch'iang and so many sheep.' Further, we have inscriptions which definitely state that the Ch'iang are men, as 'sacrifice to Grandfather Tuesday Ch'iang ten men, sheep one.' If further evidence were needed it would be provided by an inscription, on a Chinese bronze now in a European museum, which I chanced upon during the past year. It bears a special form of this character, found in the bone inscriptions, but hitherto unknown on bronzes, as the name of the maker, showing him to belong to the Ch'iang group; undoubtedly coming from a date later than Shang times, it provides final corroboration of the fact that this character must stand for men.

These Ch'iang were made captive in war, and the custom of sacrificing them probably grew up as an aftermath of warfare. But once it was established it seems to have grown, until we find expeditions deliberately sent out for the purpose of capturing Ch'iang. On the oracle bones we find repeatedly the question: 'Will we be successful in capturing Ch'iang?' It is highly probable that these captives were used as slaves as well as offerings to the gods. In the latter part of the Shang period we find that a rope has been added to the picture of the Ch'iang, passing round his neck—this is clearly a picture of a class of people kept under restraint, that is, slaves. And the word Ch'iang probably came to mean 'slave,' just as our word 'slave' is derived from 'Slav,' because at one time great numbers of Slavs were captured and sold in various parts of Europe.

It is generally supposed that the Ch'iang mentioned on the oracle bones are a single tribe or nation. Certainly there was a tribe known by that name during Shang times, but that all of the Ch'iang mentioned in the inscriptions belonged to it is very doubtful. We know the names of a number of tribes or states with whom the Shang people had wars, and some of these wars, we know, lasted for a considerable time. Numerous captives must have been taken. Yet all human victims of sacrifice, save Ch'iang, are mentioned merely as so many 'men' or 'captives'; only the Ch'iang are called by name. And whereas other sacrifices of men are rare, those of Ch'iang are frequent. Sacrifices of other men do not, so far as I know, involve more than thirty, but sacrifices of as many as one hundred or even three hundred Ch'iang are by no means rare. Finally, although we find numerous references to expeditions sent out with the deliberate intention of capturing Ch'iang, just like any other hunting party, we find no mention of such expeditions to capture any other people. All this points very strongly to one conclusion, namely, that Ch'iang, while being the special name of one tribe, was also used in a wider sense as a general term for at least a part of the barbarians of the north and west.

The name, as we have seen, primarily means 'sheep-raiser.' The Shang people themselves raised sheep, but apparently not so many sheep as cattle. There must have been more than one people, in the more arid and rocky districts of the north and west, who raised sheep primarily. Between the raiser of cattle and the herder of sheep there is an age-old enmity wherever there is unfenced grazing land. For sheep nibble grass right down to the roots, making it impossible for cattle to pasture on land which sheep have grazed for some time to come. The 'wars' between cowmen and sheep-raisers in the western United States, based on this fact, are very recent history; the battles fought for this reason on the western plains of North America may have been as large as some of those between the men of Shang and the Ch'iang. We know beyond question, from the oracle bones, that encroachment on grazing lands was a frequent source of trouble between the Shangs and their neighbours, though we cannot be sure whether the trouble was with sheep raisers. But it is quite possible that the men of Shang called all of their sheep-raising neighbours by the general term Ch'iang, and that it came to be a name of contempt meaning 'captive' and 'slave.'

In 1122 B.C. a confederation of western barbarians under the leadership of the Chous finally defeated the Shangs and put an end to their power, taking over their territory. A leading part in this conquest was taken by the tribe known as Ch'iang; the grandmother of the leader of the conquest came from this tribe, and it held an influential place in the councils of the confederacy. Descendants of this people were established as feudal lords over four states, including Ch'i. After the power of the Chou kings had waned, in 679 B.C., Duke Huan of Ch'i assumed the presidency of the feudal lords and the actual power of the king. Thus the descendants of these people, who a few centuries earlier had been hunted down, enslaved, and sacrificed like cattle, came for a time to be rulers of the whole of the Chinese world.

BOOK III

CHOU

CHAPTER XV

WHO WERE THE CHOUS?

THERE are periods in history when the human race, like a limited train nearing the end of its run, appears to decide that it has wasted time enough, and suddenly puts on such a burst of acceleration as to make both the passengers and the beholders quite dizzy. The Chou dynasty was such a period in Chinese history. Beginning from the moment of the Chou conquest, institutions and ideas were thrown into a ferment. At first it was almost chaos, but very quickly there began to crystallize out of that chaos some of the most remarkable things ever conceived by man.

According to the traditional dates—1122 to 256 B.C.—it endured for less than nine hundred years, but those years saw some of the greatest changes which it is possible to make within a civilization. Political institutions, beginning almost without theory and with the utmost actual flexibility, evolved to a point of theoretical complexity and rigidity such as has never been rivalled anywhere else in the world. At the beginning of the Chou period religion was naïve, and philosophy in any technical sense hardly existed. Philosophy became the handmaiden of practical statesmen, who developed, early in the Chou period, a code of ethical philosophy at once practical, hard-headed, and broadly humanitarian. This same philosophy developed or degenerated, according to one's point of view, into several 'schools' of professional philosophy which brought it, before the end of the Chou period, to such a degree of technical refinement and hair-splitting, and such a complete union with the religion and metaphysics of the day, that very little further advance in this direction was possible.

The whole of the so-called Classical Period of Chinese history falls within the Chou dynasty. The great works of Chinese literature which are best known in the West, such as the *Document Classic* (the so-called *Book of History*) and the *Book of Poetry*, were written wholly or in large part at this time. The great names which we know best—Confucius, Mencius, Lao Tzŭ, Mo Tzŭ—belong to this time.

Who were these Chous, whose coming to power was the brand which set off such a display of cultural pyrotechnics? They were 'barbarians.' Apparently they could not even write until they learned to do so from the Shangs, perhaps within a century of the time when they were so ungrateful as to conquer their tutors.

The early history of the Chou tribe or tribes is obscure. Presumably it was preserved in oral tradition, and we find some of that tradition written down in the *Book of Poetry*. Even this, however, carries us back little more than two centuries before the conquest. The region from which they came we know quite definitely. They flourished in the basin of the Wei River, in the heart of what is now Shensi Province, roughly three hundred miles to the west and a hundred miles to the south of the Great City Shang. This is a rich agricultural district, comparatively isolated by natural barriers. The various tribes inhabiting it seem to have had a long period of development with comparatively little interference from the more cultured Shangs and their other neighbours to the east. The Chous did not always dominate this region. Their traditions tell us that they first lived north of the Wei, near its chief tributary, the Ching River, but were forced out of this position by the pressure of other tribes. They moved southward to 'the plain of Chou,' from which, it may be, they derived their name. From here they moved, shortly before the conquest, to a place known as Fêng, south of the Wei and probably about fourteen miles south-west of the modern city of Hsian. Shortly after the conquest the capital was moved to Hao, about eight miles north and slightly east of Fêng. This remained the capital of the Chou dynasty until it was pillaged by barbarians in 771 B.C.

Nothing remains of these two Chou cities to-day, save wheat-fields. But villages near the presumptive site of each have Fêng and Hao as part of their names, and for this and other reasons there seems little doubt that they can be located with approximate accuracy.

The orthodox Chinese view is that the Chou people were essentially like the Shangs, racially and culturally. But we have abundant evidence to show that this cannot be wholly true. Alternatively we might suppose that they were a people totally unlike the Shangs. The truth seems to lie in neither of these extremes. Apparently the Chous were originally of the same fundamental North Chinese Neolithic stock as that from which the Shangs seem to have sprung. The *Book of Poetry* tells us that they still dwelt in 'kiln-like huts and caves'[1] during the life of the great-grandfather of the Martial King, who conquered the Shangs. This is a very good description of the underground dwellings of Neolithic men which have already been mentioned. Whether the Chou people had bronze before their contact with the Shangs we do not know. We do know that while they had domestic animals they were fundamentally an agricultural people. Their language was probably very closely related to that of the Shangs, for they found it possible to use the Shang system of writing with very little alteration of vocabulary, grammar, or phraseology.

On the other hand their culture shows certain marked differences from that of the Shangs. Their system of government appears to have differed greatly, but this could be accounted for on the basis of the peculiar circumstances introduced by their wide conquests. Certain fundamental differences in religion will be discussed when we come to that topic. A difference which may seem trifling, but the roots of which go to the very basis of the social system, is found in their laws of inheritance. It will be recalled that among the Shangs, when a king died, his son did not normally inherit the throne unless no brothers of the king were living. Among the Chous, on the other hand, the throne normally passed directly to the eldest son of the principal wife of the king.

A famous Chinese scholar of great erudition has recently tried to show that the Chou system, too, was originally one of fraternal inheritance, but that it was changed by the brother of the Martial King. Many bronze inscriptions prove, however, that this was not the case. We have, here, a fundamental difference of social organization. It shows beyond question that the Chou and Shang peoples, while similar in many respects, were products of two distinct lines of cultural evolution, with long, separate histories.

Exactly how much the Chou and how much the Shang people contributed to the culture of early Chou times we cannot say in the present state of our knowledge. But there is no question that by far the major portion of the contribution came from the Shangs. The chief service of the Chous was that they took up Shang culture with the enthusiasm always shown by new converts, developed many of its aspects with the intellectual vigour often shown by 'barbarian' peoples, and spread it abroad with their wide conquests.

The contact of the Chous with Shang culture came before, not after, the conquest. It is quite possible, indeed, that the Chous would neither have desired nor have been able to conquer the Shangs had they not first been tutored by them. The Chou tribesmen probably knew little of Shang culture until a short time before the conquest. The character 'Chou' occurs on the oracle bones, in inscriptions which apparently indicate some warfare between Chou and Shang, but they are few, of uncertain date, and of somewhat dubious meaning. The characters which we find on early Chou bronzes duplicate peculiar forms of characters used only in the last century of the Shang period, from which it appears that the Chous learned writing from the Shangs at this time rather than earlier.

What probably happened is that as the Chous gradually rose to a position of power and dominance among the tribes inhabiting the Wei basin they were naturally thrown more and more into contact with their powerful neighbours to the east. This contact was at first, no doubt, that of war. Captives and hostages, returning to the rude surroundings of their Chou homeland, undoubtedly told marvellous stories of the power, wealth, learning, and culture of the mighty Shang people, causing their rustic cousins to desire to emulate it. History which is not altogether trustworthy tells us that Chou chieftains even went to the Shang court, not quite a century before the conquest. From this and other things it has been deduced that the Chous were vassals of the Shang kings. But the Chinese have always had the habit of saying that anyone who was on friendly terms with them was a vassal. As late as 1793 envoys from Britain to the Chinese court were called 'tribute-bearers from the country of England.' Actually there is very little evidence that the Chous were ever in a position of political subjection to the Shang rulers. There is good reason to believe, however, that the Shangs decided that it was wiser to follow a peaceful policy with their warlike neighbour to the west, and that the Chous were quite ready to conclude an alliance with the cultivated state whose arts they wished to learn. If there was such an alliance, it may well be that the Chous willingly accepted a position of nominal inferiority.

A number of sources agree in telling us that women of noble or even royal Shang families were given to Chou rulers in marriage during the period just before the conquest. In later Chinese history the giving of Chinese princesses in marriage to powerful barbarian tribes which were feared is a well-known form of bribe; this would naturally have facilitated cultural contacts. If it is true, then the Chou conquerors were relatives of the Shang kings they deposed; this is a situation made familiar to us by European politics.

The Chou people threw themselves enthusiastically into the undertaking of appropriating Shang culture and of making themselves, in many ways at least, as much like their mentors as possible. It is not easy to say how much they changed themselves to conform to the new pattern, because we do not know much about them until after the change. But it is significant that they not only took up the system of writing, but even some of the characteristic literary phrases of the Shangs. Divination by the Shang method, the Shang system of dating, the style of architecture, and certain elements of their religion were almost certainly borrowed. Their kings even took names which had long been used by Shang rulers.

The Chous not only acknowledged but insisted upon the greatness of Shang culture, and they were proud to consider themselves its guardians and continuators. Among the instructions issued to Chou officials soon after the conquest we find repeatedly statements like the following: 'Follow the penal laws of Yin [this was the name by which the Chous usually called Shang], which were right-ordered.'[2] 'Study the old accomplished men of Shang, that you may establish your heart, and know how to instruct the people.'[3] 'Seek out extensively *among the traces* of the former wise kings of Yin what you may use in protecting and governing the people.'[4] 'Employ the ceremonies of Yin and sacrifice in the new city.'[5] On the other hand the Chou rulers, in holding up models to their people, seldom referred to their own ancestors earlier than the father of the conqueror.

That a group of barbarians should conquer their more cultured neighbours and appropriate their civilization, and that they should gradually bring that civilization to a point of achievement in many respects higher than they found it, is not unique; this has happened many times in the history of the world. Even the Romans were a rude people, as compared with the Greeks, from whom they borrowed much of their culture. The Romans, like the Chous, eventually conquered the Greeks and spread their culture over wide territories, while adding to that culture from the fund of their own genius. But self-made peoples, like self-made men, are not content with their status; they must have ancestors. The man who has made a fortune by his own efforts is often willing to part with a portion of it to the genealogist who will prove that he comes from illustrious lineage; in some strange way he feels that this proves his mettle even more than do his own accomplishments.

The Romans likewise were not satisfied with their accomplishments. They had to have a past just as illustrious as that of the Greeks. Greek culture, as every one knows, sprang in large measure from Asia Minor, and bore some of its first-fruits in the Ionic cities. The Romans, then, traced their lineage from Aeneas, the Trojan hero. This genealogy has no basis in history, but it justified itself amply for the Romans in the fact that it gave them ancestors who were cultured, perhaps, at a date even earlier than that of the rise of Greek culture.

We find this identical trick of genealogy used by the Chous. In the traditional and largely legendary scheme of Chinese history the Shang rulers compose a dynasty which held sway over all of China, and even before them there was another such dynasty, the Hsia. Even earlier than the Hsia dynasty there were still other rulers, who also ruled all of China, in fact 'every place illuminated by the sun and the moon, or reached by the wind and the rain.' The Chous traced their ancestry even back to one of these most ancient rulers, but they looked upon Hou Chi as the founder of their house, and sacrificed to him as their chief ancestor.

This Hou Chi is said to have been Minister of Agriculture under one of the ancient emperors. Actually, however, his name means 'Ruler of Millet,' and he is nothing more nor less than an agricultural deity. He was miraculously conceived, and many marvellous events surrounded his early life. He taught the people to plant and tend grain, and so on. In the days of one of his descendants the virtues of the Chinese monarch declined, and this descendant therefore fled and took up his residence 'among the Martial and the Fire-dog barbarians.' This, then, according to the good Chinese formula, explains why it may *seem* that the Chou rulers came from among barbarians. But actually, we are expected to believe, they came of the most respectable ancestry, and had continued to be good Chinese even though living for fifteen generations surrounded by uncouth barbarians.

Strangely enough, even European sinologists have taken this story seriously, and supposed that it represents a colonization by Chinese nobles among the barbarians of the west. There is no evidence whatever to support such a belief. Like the story of Aeneas, this was merely intended to show that the newly successful conquerors, though they might seem to come of obscure lineage, were really descendants of one of the 'first families.'

CHAPTER XVI

THE CHOU CONQUEST

As early as the time of the grandfather of the Martial King, who conquered Shang, the Chou chieftains had begun the process of defeating the neighbouring tribes, one after another, which was to end in giving them the undisputed leadership of the tribes of the Wei basin. For this we need not seek any special motive. The peoples of that time were commonly fighting, and they had only the choice between subduing their near neighbours or being subdued by them. This is not true, however, of the far-flung Chou conquest. It was carried out on a large scale, against peoples who probably had little desire and certainly had little ability to menace the tribesmen of the Wei valley, protected as they were by natural barriers. Such a conquest required the motivation of an idea, backed by vaulting ambition. The origins of this idea and this ambition are ascribed, and plausibly ascribed, to the father of the actual conqueror.

He is known as King Wên; this name, long used by the Shangs, we may translate as 'the Accomplished.' It denotes a devotion to civil arts and literature as opposed to force and war. Orthodox Chinese history holds that 'the Accomplished King' was his posthumous name, given after the conquest of the Shangs; since he is supposed to have been a loyal vassal of the Shangs, it is felt that he could not have called himself king. But the giving of posthumous names is a custom which apparently rose much later, and we have good evidence that he was called by this name in his lifetime. The Accomplished King is often praised as having been more peace-loving than his son, the

Martial King, and having refrained from attacking the Shang kings even though he had the power. Actually this so-called lover of peace carried out considerable conquests in the west, enlarging the territories of his state, developing his armies and consolidating his power in preparation for the eventual expedition to the east. He himself laid the plans for the great conquest and bequeathed them to his son. He would probably have carried them out himself if he had not died after a reign, it is said, of only seven years.

The mother of the Accomplished King came from a noble family of the Shangs, and it is interesting to speculate on the effect of this upon the career of her son. Did the mother, exiled among those whom she considered uncouth barbarians, try to dispel her loneliness by telling her son of the greatness of her own people, seeking to cause him to share her scorn of his father's race? Did this have the effect, unforeseen by her, of causing him to resolve to put his barbarian foot upon the neck of his superior cousins? We cannot tell, but we do know that in some way there was planted and nourished in his mind a plan of conquest, to the development of which he devoted his life.

Another and more practical reason which may have helped to motivate the excursion of tribes from the Wei valley is famine. Shensi is a pleasant and fertile region, when it rains. But when, as happens every few years, the rains fail, it suffers from famine; when this is serious, conditions are so horrible that the stories of eyewitnesses are almost incredible. To what extent such famines occurred in Shang times we do not know. Since there were undoubtedly less people and more game, they would probably not have been so serious as they are to-day. But the treacherous nature of the climate of the Wei valley may have had something to do with the raid to the east.

Long after the death of the king who laid the plans for the conquest, when his dream had been partially realized, his son, the Duke of Chou, said: 'We must go on, abjuring all idleness, to complete the work of the Accomplished King, until our reign is universal and from the corners of the sea and the sunrising there shall not be one who is disobedient to our rule.'[1] There are many passages in the literature which show that it was the Accomplished King rather than his son who planned the conquest. Whether the Shangs were ignorant of these plans we do not know, but it is probable that they were aware of them. A tradition which is not very trustworthy says that the Accomplished King was imprisoned by the Shangs because his growing power was felt as a menace, but released on the payment of a large ransom.

On his death the plan of conquest was taken over by his son, King Wu, 'the Martial King.' According to one tradition he made an expedition eastward in the ninth year of his reign, and crossed the Yellow River. After crossing, however, he declared that the time had not yet come to attack the Shangs, and withdrew his army and returned home. This may reflect a defeat suffered by his army in this first attempt to march east.

Whether the Great City Shang was still the capital of the Shang kings at this time is a question on which archæologists are divided. According to one opinion they were still there; another holds that they moved to a city called Ch'ao Kê, not far south of the same location, some fifty years before the conquest. Another change, to which the reader must become accustomed, is that the Chous ordinarily called the Shang people not Shang but 'Yin.' The origin of this name is not known. It does not seem to occur on the oracle bones at all, and apparently was not used by the Shang people in speaking of themselves. The Chous sometimes refer to them as 'Shang' and sometimes as 'Yin-Shang,' but most usually merely as 'Yin.'

In the eleventh year of his reign the Martial King mustered all of the forces he could gather from his subjects and allies and made a determined thrust to the east. He probably timed his expedition to coincide with some temporary weakness on the part of the Shangs. It may be that just at this time they were exhausted by the war with the eastern barbarians of which tradition tells us. Certainly the Chous must have been both possessed of unusual military skill and favoured by especially fortunate circumstances to enable them to conquer an enemy so far away. It may well be true that the Shangs were the victims, as tradition says, of treachery among their own subjects.

The Martial King is said to have led about fifty thousand men on this campaign. This is probably a great exaggeration, though he must have had a large army. The Shang ruler is supposed to have met him with no less than seven hundred thousand troops, which is of course absurd. This is a story told by the Chous to make their achievement look even greater than it was.

A single decisive battle, we are told, ended in the complete rout of the Shang armies and victory for Chou. The Shang king fled to his favourite pleasure pavilion, donned rich clothes, decked himself with gems, and set the building on fire, perishing in the flames. His two favourite concubines hanged themselves. The Martial King first received the submission of the Shang people, and then went to the place where the Shang king had killed himself. He personally shot three arrows into the corpse, and then cut off the head. The corpses of the two concubines were treated likewise, and all three heads were hung, as trophies, on the great banner of the Martial King.

Their success must have frightened as well as elated some of the rude tribesmen who accompanied the Martial King on this expedition. The conquest of the Shang capital did not by any means give the Chous control of the entire Chinese world, but it did put them into an exposed position of great possible danger. Many among them may well have thought that they should gather up their booty and return, while they might do so unscathed, to the familiar and safe ground of the Wei valley. But that was not the plan of the Accomplished King, and his descendants were determined, despite all opposition, to realize his dream of permanent domination. At one time during the troubles of the early years of the conquest the Duke of Chou, speaking in the name of the king, answers these counsels against further conquests as follows:

'Formerly, at the beginning of this expedition, I spoke of its difficulties, and revolved them daily. But when a *deceased* father, wishing to build a house, had laid out the plan, if his son be unwilling to raise up the hall, how much less will he be willing to complete the roof! Or if the father had broken up the ground, and his son is unwilling to sow the seed, how much less will he be willing to reap the grain! . . . I am following the Tranquillizer [the Accomplished King] whose purpose embraced all the limits of the land. . . . It is on this account that I make this expedition in force to the east.'[2]

The Martial King had still to carry his armies far afield before he could feel his position to be secure. We cannot say with certainty how large the territories included in the original Chou conquest were. One account says that they embraced 'fifty states,' but if so these states must have been very small ones, possibly only cities. These conquests probably did not extend beyond North China; whether they went east as far as the region of the coast is a question.

Whatever its size, this newly won territory was not small. To hold and govern such an area is not easy to-day; for the Chous it must have been a very great problem indeed. Distances were great, communications were difficult, and the people were hostile. The Chous had no ready-made machinery for governing such an empire, and they could not take the time to develop one. The only thing they could do was to parcel out lands to their relatives and allies. Probably they would have had to do this anyway, for these same allies and relatives had not taken part in the conquest without hope of reward, and they would hardly have allowed the Chou kings to usurp the lion's share without giving them some part of the spoils.

This apportioning of lands to various chiefs and nobles

resulted ultimately in a system much like that of medieval European feudalism—so similar, in fact, that it may properly be called a feudal system. In time this system developed elaborate rituals and rigidly graded systems of rank, but these did not exist at first. Various individuals were simply given pieces of territory; in return for this territory they were supposed to make a contribution to the revenues of the state, to prevent rebellion within their own boundaries, and to lead soldiers to fight in the service of the king when he called for them. So long as they did these things they could govern their own territories very much as they saw fit. This had the effect of placing permanent garrisons of troops of the Chous or their allies in strategic positions over the conquered territory, and making it unnecessary for the king to worry about local government. He was left free to see to the external defence of the realm, to keep the peace among his vassals, and to see that his vassals did not become so powerful as to menace his supremacy—tasks which were very soon found to be more than ample for any monarch.

Rulers of states who submitted to the Chous without resistance were apparently confirmed in possession of their territories, if they undertook to consider themselves vassals of the Chou kings and to conduct themselves as such. It may seem surprising that one of the vassals given a fief was the son of the vanquished Shang king, who was appointed to rule over at least a part of the Shang people. Actually this was good politics for several reasons. It must be remembered that the Chous and their allies were really in the east on sufferance. However great their armies, they could hardly have resisted a united and determined effort of the whole populace of the conquered territory to oust them. They knew this very well, and made every effort at conciliation. By leaving the heir of the last Shang king to rule his people as their vassal, the Chous were relieved of the care of those who might have been their most troublesome subjects. Furthermore, they thus deflected a great deal of resentment which would have been directed against them had they extinguished the Shang line utterly. Nor is the religious side of the matter to be forgotten. The most fearful aspect of cutting off a dynasty in ancient China was not human resentment, but the fact that, by cutting off their sacrifices, one concentrated upon his head the vengeful anger of a long line of most powerful spirits. But if one gave a fief to their chief descendant, enjoining him to continue their sacrifices, this absolved one of the guilt of cutting off their ceremonies and might even succeed in winning their favour. There was danger, of course, in leaving the Shang scion in a position of power; the Martial King knew that very well. To guard against the possibility that he might try to lead a rebellion against the Chou rule, the Martial King appointed two of his own younger brothers, Kuan Shu and Ts'ai Shu, to 'assist' the Shang ruler in governing his state—actually, of course, to keep watch over him and give warning if he showed signs of making trouble.

The death of the Martial King is dated in 1116 B.C., several years after the defeat of the Shangs. The Chou power was far from secure in the east, and King Ch'êng, the son and successor of the Martial King, was too young to rule with the hand of iron which the circumstances required. In this situation the Duke of Chou, younger brother of the Martial King and uncle of King Ch'êng, ruled as regent for seven years. This Duke of Chou was a very remarkable man, possibly the most remarkable man in all of Chinese history. He was an individual of tremendous intellect, energy, and force of character. Confucius pointed to him as the fountain-head of his philosophy; many Chinese have considered him greater than Confucius. We know all too little of his history, but it is quite possible that he had a large part in originating much that is most distinctive in Chinese thought and institutions. It is certain that he almost made the Chou dynasty, and with it the essential China as we think of it to-day. When the loose-knit and unwieldy fabric of the state produced by the conquest threatened to go to pieces, and others would have been content to let it go, he pulled it back together almost with his bare hands. We see him now cajoling, now threatening, now conciliating and now acting with decisive ruthlessness, all with the singleness of purpose of a strong man who has willed success and will accept nothing else.

Apparently he was not appointed regent, but simply took over the government from King Ch'êng, fearing that the young ruler would not be able to maintain his position. There was naturally wide suspicion that he intended to make himself king in name as well as in fact, and King Ch'êng himself seems to have feared this. This suspicion was shared by his two brothers, Kuan Shu and Ts'ai Shu, who had been set to watch the Shang scion. It is easy to understand their feelings. They probably felt, like many, that the Chou conquest of the east was, after all, a mere plundering raid, certain to end sooner or later in a fiasco. Living in contact with the cultured Shang people, they doubtless felt that their rude countrymen could not hope permanently to rule the east. In the action of their brother they saw what appeared to be the beginning of the end, a dissolution of the conquering band in a series of quarrels over power. They were probably quite sincere in feeling that the best thing they could do was to aid the descendant of the Shang kings in an attempt to re-establish the Shang rule, and this they did.

But they reckoned without the mettle of their brother, the Duke of Chou. Overriding apathy and opposition among the Chou people, he organized a punitive expedition and again marched east. He spent two or three years in re-establishing the Chou power in the east, put to death the Shang ruler and Kuan Shu, and exiled Ts'ai Shu. This having been done, it was necessary to dispose of the Shang people in such a way as to ensure that they would make no further trouble. The rule of the Shangs was for ever extinguished in the region of their ancient capital. Still another brother of the Martial King, K'ang Shu, was appointed to head the State of Wei, ruling the former subjects of the Shang kings from his capital at Ch'ao Kê,

PLATE XI

A HISTORIC CHOU BRONZE OF THE TYPE *KUEI*

THIS IS ONE OF THE FINEST BRONZES FROM THE WEI TOMBS AT HSUN HSIEN. ITS INSCRIPTION TELLS OF AN ATTACK ON THE SHANG PEOPLE, PROBABLY AFTER THEIR REVOLT, AND THE SENDING OF K'ANG, WHO MADE THE BRONZE, TO ESTABLISH THE STATE OF WEI. IT MEASURES SEVENTEEN INCHES ACROSS THE HANDLES.

Reproduced by courtesy of Major-General Sir Neill Malcolm.

which is not far, it will be remembered, from the Great City Shang. But this left no descendant to carry on the sacrifices of the Shang kings. A brother of the last reigning Shang king, Wei Tzŭ by name, was still living; he is supposed to have quarrelled with the king, and to have fled from the Shang court before the conquest. The Duke of Chou felt that this man could be trusted because of his grievances. He was enfeoffed with the State of Sung, in 1111 B.C.; his capital was south of the Yellow River, in what is to-day the extreme eastern projection of Honan Province. This state was appointed to carry on the honours and the sacrifices due to the Shang ancestors. It lasted until 286 B.C.

When King Ch'êng came to maturity the Duke of Chou returned the government into his hands, having governed as regent for seven years. The Chou capital was still located in the Wei valley, the early seat of the Chous, far from the centre of action in their new territories. The Martial King is said to have realized that this situation would have to be remedied by the building of a Chou city in the east, and King Ch'êng ordered such a city to be built at Loyang. The site of this city is very near the modern city of Loyang, a short distance to the north-west. Loyang is about one hundred and fifty miles southwest of the Great City Shang. After the rebellion a large number of the Shang people and officials were transported there and forced to build another city, and to live there under the watchful eyes of the Chou officials. This second city was about ten miles east of the present Loyang; its walls are clearly traccable, standing fifteen feet high in places. The Duke of Chou took a large part in superintending the building of these cities, and apparently wished the young king to move his capital to this more central location. He did not do so, however, but merely used the new city as a sort of secondary capital.

With the quashing of the Shang revolt and the building of a permanent seat of Chou rule in the east, the conquerors had succeeded in establishing themselves. There were many difficulties still ahead, and those difficulties were destined in time to get the better of them, but not before their rule had left such an impress on Chinese history that its effects are still vivid. They had succeeded, in a few years, in bringing themselves from the status of invaders to that of lawful sovereigns of the Chinese world.

*

It is to be understood that the above account of the rise and conquest of the Chous is no more than tentative, in so far as its details are concerned. The accounts vary greatly, especially with regard to chronology. Furthermore, all the accounts are heavily prejudiced in favour of the Chous. The Chou people and their allies are depicted, literally, as Heaven-appointed saviours; the Shangs and those who aided them are as literally painted as no less than devils. I have tried to select from the conflicting accounts and the heavily biased testimony that which is most plausible, and to pass over in silence what is most dubious. Future investigation will give us certainty on many points which are at present unclear. But while it is quite possible that the account given here fails of complete accuracy in some of its details, there is no doubt that the main trend of events and the underlying motives were substantially as depicted.

CHAPTER XVII

POLITICAL HISTORY

For the first centuries of the Chou dynasty we have no connected history. Even the orthodox Chinese histories give only scattered anecdotes and the names and order of the kings, not attempting a continuous narrative. All that we shall do in this chapter is to depict the large outlines of political events, down to about 600 B.C., as a background against which to throw the culture of the period.

In the early days of the Chou dynasty it was comparatively easy for the king to keep even the most powerful of his vassals loyal and submissive. It must be remembered that these feudal lords, appointed by the house of Chou, had to establish and maintain themselves among strange and often hostile subjects. These would often have been only too glad to seize any opportunity to rebel against their masters, and a break of the feudal ruler with the king would have provided such an opportunity. The vassal needed the support of the king's army, and the fear of it to hold over his subjects, to help him keep his position. Furthermore, if he were disobedient to the king the king might order one or more other vassals to seize his territory and appropriate it to themselves, and they would ordinarily have been more than willing to do so. Thus, between the king on the one hand and his people on the other the feudal noble was constrained to loyalty; the king, by playing the nobles off against each other, had no great difficulty in maintaining himself.

But this condition could not last for ever. A few generations were sufficient to make the Chou nobles seem indigenous to their eastern territories, and their subjects often became as loyal to them as they had been to their former rulers. Nobles built up their wealth and their armies, enlarged their states at the expense of weaker neighbours, and gradually came to a point where they could disregard the king's commands with impunity. Gradually they began to stop going to court, as they were supposed to do, and to cease contributing to the king's revenues.

We know both from the recorded history and from bronze inscriptions that there was constant trouble with barbarian peoples living on the borders of the Chinese territories. Some of these were people who later became thoroughly Chinese, but at this time they were constantly at war with the subjects of the Chou house. The kings often ordered their vassals to attack them, rewarding them if they were successful; sometimes they led punitive expeditions in person. The fourth Chou sovereign, King Chao, 'did not return,'[1] it is said, from an expedition to the Yangtse River in 1002 B.C. The circumstances of his death are surrounded with mystery; it is impossible to say whether he was killed in battle.

Since the king was menaced by ambitious vassals within his territories and warlike barbarians from without, it will be understood that his power depended very much upon his character and ability, and rose and declined with them. It is a familiar weakness of hereditary monarchies that they cannot guarantee that every legitimate heir shall be equally worthy of the throne. King Li, who succeeded in 878 B.C., is said to have been avaricious, cruel, and arrogant. There was much murmuring against him among the people, and one of his ministers warned him of this. The king responded by employing a sorcerer to point out those who were criticizing him; all whom the sorcerer indicated were put to death. After this there were few who murmured, but the nobles ceased coming to court. Later King Li redoubled the severity of his suppressive measures; the people did not dare to speak, merely eyeing one another as they passed on the road. The king was greatly pleased, and told his minister, the Duke of Shao, 'I have succeeded in stopping that slandering; they don't even dare to talk now.' 'You have dammed it up,' the duke replied. 'But to stop the mouths of the people is as dangerous as to prevent the flow of water. Finally it will break through, and those who are injured will be many.' King Li refused to listen to his remonstrances. Three years later there was a serious revolt, during which King Li was attacked and had to flee. He spent the remaining fourteen years of his life as a refugee in the state of Chin, shorn of his royal power.

At the time of the revolution the son and heir of King Li took refuge in the house of the Duke of Shao, the minister who had remonstrated against his father's course. When the revolutionaries surrounded his palace and demanded that he surrender up the young heir, he was placed in a quandary. If he gave the boy over to be killed it would look as if he had done so out of revenge, because the king had refused to follow his advice. This would have violated the code of feudal loyalty. Finally the duke turned over his own son in place of the heir, who escaped the wrath of the mob. The Crown Prince was reared in the family of the Duke of Shao. The government was administered jointly, according to one version of the history, by the Duke of Shao and the reigning Duke of Chou for fourteen years. In 827 B.C., King Li being dead and the Crown Prince being of age, he was enthroned as King Hsüan.

Such events could not but leave the prestige and the power of the Chou house at a low ebb. The days of Chou greatness were rapidly drawing to a close, and that close was being accelerated by many agencies. King Hsüan is said to have been able, and to have considerably increased the respect and the allegiance of the feudal nobles to the throne, but he was constantly under the necessity of waging war with the barbarians of the west, in which he was by no means always successful.

Selections in the *Book of Poetry* and passages in other literature give the impression that the latter days of the Western Chou dynasty were fraught with wide dissatisfaction, of the poor against the rich, of the people generally against the exactions of those in power, and of the east against the west. Sectional rivalry between north and south China is a potent factor in Chinese politics to-day; there was similar feeling between east and west at that time. The Chous, as conquerors from the west, had naturally given the lion's share of things to western men, but protest against this gradually reached the point of becoming articulate. A poem probably written in the latter part of the Western Chou period says:

'The sons of the east
Are only summoned (to service), without encouragement;
The sons of the west
Shine in splendid dresses.
The sons of boatmen
Have furs of the bear and the great bear.
The sons of the poorest families
Form the officers in public employment.

If we present them with spirits,
They do not look on them as liquor.
If we give them long girdle-pendants with their stones,
They do not think them long enough.'[2]

The story of the collapse of the Chou power is worth repeating in full, because it shows how almost inextricably fact and legend are interwoven in the history. Most of it occurs in the *Discourses of the States*, which quotes a still older work. It begins in the Hsia dynasty, which, it will be remembered, the orthodox history holds to have preceded the Shang. One day during the declining years of the Hsia dynasty two ghosts of former rulers of the State of Pao turned themselves into dragons and presented themselves in the court of the king, announcing their identity. The king forthwith divined, asking whether to put them to death, to oust them, or to detain them, but the oracle said that none of these courses would be fortunate. He then asked if they should be requested to expectorate, and the spittle preserved, and it was replied that this might be done. A cloth was spread before the dragons and the request presented to them in writing. The dragons immediately disappeared, but the spittle remained; it was placed in a coffer which was carefully laid away, and handed down among the royal possessions from generation to generation and from dynasty to dynasty.

The resemblance of this story to the Greek myth of Pandora's box is interesting. The casket containing the dragon's spittle passed from the Hsia sovereigns to the Shang, and from them to the Chous, never being opened. But during the latter part of the reign of King Li (who later had to flee from revolution) curiosity overcame caution, and the box was opened. Immediately the contents flowed out into the court, and could not be stopped. The king ordered his women to shout at it, whereupon it turned into a small reptile and entered the harem. There it was found by a little girl of about seven years of age. When this girl came to the age of assuming the hairpin (the age of puberty) she was found to be pregnant, although the child had no father. When it was born the young mother was afraid, and abandoned the baby.

The songs sung by boys were believed by the ancient Chinese to be infallibly prophetic. For some time they had been singing this jingle:

> 'A basketry quiver and wild mulberry bow,
> These surely will be the end of Chou.'

King Hsüan heard of this and was troubled. There were a man and woman in the capital selling just such bows and quivers, and the king ordered that they should be seized and put to death. They made their escape, however, and as they fled in the night they heard a babe crying by the wayside. This was the infant born under such strange circumstances in the palace.

The man and woman took pity on it, and carried it with them to Pao. It grew to be a most attractive woman. Later, when the ruler of Pao was about to be punished by the king, he presented this woman as a bribe to excuse him for his fault. She was Pao Szŭ, who became the favourite concubine of King Yu.

Yu, last king of the Western Chou line, made himself thoroughly unpopular, but he is supposed to have met his end, like many another man, all because of a woman. Pao Szŭ dominated him, and he was willing to do anything to please her. She was not easily amused, and the king wished to make her laugh. He used ten thousand devices, but was not rewarded with so much as a smile. King Yu had a system of beacons for summoning the feudal lords, by means of smoke signals, to repel attack in case of invasion. One day he had them lighted. The nobles came, with their armies, post-haste; there was no enemy to be fought, but the spectacle did succeed in making Pao Szŭ laugh. This pleased King Yu greatly, and he did it over and over again, until finally nobody believed in the beacons.

The infatuation of King Yu for Pao Szŭ became greater and greater, and when she bore him a son he wanted to set aside the heir-apparent and put her son in his place, at the same time making her his queen in place of the rightful holder of that place. The fact that his queen was the daughter of the Marquis of Shên made him hesitate, but finally, influenced by a flattering minister, he did so, sending the rightful heir back to the state of Shên. The marquis was made furious by this insult and allied himself with another state and with several barbarian tribes to punish the king. This gave the barbarians just the chance for which they had been waiting. It is said that when the beacons were lighted by the king's orders, the nobles failed to rally, having been fooled too many times. King Yu was killed, Pao Szŭ was taken prisoner, and the ruling house was looted of all its treasures. The Western Chou dynasty was at an end, and the glorious days of the House of Chou were over.

The official end of the Chou dynasty was not until 256 B.C., however, while this catastrophe occurred in 771. The feudal lords set up the rightful heir of King Yu as King P'ing. The defeat of the Chou arms had shown how exposed was their western position to the attacks of the barbarians. The royal capital was moved to Loyang, which had long been their eastern seat, and the Chou line was continued there with a royal domain smaller than the possessions of some of the individual feudal lords. This was known as the Eastern Chou dynasty.

From this time forward the Chou kings were little more than puppets in the hands of their nominal vassals. At best their power was not greater than that of one of the nobles, and they attacked and were attacked, intrigued and were intrigued against, very much like any other chiefs of petty domains. The powerful nobles took advantage of the decline of the royal power to enrich themselves and enlarge their territories by seizing the weaker states on their borders. Out of this process there emerged four states of especially large territory and great power, dwarfing their smaller neighbours, who continued to exist, as it were, on sufferance. The State of Ch'i, on the north-east, included much of what is now Shantung Province. The State of Chin, north of the Yellow River, took in large portions of the present provinces of Shansi and Hopei (formerly Chihli). The State of Ch'in held large territories to the west, including the Wei basin, the former home of the Chous. Ch'u, largest of all, had the whole Yangtse region and territories running north more than half-way to the Yellow River. At this time Ch'u had only partially entered the fold of Chinese culture; it was still considered a more or less 'barbarian' state, but it was very powerful, and played an increasing part in Chinese politics.

We now speak of the Eastern Chou period as the latter part of the Chou dynasty, but men living in early Eastern Chou times considered the Chou dynasty to have ended with the death of King Yu in 771 B.C. They speculated on the question of who would succeed to the royal power, some predicting that one, some that another powerful noble would establish the next dynasty.

In fact, however, none of them took over the title of 'Son of Heaven,' which was at this time understood to go with the rule of all China. Many of them would have been willing to, but none was quite powerful enough. Had anyone tried to do so, the others would have banded together to prevent him, determined that no one else should have what none of them individually was able to attain. The result was a sort of deadlock, in which the Chou successors were allowed to wear, harmlessly, a title which no other dared to take.

But greedy and mutually distrustful though they were, the Chinese nobles realized that there was some need of co-operation. Much as they fought among themselves, and wars at this time were almost constant, they recognized that it was still more necessary that the representatives of Chinese culture should present a united front against the barbarians who were pressing against them from every quarter. To do this without a leader was difficult, and the Chou kings were quite unable to lead. To meet this situation a curious institution developed. The noble possessed of the greatest power and prestige came to be known as 'Pa,' a term which we might translate as 'First Noble.' This title was held now by one, now by another of the rulers of states, depending solely on their possession of power and prestige. This First Noble arrogated to himself, in practice, nearly all of the powers and functions of the king. He repelled invasions and directed punitive expeditions, acted as arbiter of differences between the feudal rulers, punished those who disobeyed his orders, and received the revenues which had formerly gone to the king. The first holder of this place was Duke Huan of Ch'i, who actually assumed it in 679 B.C. Twelve years later the Chou king, Hui, conferred the title of First Noble upon

Duke Huan, thus adding official recognition to what already existed. There were five who held this title between then and the time when it ceased to be used in 591 B.C. Their power was at times so great that they casually made gifts of lands in states other than their own. The Chou kings not only perforce recognized their power, but even asked them to adjudicate quarrels between members of the royal house.

The history of China on its political side from this time to 221 B.C. is largely the history of the struggle between the various states, on the one hand to preserve and on the other to break the 'balance of power' which prevented any one of them from swallowing the others and establishing its rule over all China. This struggle had many phases; among its by-products was a large portion of Chinese philosophy. The story is an interesting and an important one, but one with which this book has nothing to do.

By the time which we have now reached, about 600 B.C., China and the culture, ideas, and institutions which we know as Chinese, had been born. Important as the later portion of the Chou period was, many phases of its culture and institutions were no more than logical and almost predictable developments from what had existed prior to 600 B.C. The same thing is true, in lesser degree, of certain aspects of Chinese history almost down to the present. The remainder of this book will be devoted to an examination of Chinese culture, ideas, and institutions during this formative period.

CHAPTER XVIII

ARCHÆOLOGY

ALTHOUGH the Chou period is more recent than the Shang, it is less well known from the point of view of excavation. No extensive scientific excavation has yet been carried out in any dwelling-site of Chou date. A number of Chou tombs have been excavated in the last few years, however, in Hsün Hsien in northern Honan. That the place of the people buried in them may be thoroughly understood, it is necessary to recapitulate a bit of history.

It will be remembered that after the Chous had conquered the Shang people, at least a part of them were allowed to remain under the rule of the son of the last Shang king, who became a Chou vassal. After the death of the Martial King they rebelled, and the revolt was put down with some difficulty by the Duke of Chou. This had shown plainly that the Shang people constituted a danger, and a number of them, probably including the prime movers in the revolt, were moved to Loyang, where they could be kept under direct surveillance of the Chou officials. But the Chous still had no desire to antagonize the powerful spirits of the Shang ancestors, nor did they wish to be in the position of cutting off the sacrifices of a line for which they professed to have the greatest admiration. They therefore enfeoffed a brother of the last Shang king, as ruler of the State of Sung south of the Yellow River, to continue the sacrifices of the Shang line. But they could hardly have transported all of the people from the general region of the Great City Shang, even if they had wished to, nor would they have cared to depopulate a district so fertile. Instead, they appointed a member of their own house, K'ang Shu, a brother of the Martial King, to rule the newly created State of Wei in this area. He is supposed to have made his capital at Ch'ao Kê, some thirty miles south of the Great City Shang.

Eighty-six tombs, of Chou date, were excavated in Hsün Hsien, at a place a few miles north of the site of Ch'ao Kê, in 1932 and 1933. For various reasons it is believed that these tombs must be those of the rulers of the State of Wei, just mentioned. One of the best of these reasons is the bronze vessel illustrated in Plate XI. It was not excavated scientifically, but came into the Peiping market in 1935 as being from Hsün Hsien; there is little doubt, from its style and patination, that it actually does come from there. From its inscription, twenty-four characters long, it appears that the vessel was made by the same K'ang Shu who first ruled Wei; the war against the Shang people, apparently after the rebellion, and the appointment of K'ang to rule Wei are recounted on the bronze. The name of the State of Wei also appears in inscriptions which were scientifically excavated at Hsün Hsien. The bronze just mentioned must have been made in the first years of the state, so that these tombs must include some which give us materials from the very beginning of the Chou period.

They were excavated by the Honan Archæological Research Association, in co-operation with the National Research Institute. No complete report of the excavation has yet been published, but Mr. Kuo Pao-chün, the Director, kindly showed me the recovered objects and explained the finds.

Of the eighty-six tombs ten were large, the largest being about forty-six feet deep and thirty-two feet square. These are believed to be the tombs of ruling nobles. The remainder were small, ranging in size down to six which were only a little over a yard in depth. There was no sign of a tumulus over any of the tombs. Like the Shang tombs at Anyang, they had been filled up with pounded earth—as many as ninety layers of it in some cases—and left level with the surrounding soil, from all appearances. The large tombs had sloping approaches on the north and south, usually a smooth ramp on the south and steps on the north. The tomb chambers were not so large and splendid as those at Anyang. A board room about six and one-half feet wide by ten feet long was built at the bottom of the larger tombs, and the corpse was apparently placed in this without a coffin. All but two of the tombs had been robbed, and grave-robbers frequently break up the skeleton to prevent the dead from harming them; for this and other reasons, only about three skeletons were obtained in good condition.

Two pairs of tombs are believed to be those of nobles and their consorts. In the case of the larger pair, the man's tomb is somewhat larger than the woman's; the other pair are of the same size. The man's tomb in each case was on the west, the right-hand side as one faces south. The right was the honoured position in ancient China, as the left is to-day.

Valuable objects buried with the dead in the tombs had a fixed order. What look like grotesque bronze masks, having some resemblance to human faces, were affixed to the south wall of the tomb, on either side of the approach. Chariots were also buried on the south. Armour was buried on the east, and weapons on the west, according to Mr. Kuo. Ritual vessels were buried on the north. This has been a great convenience to the grave robbers, whose chief interest is in the ritual bronzes. They simply dig out the north end of the tomb, and often leave the south half untouched. This has resulted in very rich finds of chariots and chariot-fittings by the scientific excavators. More than five hundred pieces of chariot bronze and many of the wooden parts of chariots have been found, and from them Mr. Kuo has been able to make the best reconstruction of the Chou chariot to date.

The excavators have found a number of ritual vessels, some of them inscribed, and a great many miscellaneous objects of various sorts. The Hsün Hsien tombs and the objects which come from them give us an unusually good opportunity to study the effects of the Chou conquest on both the Chou and the Shang people.

Since the Wei rulers were members of the House of Chou we should expect them to follow Chou customs. It is interesting, however, to note that what appear to be the earliest Wei tombs have considerable resemblance to the Shang tombs at Anyang. Particularly noteworthy is the fact that, whereas the early Chou tombs north-west of Hsian are surmounted by tremendous tumuli which still dominate the whole valley, all of the Wei tombs seem to have been constructed without tumuli, just like the Shang type. Likewise, the bronzes and other objects found in the Wei tombs show strong and striking Shang influences, both in motif and in style. Of the bronze vessels from Hsün Hsien which I have seen, there have been perhaps three or four which might have passed as Shang productions, and one of these was of very high quality indeed.

On the whole, however, the Chou influence produced a marked and immediate change. The objects from Hsün Hsien have many of the same motifs, and some of the same general style, but with a difference. In May, 1935, I went in one day from Anyang, where I had seen the most recent and the richest Shang finds, to Kaifêng where I saw the things excavated at Hsün Hsien; this provided a peculiarly good opportunity to compare and contrast the cultures. The dominant impression was that the Hsün Hsien things had been made as if in an attempt to copy the Shang productions—an attempt which did not quite succeed. Motifs were often identical, but the execution was very different indeed. What were subtly compound curves in Shang design had a tendency to become simple curves, hard and obvious, in the work of the later craftsmen. Spaces which were covered with delicate traceries by the Shang designers were left blank or covered with heavier and cruder patterns by those of Chou. All in all, the articles from the Wei tombs, although later, seemed somewhat primitive as compared with those from Anyang.

It is doubtful that this can be explained merely by the obvious statement that the Chous were primitive as compared with the Shang people, for there is every reason to suppose that many, at least, of these objects were made by the same artisans who produced the Shang things, or their descendants. The reason for the difference of quality we can only guess. It may be simply that the spirit of the Shang people was broken by their defeat, and that this was reflected in their work. They may have refused to put their best efforts into producing luxuries for the conquerors. Or the latter, not possessing the æsthetic appreciation of their more cultured predecessors, may have demanded quick results. There is reason to believe that the Shang bronze casters, for instance, may have made several unsuccessful trials for each vessel which they adjudged to be perfect enough to be kept, rather than melted down for another attempt. Such care may not have appealed to the hearty, martial temperament of the Chous.

Yet some of the typically Chou things from Hsün Hsien have decided merit. The vessel illustrated in Plate XI is an example. Although from the very beginning of the Chou period, no one would take it for a Shang bronze, despite the fact that it employs several typical Shang motifs. The whole piece is designed with great boldness and strength. Even the plain grooved effect, on the body, which replaces what would be a wealth of decoration in a Shang vessel of this sort, is strong and pleasing. But the art of design degenerated rapidly in the Chou period; strength became mere crudeness, and simplicity became mere plainness. But both of these were better than most of their attempts to be elaborate, for they too often succeeded in being merely florid. The Chous were endowed with many virtues, but artistic perceptions were not conspicuous among them. And although they conquered the Shang people they never succeeded in acquiring their superlative taste—although they

PLATE XII

THREE WEAPONS OF THE SHANG PERIOD

THE TWO ON THE LEFT ARE DAGGER-AXES, SHOWING TWO DIFFERENT STYLES OF HAFTING; THAT ON THE RIGHT IS A SPEAR-HEAD. THE AXE ON THE LEFT WAS PROBABLY DESIGNED FOR USE; THE CHARACTER INSCRIBED ON IT IS A PICTOGRAPH MEANING 'BATTLE-AXE', AND THE THREE FEET AT ITS BOTTOM REPRESENT A STAND TO HOLD IT ERECT. THE WEAPONS IN THE MIDDLE AND ON THE RIGHT ARE TOO THIN AND WEAK TO HAVE BEEN INTENDED FOR ANYTHING BUT CEREMONIAL PURPOSES; THEY ARE INSCRIBED WITH THE SAME CHARACTER, AND THEY MAY HAVE BELONGED TO THE SAME PERSON OR FAMILY. THE DAGGER-AXE IN THE CENTRE IS FOURTEEN AND THREE-EIGHTHS INCHES HIGH (OTHER PIECES NOT TO SCALE).

Reproduced by courtesy of Mr. P. C. Huang.

seem, strangely enough, to have extinguished it among their descendants.

It will be noticed that the method followed in discussing early Chou culture, in the succeeding chapters, differs considerably from that which was used in the Shang section. For the earlier dynasty much attention was devoted to actual objects yielded by excavation and to handicrafts, while in that which follows little will be said about material objects. There are two reasons for this. In the first place, whereas for the Shang period we have only the oracle bones, a comparatively full and rich literature is preserved from the early Chou period. This makes it unnecessary to depend chiefly upon inferences from objects; we can concentrate our attention directly upon the ideas and institutions of the time. In the second place, we have no such excavation of any Chou dwelling-site as has been carried out at Anyang.

It is planned, in the near future, to excavate the ancient city at Loyang. When this is done it should add greatly to our knowledge. To what extent this and other planned excavations may be delayed by the unsettled political condition of north China is a question which it is impossible to answer. Another important spot at which it is planned to excavate is that of the Chou tombs.

Unlike the reputed burial-places of some earlier and mythical Chinese rulers, there is good reason to believe that these tombs are just what they are supposed to be. They are located northwest of Hsian, north of the Wei; the main group of Chou tombs is about four miles north of the present site of the city of Hsien Yang. The tombs of the Duke of Chou, the Accomplished King, the Martial King, and their successors King Ch'êng and King K'ang are grouped in an area of about four square miles. The tumuli are flat-topped earthen pyramids, which appear to have suffered far less from the erosion of their three millennia than one would expect, but this is doubtless due in part to repairs. I did not try to measure them on my visit, supposing that it would be possible to obtain accurate data on their size. This proved not to be the case, and I can only estimate that they range from twenty-five to forty feet in height, and are probably twice this dimension in length at the base. The tombs of the Accomplished King and the Martial King, very close together, are an impressive object lesson in filial piety. The Accomplished King was really only the chieftain of a few tribes in the Wei valley, and had no direct part in the conquest of the east. Yet his tomb is much the larger of the two. That is, of course, because the Martial King built it, doing his father, and indirectly himself, honour by this act of filial piety. To the credit of the Chinese Republic be it said that these two tombs are still fronted by a temple, in excellent repair, which is a shrine of pilgrimage for those who go to pay their respects to these ancient rulers who played so large a part in laying the foundations of China's greatness.

Although they cannot be compared in size, these Chinese pyramids are strangely reminiscent, when seen in the distance, of those of Egypt. Located on the ancient plateau of Pi, they are visible far south of the Wei, near the site of the little city which was the early Chou capital. It is impossible for one who knows their story to see these tombs, looming mistily across the valley, without a feeling of awe and a catch in his throat. As one approaches the Wei, and they stand out more clearly, the whole panorama of Chou history lies unrolled. To the north lie the mountains, in which was their early seat from which they were forced out by the pressure of other tribes. By a turn of the head one can see the southern mountain range which provided a natural defence for the Wei valley, and allowed them to consolidate their power and lay their plans. Within easy walking distance are the fields where once stood the city in which they dreamed their dreams of conquest. At one's feet lies the Wei, the stream which led them eastward, to the Yellow River, to civilization, to the world. They were a young people, the Chous, a crude people if you like. But they were an immensely vital people, and they succeeded in disseminating widely a culture, and laying the foundations of a political state, which have persisted longer, with less of fundamental change, than any others ever created by man. And there, on the plateau above the valley, lie the kings and the duke who did it, sleeping still in silent majesty.

CHAPTER XIX

LITERATURE

It has sometimes been thought that the Chinese of the Chou dynasty used writing but little, producing books by laborious and time-consuming methods. This is not true at all. The number of documents written even during early Chou times must have run into the tens or hundreds of thousands.

It is recorded that in the tomb of one king, buried in 296 B.C., there were found enough books, written on bamboo slips, 'to fill several tens of carts.' The *Annals of Lü Shih* tell us that in 408 B.C., when the State of Wei finally succeeded in conquering the small but powerful State of Chung Shan, the general who had directed the final campaign returned full of swaggering pride, taking full credit for the achievement. To humble this bumptious warrior his ruler had the Keeper of the Archives bring into the court, and show to him, two chests full of books. Each of these books was a special treatise discussing the strategy to be used in attacking the State of Chung Shan, which had a territory of only a few square miles.

These incidents come from a time slightly later than our period, but we have abundant evidence that from the very date of the Chou conquest, writing, literary writing, was used with a frequency which is almost astounding. One of the books in the *Document Classic* is a plea addressed by the original Duke of Chou to his brother, Duke of Shao, exhorting him to continue to aid in the establishment of the new dynasty.[1] That such a request should be put into writing at all is remarkable, but the high-sounding phrases in which it is couched make it seem, at first sight, an obvious forgery. Yet if we check its style by the bronze inscriptions and its matter by history there is no reason to question its genuineness. We simply have to accept the fact that the Chous were a people who liked to write books. One almost wonders if, having learned writing recently from the Shangs, they took pride in using it on every possible occasion.

On the death of a king the regulations for his funeral were drawn up in writing. Written deeds of gift were drawn up and presented by the donor along with objects which were sometimes of no very great value. Sometimes these deeds recited the merits of the recipient and his ancestors, and the reason for the gift, and were read aloud in a presentation ceremony. The fidelity with which records and vouchers were sometimes kept would win the approval of an accountant. The *I Li* describes the procedure followed in preparing for a diplomatic mission to another state as follows: 'The steward writes out a list of the presents to be taken. He then orders the officials in his department to get them ready. . . . Then the recorder goes over the list and examines the presents. The steward takes the list and, announcing that everything is in order, hands the list to the commissioner, who receives it and hands it to his chief of suite. . . . The chief of suite scrutinizes the loads, checks them against the list he has received, and lets them go.'[2] Records of almost every conceivable sort were kept. It appears from at least one bronze inscription and one literary reference that the names of slaves were kept in registers, and that their status was in some way bound up with this record. In one recorded incident a slave agrees to perform a special service only on condition that the record of his servile condition shall be destroyed. Naturally most of the records, which dealt with trivial affairs, have perished. It is only through the inscriptions on bronzes and occasional mention in books that we are able to infer that they must have existed in very great numbers. Even the deities kept account-books. We read in the *Document*

Classic: 'Heaven, looking upon men below, keeps a record of their righteousness';[3] here is a Chinese Recording Angel!

Simple routine orders, which could easily have been delivered verbally, were written down and then read, with great ceremony, to the recipients. This was probably done so that they would make a greater impression, as well as from sheer love of ceremony; the latter trait was certainly present in the Chinese of that time, as it is in their descendants to-day. The virtue of written orders covering important matters is obvious; they fix responsibility and prevent error. To issue orders in writing was the regular procedure, from early Chou times. A soldier, lamenting his long absence from home, writes in the *Book of Poetry:*

> 'When we went away,
> The millets were in flower.
> Now that we are returning,
> The snow falls, and the roads are all mire.
> The king's business was very difficult,
> And we had not leisure to rest.
> Did we not long to return?
> But we were in awe of the orders in the tablets.'[4]

We have no evidence that there was a regular postal service, but letters were sent by messengers with great frequency. They passed between allies and enemies, individuals and officials. Parts of the *Document Classic* are made up of letters. As has already been mentioned, the Chinese sometimes 'wrote to Shang Ti' and other deities, sending letters to the gods. Mundane letters were sometimes intercepted and altered to accord with the plots of those making the alteration; this indicates that there was no very effective method of affixing seals or signatures so as to identify the sender of the letter beyond question.

The proportion of literate persons to the whole population was undoubtedly small, yet not so small as one might imagine.

There is considerable indication that the ability to read and write was expected of every member of the privileged or aristocratic class, which was not small. The *I Li* lists a bamboo writing-tablet among the articles of clothing with which the corpse of every member of this class was to be dressed.[5] It was apparently worn at the girdle, and used as a sort of notebook. The Chinese, like the ancient Greeks, had the admirable habit of taking notes. It is recorded that Duke Wu of Wei (812-758 B.C.) insisted that his ministers admonish him, despite the reverence due to his age, and on one occasion said to them: 'If you hear the slightest thing which may serve to correct me, remember it or write it down, and tell me.' It would be possible, of course, for such notebooks to be worn as a sign of learning which was not actually possessed, but it is clearly indicated in the literature that even rulers of states, such men as have in some cultures considered themselves above clerkly attainments, had not a little of 'book learning.' And the traditions which ascribe the composition of great books to emperors and their chief ministers show clearly that the arts of literature held a place of no slight respect.

This is not to say that kings ordinarily wrote their own edicts. Even to-day kings and presidents do not always write their own speeches, although they are almost invariably literate. But the composition of state documents is an art which requires special talent and special training like any other art. This was so in ancient China as it is to-day. Therefore there were special ministers whose business it was to put into appropriate words the sentiments to which the ruler wished to give expression. Inevitably these authors were able to influence the content as well as the form, and their influence in the government grew apace. We can often distinguish documents written by such ministers rather than by the ruler himself, for they frequently begin with a phrase which may be translated, not as 'The King says . . .' but 'It is as if the King said . . .' or 'The King agrees in saying . . .' The individuals who produced these documents were usually known as Shih; this is the office, it will be remembered, which began as that of score-keeper in the archery contest. The Grand Shih, who served the king, was a very important functionary indeed. Another official title, much used in bronze inscriptions, is 'Maker of Books.' Lesser rulers also had such attendants, and indeed it appears that every household of any aristocratic pretensions had one or more retainers whose duties were chiefly literary or clerical.

The official documents of the State of Chêng in the middle of the sixth century B.C. were produced by no less than four ministers working in co-operation. Confucius described their work as follows: 'P'i Shên made the rough draft; Shih-shu discussed and revised it; Tzŭ-yü, the manager of foreign intercourse, then polished the style; and finally Tzŭ-ch'an of Tung Li gave it the proper elegance and finish.'[6] The diplomatic and rhetorical skill of this team of ministers is given a large share of the credit for the fact that their state, though small and weak and surrounded by powerful neighbours, was able to maintain its separate existence.

Literature during our period (i.e., prior to 600 B.C.) was largely a practical matter, an adjunct of statecraft. Even poetry, as we shall see, was pressed into the service of the state. Yet poetry gave most of what scope there was for the indulgence of the imagination in literature. Stories of one sort and another and legends there doubtless were, but they were probably considered too unimportant to write down, and if written they were not considered worth the trouble of preserving. Some of the popular stories collected in later times seem to bear the stamp of age.

Yet if literature at this time was practical, it was not narrowly so. It was not merely documents of immediate utility, such as decrees and treaties and notes to foreign states which were considered worthy of the pen and the perusal of the aristocrat. Treatises on ceremonial, on poetry, on discourse, on music, and especially on history were prized and were studied, along with archery and charioteering, by youthful aristocrats.

It is doubtful that any other people living in the world of 1000 B.C. had such a regard for and such a sense of the value of history as did the Chinese. Documents in the *Document Classic*, written just after the conquest of the Shang dynasty by the Chous, point out that the Chou rulers must study the history of the former dynasty in order to be able to avoid its mistakes. One of these draws lengthy illustrations from the history of former times to be a guide and a warning to the reigning king. The exhortation to look at history and shape their conduct accordingly is a favourite theme of ministers addressing their rulers. The downfall of former rulers is ascribed to their inability to use history as a mirror in which to examine their own times. In a warning against the danger of feminine influence, Shih Su, of the seventh century B.C., tells in detail how three dynasties have been ruined, all by women. History was taught to young princes 'to stimulate them to good conduct, and warn them against evil.'

The practice of keeping detailed annals at each of the feudal courts was in full swing well before the close of our period. A minister protesting against the licentious actions of Duke Chuang of Lu said: 'Every action of a ruler must be recorded. If your recorded actions are unlawful, how can your descendants look upon them?'[7] Not only internal affairs but also events in other states were recorded by the various court historians. The result of this has been to give us such detailed history of ancient China as exists for very few other places of that day. As it has been transmitted to us there are many gaps and many interpolations; nevertheless it stands as one of the wonders of the ancient world.

That only a very small proportion of the literature of the early Chou period has come down to us is not surprising. It was written on very fragile materials, and the Chinese climate destroys all but the most durable with great rapidity. Much of it was copied, and handed down from one scribe and scholar to another. When we consider, however, that a great many of the documents were produced only for a particular occasion, it is evident that there was little reason why anyone should have bothered to transmit them. Again, the disorders, plundering and burning which attended the fall of dynasties and the frequent civil wars, were very destructive to archives. Finally, in 213 B.C., the First Emperor of the Ch'in dynasty had such copies as he could seize of most of the books then extant burned, as a political measure, and their preservation was made a crime with severe penalties. Of the works which yet survived, many were destroyed in the general disorders which attended the end of the short-lived dynasty.

Despite this fact, we have not a little of literary material which dates from the period before 600 B.C. There are many works of which we know only their names, and the fact that they existed, but others have come down to us whole or in part. To work with these books is very difficult for several reasons. The practice of pious forgery has flourished in China as elsewhere, and the Chinese have such reverence for antiquity that a number of books, really written very late, are ascribed to a very early period indeed. Such complete works are not so hard to distinguish, but when later passages are interpolated into genuinely early books the task of discrimination becomes more difficult.

Chinese scholars have worked for centuries, and Western scholars for a few decades at the task of discrimination. Their efforts have met with considerable success, but they have been greatly handicapped by the lack of standards of judgment. It is all very well to say that a certain book dates from the Shang dynasty or from early Chou times, but if no one has ever seen what is certainly a piece of Shang or early Chou writing, the whole matter remains one of theories based on theories. The new archæological research of the last few years has now given us standards by which to judge. In the Shang oracle bones and in a number of early Chou bronze inscriptions we possess writing which certainly dates from those times, and has undergone no later alteration.

Let us examine, one after another, the various literary materials which have come down to us from early Chou times, and the tentative conclusions which recent study allows us to draw about them.

INSCRIPTIONS ON BRONZES

We have seen that, speaking generally, the bronzes of the Chou dynasty are inferior to those of the Shang period, from the artistic and technical points of view. But as regards their inscriptions the Chou bronzes are of far more interest than the Shang, and the earlier Western Chou bronzes are better in this respect than those of the later Eastern Chou. Indeed there is a sequence which seems almost ordained by providence for the benefit of the archæologist. In the Shang period we have the oracle bones, in the Western Chou period we have many long and informative bronze inscriptions, and in the Eastern Chou period, when the bronze inscriptions become shorter and less interesting, the transmitted literature is much more abundant.

Nearly all of the inscriptions of length and importance occur on vessels. Bronze vessels were cast for a variety of reasons, on a great variety of occasions. Sometimes they were simply made for the purpose of providing an eating or drinking utensil for use on gala occasions, and merely inscribed with the statement that 'So-and-so made such-and-such a vessel at such-and-such a time.' But these seem to have been more common in the later period, when we may suppose bronze to have been more plentiful. For the most part these vessels, made of a precious material and executed by craftsmen of great artistic and technical skill, were prized in those days very much as they are prized now. The fact that a very large proportion of the inscribed vessels we know were made by royal officials, and mention the king, show that they were not a common possession. Such bronzes were considered as among the greatest treasures of a state, and they are usually mentioned as the chief objects of loot carried off by invaders. A single *chüeh*, one of the smallest and commonest of vessels, was enough to cause a quarrel among nobles; a large *ting* had sufficient value to bribe the ruler of a state. On one occasion, when attacking enemies seemed on the point of extinguishing one state, its chief minister urged the ruler to buy off the enemy with the bronze vessels. When he refused, the minister asked for what else he had laid up such treasures. As a matter of fact bronze vessels were frequently used to bribe attacking armies to withdraw.

Occasions on which bronzes were cast ranged from the successful conclusion of military raids, when captured metal was made into vessels, to weddings. When a feminine member of a family of rank married it was customary for one of the male members of her family to have made for her a bronze vessel, which was given to her as a wedding present. It was apparently intended for sacrificial purposes. It carried a brief inscription, ordinarily including the name of the donor and the recipient, the name of the kind of vessel, and a wish that her sons and grandsons would for ever preserve and use it. Sometimes it included the hymeneal hope that she would have 'sons and daughters without limit.' Occasionally these vessels were made for sacrificial purposes, without any other motive, in which case the maker often set forth the various blessings he hoped to receive as a result of his piety. Such a vessel was usually dedicated to a particular ancestor, though it does not seem that the sacrifices made with it were directed to him or her exclusively. Other vessels, made for various occasions, quite usually included such a dedication to an ancestor and such hopes for blessings to be received in recognition of the sacrifices to be rendered with the vessel.

Most of the uses of these inscriptions are such as take advantage of their durability. It is no accident that many of these bronzes have persisted and come down to us through three millennia; they were intended to last longer than this. The usual formula is 'for ten thousand years, for ever,' whatever that may mean. When they wished to put a record into such form that it was sure to be preserved, they cast it on a bronze. Thus one bell (bells were used for this purpose much like other bronzes) preserves its maker's genealogy. A treaty defining the boundaries between states, and a record of the adjudication (with an army!) of a dispute between two feudal lords by the king are among our bronze archives. The *Tso Chuan* says that in 536 B.C. the code of criminal law of the State of Chêng was cast on a set of bronze vessels.[8] We have several inscriptions recording the details of transfers of lands. Apparently they performed the function of deeds, cast in 'deathless bronze'—witnesses which have outlasted every title to property which existed in their world. These bronzes are not always limited to recording one event or one set of facts. Some of them suggest that items were saved up for a space of several years, and then thriftily cast consecutively in one inscription.

Vanity outranks almost every other human passion, and the ancient Chinese were human in this as in other respects. The desire to be thought well of and considered important by later generations as well as by their own was very strong in them. One of the strongest arguments used by ministers in trying to persuade their recalcitrant sovereigns to act morally was the fact that posterity would condemn the reprehensible, but praise the good. And whenever anything which seemed to enhance his prestige happened to an ancient Chinese he appears to have cast a bronze to record the fact, if he was rich enough. Thus we read in one inscription that a noble failed to send his due quota of soldiers to aid the king in an expedition, for which he should have been fined three hundred *lieh* of metal. But it was not possible so to fine him, probably because he was too powerful, and the offending noble cast a bronze telling all about it, apparently for the purpose of showing his descendants that their ancestor had been 'beyond the law!'

Not all of them are so forthright, however. Some of the devices which the more modest use to cloak their ostentation would do credit to a practised social climber. It is quite usual to dedicate vessels to the father and mother of the maker, and sometimes also to his grandfather and grandmother. But one vessel which is dedicated only to the grandparents of the maker omitting all mention of his parents, is a little surprising until one notices that the surname of the grandmother is that of the royal family—a fact with which all who read the inscription were no doubt expected to be duly impressed.

More numerous than all other sorts are those which record the receipt by their makers of gifts or marks of favour from the king or some other superior. Sometimes it is no more than a word of praise from the king which is thus celebrated. One inscription tells us that on a certain day when the king went fishing one Ching had the honour of attending him in this sport, and the king gave Ching a fish, whereupon Ching cast a *ting* to preserve this signal instance of royal condescension from oblivion. On another occasion it was the bestowal of a deer, spoil of the royal chase, which was the cause of such a vessel.

Ordinarily, however, the presentations thus commemorated were more substantial. For an evening's entertainment, the conquest of a principality, or years of loyal service, the king and other rulers bestowed money, horses and chariots, weapons, badges of rank in the form of clothing worn only by the nobility, offices, slaves, and territory. There was a regular ceremony used for presentations of importance, and corresponding to this we have a general formula for bronze inscriptions telling of them.

This formula occurs complete on the set of vessels made by the officer Sung, probably in the ninth century B.C., or earlier. The inscription begins with the date, the third year (of the king) and the fifth month, the phase of the moon, and the day. The king was at Chou, at a certain palace. At dawn, he went to the 'great house' (temple), and took his place. One of his attendants took his place on the right, and Sung entered and stood in the middle of the court. A minister handed the king the document (previously prepared) containing the royal orders. The king handed this document to another minister, and ordered him to read the contents to Sung. 'The king says': Here follows the contents of the document, appointing Sung to office and defining his functions. It also bestows upon him certain gifts, clothing and ornaments worn by nobles and a banner. It ends with the exhortation 'use these in performing your service.' Sung bowed, received the document containing the royal decree and suspended it from his girdle, and retired. Thereafter he 'dared to respond to the very illustrious, magnanimous generosity of the Son of Heaven' by making a sacrificial vessel dedicated to his father and his mother, to be used in sacrificing and to pray for the blessings of tranquillity, spiritual aid, prosperity, and long (eternal?) life. The inscription ends with the following prayer: 'May Sung enjoy longevity for ten thousand years, serving the Son of Heaven, and finally coming to an auspicious end. May his sons and grandsons treasure and use (this vessel).' This particular event was celebrated by the casting of no less than four vessels of which we know, different in form but having the same inscription. There is another inscription which tells us that its vessel was duplicated twelve times.

The important point to note is that a book, prepared in advance by the secretariat of the king or other ruler, was given to the recipient of the gift, who copied that book into the inscription. This means that *in these bronzes we have exact copies of the texts of books nearly three thousand years old which have undergone no alteration since that time.* Among well-authenticated early Chou inscriptions there are at least twenty-nine such books.

In so far as possible I have studied the vocabulary, grammar, style and ideas of these inscriptions, comparing them with the literature which is supposed to have been produced at the same time. A thorough study of these things will require the co-operative work of many students for many years. Such study shows that much of the literature corresponds exactly with what we find on the bronzes. Some sections of the *Document Classic* might almost have been copied directly from a bronze, or vice versa. Other books and portions of books are completely different. Furthermore, the books which are alike in style are also alike in ideas, while those which differ in language are, for the most part, books which scholars have long suspected to be forgeries because their ideas did not appear to fit the period to which they were assigned.

To date these bronzes accurately is very difficult. They often specify 'In the —th year of the King,' but they fail to say what king. From names mentioned, historical data and other criteria, it is possible to date a few with considerable accuracy. For the rest we must depend on the form of the characters, which changed very greatly in the course of a few centuries, and on language, and content. From these it is possible to date them with a possible error of one or two centuries, which is closely enough for a study of the history of culture rather than of events. It is not to be supposed that long inscriptions can commonly be read from one end to the other with complete certainty. There are usually gaps in our understanding, and there is much which is doubtful. All that one can do is to use the things which are certain and discard the rest. Nor can one accept every inscription as genuine. There are many fake inscribed bronzes, and many fake inscriptions which have been cut on good bronzes. Only long and careful study by many scholars can separate the good from the bad. My study of bronze inscriptions is based on detailed analysis of two hundred and nineteen inscriptions from the western Chou period and one hundred and thirteen eastern Chou inscriptions. These include all of the most important inscriptions which are current, and all of them have been authenticated as genuine by the concurrent opinion of experts.

Imperfect though our understanding of ancient bronze inscriptions may be, they constitute a source of material which cannot continue to be disregarded, to the extent to which it has been disregarded up to this time, by those who study ancient Chinese culture. The longer inscriptions not only deal with such routine matters as those mentioned, but often contain long moral discourses and accounts of ceremonial procedure which shed a great deal of light on the philosophy and religion of the times. It is true that many of the inscriptions are brief, but we have well-authenticated Chou inscriptions of the following lengths: from seventy-five to one hundred characters, fourteen; from one hundred to one hundred and fifty characters, fifteen; from one hundred and fifty to two hundred characters, five; two hundred and ninety-one characters, one; three hundred and fifty-seven characters, one; more than three hundred and ninety characters, one; four hundred and three characters, one; four hundred and ninety-seven characters, one. To get the equivalent length of these in English words the figures would have at the least to be doubled.

The remainder of this chapter will be devoted to a brief description of the nature and contents of each of the books on which our account of the Chou period is chiefly based. The reader who finds these details uninteresting may omit them, turning at once to page 276, without missing anything vital to his understanding of the rest of the book.

The *I Ching*, or *Book of Changes*

The *Book of Changes* was probably the first complete work of Chinese literature, among those which have come down to us, to reach its present form. This applies only to the original text, not to the commentaries which are usually published together with it as if they were one work. Tradition says that it was written by the Accomplished King while he was in prison, held there by the last Shang ruler. There is little reason to believe this, but the book does reflect the conditions of the last years of Shang and the first years of the Chou period.

It is a book of divination, a sorcerer's manual as it were, used to foretell the future. The diviner first manipulated a number of stalks of the milfoil plant, by a method which indicated one or another of the sixty-four diagrams which can be made by combining six lines, either straight or broken, thus ䷾ Having obtained a particular diagram, he turned to the section discussing that one in the *Book of Changes* and from its explanation gave the prophetic information desired. This method was used along with divination by the tortoise-shell in the Chou period.

The language of this book is very concise, even cryptic. This has given rise to various theories that it contains a secret language or an occult symbolism. It makes one wonder if it was written at a time when the Chous had not yet learned to write very clear Chinese. But probably, being a book for wizards, it was intended to be cabalistic. He is a bold man who would pretend to understand all of this book, but some of its material can be used none the less, to throw light on the culture of the time. A reference to ox-carts in this work shows that they existed just as well as it would in another.

Some aspects of the *Book of Changes* are illuminated by the recently discovered Shang oracle bones, with whose inscriptions it has much in common. Future study along this line may make its meaning clear to us. The translation by Legge is perhaps the best we have. But the following quotation from his rendering shows that even when translated this book is a bit puzzling:

'The topmost line, undivided, shows its subject solitary amidst the (prevailing) disunion. (In the subject of the third line, he seems to) see a pig bearing on its back a load of mud, (or fancies) there is a carriage full of ghosts. He first bends his bow against him, and afterwards unbends it, for he discovers that he is not an assailant to injure, but a near relative. Going forward, he shall meet with (genial) rain, and there will be good fortune.'[9]

The *Shang Shu*, or *Document Classic*

This work is commonly known in English as the *Book of History*. This name is misleading, for it is in no sense a history, but only a collection of documents. The Chinese call it by two names, *Shu Ching*, which means 'Document Classic,' and the older and more common name, *Shang Shu*. Many theories have been advanced as to the meaning of the latter; from the use of these words in bronze inscriptions I am convinced that it means simply 'Preserved Books' or 'Treasured Books.' These were documents, written for a particular occasion, which were considered important enough to be preserved in the state archives. But this book as we have it now cannot be considered to be the Chou archives. Many documents have been lost, and in some cases parts of one document have been put with parts of others. In one or two cases documents of very minor importance have found their way more or less by accident into the collection.

The latest of these documents is supposed to date from around 600 B.C., but the collection as we have it now consists chiefly of forgeries, some of which were probably written as late as the third century A.D. Comparison with bronzes and examination by other standards indicates that not more than fifteen documents, about one-quarter of the whole book, can be assigned with confidence to a date before 600 B.C. It was thought, until very recently indeed, that at least one of these documents was a genuine work of the Shang period. But I have proved, by comparison with the language and ideas contained in the Shang oracle bone inscriptions, that every book in this collection which has been supposed to date from Shang times was really forged at a later date. Some of the supposedly Shang books do date from before 600 B.C., however; they were forged in early Chou times for political purposes.

The genuine pieces include speeches made at various crises by kings and other rulers, exhorting their subjects to support them; moral and admonitory communications made to newly established feudal lords; a proclamation denouncing the use of intoxicating liquors save for sacrifices and on other very rare occasions; a collection of documents concerned with the building of the city at Loyang; two lengthy exhortations addressed to the conquered subjects of the Shang dynasty, warning them against rebellion; a harangue addressed by a duke to his army at the beginning of a military expedition; and so forth. Together they form much of our most important material.

The *Shih Ching*, or *Book of Poetry*

The *Book of Poetry* is the only literary work of our period in which there is a great deal of expression of emotion and imagination. The remainder of the literature is primarily documentary in style, although it does rise to heights of rhetorical majesty which almost lift it out of this category at times. The earliest poems in this work are chiefly of a religious nature, intended to be used in connection with sacrificial ceremonies, so that even they are of a practical nature.

None of these poems is earlier than Chou times. The last section is called Praise-Odes of Shang, and consists of poems used in sacrificing to the kings of the Shang dynasty. Although sometimes ascribed to the Shang period, they were written in the State of Sung, which continued the Shang sacrifices under Chou. The brief section called Praise-Odes of Chou, and parts of the so-called Greater Odes of the Kingdom and Minor Odes of the Kingdom are considered to have been composed in western Chou times. The remainder is later, but every piece in the book is supposed to have been written earlier than about 600 B.C.

This book is an anthology of three hundred and eleven poems, selected from a much larger number which existed at that time. Tradition says that Confucius made the selection from three thousand pieces, but it was probably done before his time. The authors of the poems are for the most part unknown, though one poet signs himself, in the body of his poem, as follows:

> '(I), Chi-fu, made this song,
> An ode of great excellence,
> Of influence good,
> To present to the chief of Shên.'[10]

Not all of these poems are sacrificial odes. Laufer has said that the Chinese have produced no epic poetry,[11] and this is doubtless true. But some of these pieces, reciting the birth and exploits of heroes, seem to verge on the epic style; they are all, however, rather brief. Many, perhaps all, of the poems were once set to music, but the music has long been lost. A large proportion of them are lyric poetry, in the sense of being the expression of the private emotions of individuals. Lovers exulting over their beloved; lovers disappointed; honest toilers sneering at the idle rich; women who helped to make their husbands' fortunes, cast off in favour of some more youthful favourite; concubines lamenting that they receive so little of the company of their lord; soldiers kept long from home on frontier duty and their wives wondering if they will ever see them again; retainers celebrating the prowess of a bonny princeling; ministers, whose counsels of prudence have caused them to be cast off to make place for flatterers; a recluse, praising philosophy which makes sweet the uses of adversity; greybeards who lament that the 'good old days' are gone, and that there are no longer any real ladies and gentlemen; prophets who damn the corruption of their times and foretell disaster; all these and others find outlet for their feelings in these verses.

Very early this poetry was 'interpreted,' which means that it was often understood to mean what it did not mean at all. Thus the most obvious love poems were supposed to have deep philosophical meaning. Because of this fact, there grew up a curious use of poetry in diplomacy. A diplomat to-day may have an extensive repertoire of poetry at the tip of his tongue, but if so he employs it in making pretty speeches to ladies rather than in discussing the serious business of statecraft with diplomats themselves. But such was not the case in ancient China. When negotiations were going forward, and especially at banquets, apt quotations of poetry were sung or recited to illustrate the sentiments or to reinforce the points of the various parties. Not only was the statesman required to know poems to advance his own argument, but he was expected to be sufficiently learned and quick of wit to be able to recite appropriate verses in response to those quoted by others. That is why Confucius said: 'Though a man may be able to recite the three hundred odes, yet if, when entrusted with a government charge, he does not know how to act, or if, when sent to any quarter on a mission, he is unable to respond without being prompted, although his learning may be great, of what practical use is it?'[12] This use of poetry in government has had the unfortunate effect of causing these pieces to be explained by the commentators in the most fantastic manner. The puritanism which has cursed much of Confucian orthodoxy has not made matters better in this regard. Thus we are expected to believe that some of the daintiest and most light-hearted of love lyrics or descriptions of the amusements of the peasantry were written 'to condemn the licentiousness of the times.'

The *Book of Poetry* gives us our best and almost our only picture of the unofficial thoughts and feelings of individuals of various classes in this period. Chinese poetry does not lend itself to translation, which at best gives only a most pale and distorted image of the original. Read in Chinese, these verses are often charged with the greatest beauty, fire, and delicacy.

The *Tso Chuan*

The meaning of the name of this book is uncertain; perhaps it should be translated as the chronicle of a person named Tso. It was written in its present form some time after 468 B.C. It is supposed to be a commentary on the annals of the State of Lu, and these annals are supposed to have been revised by Confucius; both of these propositions are doubtful.

There is no question, however, that it is one of the most important of all sources of ancient Chinese history. It draws heavily on the state chronicles which have been mentioned, and its material appears to be, for the most part, authentic, though there are exceptions to this. It covers the time from 722 to 468 B.C., so that only its first half falls within our period.

The *Kuo Yü*, or *Discourses of the States*

A large portion of this book is based on material written during our period, but it was not itself written at that time. Its value lies in the fact that it embodies material from the various chronicles kept in the various states. Some of its stories go back as far as the tenth century B.C., but most of them deal with the seventh and sixth, and a few with the fifth century B.C. The date at which the book was put together is uncertain, but it was long after the end of our period.

Some of the stories and conversations appear to have been copied exactly from older sources. Different points of view are represented, as they would not be if all of the material had been revised and edited by one person. On the other hand, much of the material is obviously false. Whole movements of history are predicted in detail in conversations supposed to have taken place long before the events occurred. Late philosophical ideas are introduced into conversations which took place before these ideas had come into existence.

The *Discourses of the States* is a book which may be used

to give us details about events which we already know to have occurred or to be highly probable. But it is not reliable enough to be used as first-hand evidence by itself, and incidents quoted from it in the following pages will be understood to be subject to a certain degree of possible doubt.

The *I Li*, or *Book of Etiquette and Ceremony*

We have already seen that the Chinese of the Chou period loved ceremony. Even to-day in the West we have set rituals for the performance of the marriage ceremony, religious and legal procedure, etc.; the ancient Chinese carried the same principle much farther. Since the regulations were many and detailed, it became necessary that they be written down, so that they could be referred to. There are three ancient books of regulations for ceremonial procedure. These are the *Li Chi*, or *Ceremonial Records*, the *Chou Li*, or *Ceremonies of Chou*, and the *I Li*, or *Book of Etiquette and Ceremony*. All three of these books were put together later than our period. The *Li Chi* and the *Chou Li* are completely permeated with ideas and phraseology which are never found in the literature or inscriptions of the early Chou period; if they contain early material, it has been so thoroughly edited and altered that it is of little use as evidence concerning that time. But the *I Li* falls into a different category. Certain of its passages are easily distinguishable as late additions to the work, and it is a question whether any portion of it existed in its present form earlier than or even as early as the time of Confucius. Nevertheless, the book in general bears the unmistakable stamp of an earlier day, as compared with the other works on ritual. This does not mean that it can be used as a primary source for the early Chou period. But it can be used to provide corroborative detail concerning matters of which the fundamental authenticity is established by more completely reliable works.

The book is chiefly concerned with describing the rituals to be used by 'ordinary officers,' that is, the least exalted members of the aristocratic class. It tells in detail what is to be done in connection with the following events in the lives of such persons: capping (i.e., the giving of the cap worn by aristocrats to the young man coming of age); marriage; visits between ordinary officers; death; mourning; burial; and sacrifice. In addition it gives directions for the conduct of banquets, less important and more important archery meetings, and embassies sent to foreign states. It cannot be said that this book makes very interesting reading, for it goes into such minute details as at times seem almost absurd. But it does give us intimate pictures of many phases of the life of the time about which we should otherwise know little more than the bare fact of their existence.

*

All of the above works, with the exception of the bronze inscriptions and the *Discourses of the States*,[13] have been translated. These translations are uniformly the result of careful, conscientious work, and are very valuable. But they suffer from too much dependence on commentaries. The commentators were Chinese scholars, living many centuries after the writing of the books which they undertook to explain, who very frequently knew far less than the Chinese scholars of the present do about very ancient China. Very often their explanations are very valuable; very often they are bad guesses. If there was anything in a book which did not agree with the commentator's previous ideas, it did agree by the time he had finished explaining it. Therefore, it is impossible to place any reliance on translations for scientific work.

CHAPTER XX

CHOU SOCIETY

In China in the early Chou period power and position depended upon the holding of land. When the Chou conquerors established themselves, they parcelled out territory to the relatives of the royal family and to the allies who had aided in their conquest. These individuals, possessing large tracts of land and holding the power of life and death over the human beings living on that land, held the highest social position next to the king. They gave out lands to ministers and other smaller vassals in return for services. There was no regularity in the system, no provision of so many steps from king to commoner, but finally, under the vassal who actually supervised the farming of his own land, there were the common people, who did the agricultural and other work of the community. Their position was virtually that of serfs or slaves, and they occupied the bottom of the social scale.

It is not to be supposed that land-holding in those days was a simple matter of having a clear title and a registered deed, and paying one's taxes regularly. Lands were given 'to have and to hold,' and the latter was the more difficult part of the undertaking. These were rough-and-ready days. Virtually all land titles had recently changed hands as a result of military invasion, and if one found himself with a strong army next to a weak neighbour with too much land, why not relieve him of some of it? Of course, one might get into trouble by doing so, and be punished by the superior of both the landholders concerned. We have one bronze inscription which tells of such an incident, in which the king interfered and stopped the robbery. But even so, the king had to send an army to enforce his demands, and the king and other nobles would not always bother to do that. They were too busy with their own affairs, and it looks as if they sometimes welcomed quarrels among their inferiors as a means of keeping them divided and harmless. For it was not only the superior who had the legal right to take one's land if he wished, or the equal who might be powerful enough to take it, who were to be feared. One's inferiors, who could be oppressed at will so long as they would tolerate it, might band themselves together, revolt, and set up one of their own number in his place.

The mere possession of lands, then, meant little. Eternal vigilance was required of him who would keep them. Practically every landholder had an army, since he was expected to send or lead it to fight for his superior who had given him the land. For his own safety it was necessary that he make his army as strong as possible. But there were many things which were important for the strength of his position apart from sheer military force. Ties of birth or friendship with other feudal lords, which would assure him of aid in times of danger, were very important; unpopularity with his equals was an expensive luxury. Good advisers were worth much to him. Even the goodwill of the peasants who tilled his fields was of value. They made up the rank and file of his army, and by rebelling or deserting him in a crucial moment they could ruin him. This was a powerful motive to the development of humanitarianism toward the common people.

Birth, the fact of being descended from persons of consequence, is always a factor in fixing social position. In ancient China it was especially important because ancestors were not merely a memory of departed glory; they were active, powerful spirits who could give supernatural aid to their descendants. Birth into a powerful family was also important because it gave one relatives who could ordinarily be depended upon to assist him in maintaining himself and his possessions. This was especially true in the case of members of the ruling Chou family and of the few other families which emerged as very powerful after the conquest.

There was a hereditary aristocratic class. Toward the end of our period it could occasionally be entered by persons of humble origin, but ordinarily its members were born into it. The members of this group were known as *shih* 士 (this is not to be confused with *shih* 史, the name of an office). The *shih* were a group who might be compared very roughly with the knights of medieval Europe. Their life and customs were very different from those of the common people. They did not, it appears, do agricultural labour, work as artisans, or engage in trade. They were military officers and government officials. The sons of members of this class were initiated into it upon reaching an age which varied, but was often around twenty. This initiation was known as 'capping,' i.e. the bestowing of a cap. It was a ceremony of considerable elaboration, which included sacrifices and the giving of a special name or 'style.' Sons of *shih* by concubines were capped, but with ceremonies of inferior dignity.

From these circumstances some have supposed that the *shih* were not merely an aristocratic class, but rather a caste, of different racial origin from the common people. It has been suggested that they were the descendants of a group of invading, bronze-using warriors who came into north China from some place in the West, and settled down as predatory overlords of the Neolithic aborigines, whom they reduced to the status of virtual slaves and compelled to provide their masters with a living. But we have already seen that there is no evidence of an invasion of people of differing racial type among the ancient skeletal material which has been studied. And most of the evidence points to quite a different origin for the *shih*.

What really happened seems to be that a ruling, fighting class gradually separated itself out from the general Neolithic population. As fighting became more common, and the Neolithic and early bronze-using people began to make raids on each other, it was necessary that some of the men of each village should specialize on defence and on fighting. Perhaps whole settlements sometimes found that it was easier to set up as warriors, and let the people around them work for them, than to labour in the fields. The chiefs and their groups of warriors, no doubt, provided the farmers with 'protection' whether they wanted it or not, and in return for that service they took a share of the peasant's crop. The size of that share was fixed by the warriors, since they had the power to fix it and the peasants were helpless.

We know that the word *shih* 士 meant 'a young man,' 'a stalwart.' Its original sense was probably much like that of the word 'brave' used of the warriors of an American Indian tribe. It was natural that such men should form an intimate group around the ruler, and that they should enjoy special privileges in the community. As territories enlarged, and petty chiefs became petty kings, it was natural that the officials and administrators should be chosen from among the members of this group who had passed the age of active fighting and developed in experience and wisdom. That such a group should become hereditary is altogether to be expected.

Inevitably the *shih* developed customs and a whole manner of life quite different from that of the commoners. The two groups had little in common. The *shih* were interested in fighting and government, not in tilling the soil except as supervisors of it. Being fed, clothed, and sheltered by others, they had time to develop elaborate ceremonies around such details of their life as coming of age, marriage, and sacrifices to ancestors. They had time for elaborate banquets and archery contests in which the commoners could take no part. The advent of books and writing made a still greater difference, for the ordinary peasant had neither leisure nor opportunity to cultivate these. Finally we have two extremes: the commoner, a ground-tilling clod who knows nothing but his labour, his rustic merry-makings, and the occasional fighting for which he is conscripted; the aristocrat, wearing fine clothing and eating fine food, skilled in archery and charioteering, accustomed to command, schooled in an elaborate etiquette, able to quote verses appropriate to any occasion, smooth, polished, sometimes witty. As different as the poles, but for all that we need not assume that they are descended from different ancestors.

The *I Li* lists, among the 'articles of utility' to be buried with the dead *shih*, the hoe of the farmer as well as the bow and arrow of the warrior.[1] I do not think that this means that the Chou aristocrats personally tilled the soil as a serious business, but I do think that it indicates that the time was not far distant when they had been prosperous farmer-warriors, and that their burial customs had survived from that time. Another evidence of this is the symbolic tilling of the soil, done as a religious ceremony, by the king himself in the spring. This custom persisted until the end of the Manchu dynasty; we do not know how old it is, but there is literary evidence that it was an old-established practice before 800 B.C., and it is referred to in a bronze inscription which was probably cast within a few decades after the Chou conquest.

Members of aristocratic castes commonly refuse to do menial tasks, leaving them to their inferiors. But in ancient China we find nobles of lower rank serving food, with their own hands, to those of higher station, while high officials serve feudal lords and important guests. The lower nobles are served, of course, by commoners or slaves. But what we have is a series of gradations, not an abrupt cleavage.

The original meaning of the word *shih*, a young, able-bodied man, was not entirely lost; the *Book of Poetry* speaks of field-workers as *shih.*[2] In the aristocracy, the *shih* were the lowest class, those with no special rank. The *I Li*, in speaking of slaves, mentions 'the head of the slaves' and 'the *shih* of the slaves,'[3] that is, the common slaves with no special rank. On every hand there is evidence that *shih* was not a term standing for a caste.

The *Ceremonial Records*, a book written much later than our period, says: 'The ritual does not extend down to the common people; punishments do not extend up to the great officers.'[4] This passage has been quoted countless times as showing the vast gulf which lay between the aristocracy and the common people. The passage is perfectly authentic, but mistaken. It was written by a member of the official class, who probably wished to impress the rulers with the idea that 'punishments should not extend up to the great officers.' Perhaps it has some validity for later periods; it has little for ours. The severest punishments, not merely torture and death, but even the exposing of the body to public contempt, were visited on persons of the highest rank, when their superiors wished to punish them and the persons to be punished were not too powerful.

Costly and complicated ceremonies did not commonly extend down to the peasants for obvious reasons; they had neither time nor money for them. But the lowest class was not outlawed, from a religious point of view, like the untouchables of India, who would pollute a religious service by going near it. In the sacrificial ceremonies of aristocratic households the servants and slaves had their place, prescribed in the book of ritual, like anyone else. It was a subordinate place, to be sure. But they were served by the head of the house, who conducted the sacrifice in his turn just like every one else; their chief bowed to the head of the house, who bowed in reply to him. They received a share of the sacrificial meat, relishes, and in fact everything, and apparently as much of everything, as the most blue-blooded noble present. Servants or slaves even acted as priests, at times, in the sacrificial ceremonies of noble families.

Furthermore, individuals were raised to the aristocratic class from the plebeian, and sank to plebeian status although they had been aristocrats. Kuan Tzŭ, the statesman who is credited with having brought the State of Ch'i to prosperity, urged that all of the exceptionally able among the common people should be selected, by the officials who supervised them, and raised into the *shih* class. On the other hand, wholesale reduction of families to the enslaved class, because of a crime of one of their members, was a penalty which always hung over the heads of the aristocrats. The *Discourses of the States* quotes the son and heir of King Ling who, after reflecting that the sons and grandsons of many who formerly occupied high places were now tilling the soil while others who started as peasants were now in the government, concluded that 'really, there is no difference' between the people of various classes.

When we seek to understand clearly the position of the people outside the aristocracy we have a difficult task, for two reasons. In the first place, the whole early Chou period is one in which institutions were developing, but in which they had not yet come to be fixed in clear forms which we can describe, and say that it was thus and so always and everywhere. In the second place, not one of our sources of information, with the possible exception of a small part of the *Book of Poetry*, comes from the common people, and therefore what they tell us about the common people is only incidental.

At the bottom of the scale we have slaves. People became slaves in two ways that we know of. Prisoners of war were enslaved as a matter of course, and war was frequent and common. Persons who had offended their superiors, which in those days was equivalent to having committed crimes, were often condemned to slavery. Frequently the offender himself was executed, while his relatives were enslaved.

In all our material there is only one mention of the sale of men by one owner to another. An inscription on a bronze *ting*, said to date from about 900 B.C., seems to record the exchange of five men for one horse and a roll of silk; it is difficult, however, to be completely sure of its meaning. Gifts of slaves, by the king and others, are very frequent indeed. They are often enumerated, not as so many individuals, but as so many families. A number of different terms are used as names for people who are apparently slaves or virtual slaves. Some of them are evidently serfs, attached to certain pieces of land and given along with the land to whoever owns it.

But if we turn from those who are called slaves and bondsmen to the people at large, can we say that they were free? Only in a very limited sense. The work that they must do was assigned by their superiors or their officials, and if they did not do it they were punished. The houses in which they must live were assigned to them. The very clothing which they might wear was prescribed, and the wealthiest merchant was not allowed to wear finer clothes than his rank would entitle him to. The taxes which the people paid to their rulers were regulated to some extent, no doubt, by custom, but when a noble wished to increase his exactions the people had no recourse save rebellion. It was stated as a principle that no one had the right to appeal over the head of his immediate superior, which meant in effect that every command of one in authority was absolute.

It might be said, then, that virtually the whole non-aristocratic population was in the status of slaves or serfs. But it must be remembered that the aristocrat who held a small territory was almost as much at the mercy of his superior as his underlings were at the mercy of himself. In the case of each, revolt or flight were the only alternatives to obedience. The slave and the peasant could run away, if they were not apprehended, and often did so, so that the territories of very oppressive landlords were almost depopulated. But for the petty noble, to leave his lands was to ruin himself; in this sense he was more helpless than the common man, though he had an army and could fight if he thought he had a chance of success.

It was not, then, a social system in which one portion of the population lived in slavery or near slavery while the privileged class luxuriated in absolute freedom. There was great difference in the lot of the aristocrat and of those outside his charmed circle, but the situation was fundamentally one of a graduated hierarchy of power, in which each man could do as he pleased with those under him, putting them to death if he liked, while he stood in fear of the same absolute power over himself which was wielded by his superior. Only the king had no such superior in theory, and even he was often at the beck and call of some more powerful noble in actual practice.

Merchants and artisans fall outside this scheme of agricultural labour controlled and supervised by the nobility, and it is very difficult to deduce, from our evidence, where they should be fitted into the system. It is said that at about 650 B.C. five-sevenths of the population of the capital city of the State of Ch'i was composed of *shih*, chiefly army officers, while two-sevenths were artisans and merchants. We have no accurate information as to how the artisans were supported, but it would appear that they were given a living for doing what work was required of them by the nobles, and that, as a class, they were largely, though not wholly, hereditary. The merchants seem to have traded with a good deal of freedom and amassed considerable fortunes.

No examination of social conditions can be complete which neglects the female portion of the population. The majority of women were outside the aristocracy, of course, and as such lived lives of toil. Yet they seem not to have worked regularly in the fields. They prepared and carried food to their men and did the various tasks of housekeeping, making clothing, and so on, which are necessary in a civilization without machinery. A great many women of servile status were attached directly to the great households, doing various sorts of work, including silk culture. Like every one else in that culture, they were at the mercy of those above them, and that meant that the lord of the household had a perfect right to use them as he pleased. Such women were known as *ch'ieh*, the word which, as has been pointed out, now means 'concubine.' If one of them bore him a child, this improved her status; a male child of such a woman could even be made his father's heir, though this was not usual.

The institution of concubinage, with its special position of the woman as a subsidiary wife, grew out of this situation. Yet such women were regarded as little more than a means of amusement. A prime minister of Lu was praised for his honesty and frugality; 'his concubines never wore silk and his horses never ate millet.'

The difference in the lot of men and women of the aristocracy is summed up in the following verses in the *Book of Poetry*, concerning a king:

'Sons shall be born to him—
They will be put to sleep on couches;
They will be clothed in robes;
They will have sceptres to play with;
Their cry will be loud.
(Hereafter) they will be resplendent with red knee-covers,
The (future) king, the princes of the land.

Daughters shall be born to him—
They will be put to sleep on the ground;
They will be clothed with wrappers;
They will have tiles to play with.
It will be theirs neither to do wrong nor to do good.
Only about the liquor and the food will they have to think,
And to cause no sorrow to their parents.'[5]

Woman's place was in the home and her career was marriage. 'A woman,' another verse tells us, 'has nothing to do with public affairs.'[6] She was expected to be meek and submissive. 'It will not be good,' predicts the *Book of Changes*, 'to marry a female who is bold and strong.'[7] Then, as among conservative Chinese at the present day, women lived in a considerable degree of seclusion in the women's part of the household, though this was evidently not true at all times in all places. The *Tso Chuan* declares that if a woman had not died in her own chamber, the tablet for her spirit could not properly be placed with that of her husband.[8] As is often the case, women appear to have insisted upon the rigid enforcement of their seclusion even more than the men did. When the chief minister of the State of Lu went to call upon the mother of a colleague, who was his own aunt somewhat removed, the lady (who was something of a Tartar, anyway) made him stand outside the door while he talked to her. Women were not ordinarily present at public ceremonies, but sometimes they were placed behind a screen in the audience chamber, so that they could observe without being seen. An inopportune laugh by a woman in such a position, who was amused by the physical deformity of an envoy, caused him to vow vengeance and led to a serious war between the States of Chin and Ch'i.[9]

Married women were expected to supervise their households and to busy themselves with silk culture, weaving, and other such occupations. Even the wives of noblemen and the queen herself were supposed, it is said, to perform such tasks. But to require much work of one's wife did not help his reputation, according to the *Book of Poetry*.

> 'The delicate fingers of a bride
> May be used in making clothes.
> (His bride) puts the waistband to his lower
>   garment and the collar to his upper,
> And he, a wealthy man, wears them. . . .
> It is the narrowness of his disposition
> Which makes him a subject for satire.'[10]

The wife had her part in sacrifices, often almost identical with that of her husband. When envoys carried presents to a ruler, they usually took gifts to his wife as well.

From what is said about women generally one would suppose that they were without education, yet many incidents show that this was not always true. Women, like men, quote aptly from the *Book of Poetry* on more than one occasion, and sometimes quote extensively from other books. An old woman of an official family of Lu, who discusses statecraft quite in the manner of the learned scholar, says that she fears for the future of the state when it has such ignorant boys for officials.

Not all women submitted meekly to the taboo which forbade them to take part in public affairs. The *Book of Poetry* preserves the protest of a woman who, involved in the disaster of her state, sees the course which she thinks would save it, but is prevented from acting because people say that she is 'only a woman, full of notions.'[11] It must be admitted that the history of the times in general amply justifies her protest. Time after time it is recorded that men were saved from disaster by following the shrewd advice of their wives or other women. Occasionally men in positions of influence candidly sought the advice of women whose judgment they respected. Occasionally women were able to exercise direct influence in public affairs, but usually this was when they had reached old age, which in itself commands respect in China. Several bronze inscriptions tell us that the wives of kings and other rulers sometimes held the reins of power while their husbands were away on military expeditions; this fact, if fact it is, we should hardly learn from the histories.

Yet all of these things which could be said for women did little to change the current, general opinion about them. Moralists had little good to say of women, but they delighted to tell of kings and princes who met their doom through feminine intrigue. One of the worst things which could be said of a man was that 'he follows the words of his woman.' Of one who lost his life because his wife did not keep his secret, it was said: 'He told his wife; indeed, he deserved to die!' The *Book of Poetry* sums up the popular masculine judgment:

> 'A wise man builds up the wall (of a city),
> But a wise woman overthrows it.
> Admirable may be the wise woman,
> But she is (no better than) an owl.

A woman with a long tongue
Is a stepping-stone to disorder.
Disorder does not come down from Heaven—
It is produced by women.
Those from whom come no lessons, no instruction,
Are women and eunuchs.'[12]

CHAPTER XXI

MARRIAGE

MARRIAGE was considered a woman's natural destiny to such an extent that when she left her home to go to that of her future husband it was said, not that she went away, but that she was 'returning'[1]—to the place, that is, where she properly belonged.

Any persons of different surnames might marry. This, of course, permitted marriage of first cousins on the distaff side, but forbade that of persons very distantly related or not related at all if their surnames were alike. It was said that marriage between those of the same surname produced inferior children; nevertheless the prohibition was sometimes disregarded, and one case is recorded in which the resulting offspring was exceptionally fine.

We have no early data on the age at which people usually married. At the beginning of the fifth century B.C., when the State of Yüeh was doing everything possible to prepare for war, it was decreed that all men must be married by the age of twenty, and all women by seventeen, under severe penalties. Since the object was to increase the population, it is safe to infer that this was considered near the youngest marriageable age. This indicates that the man was to be three years older than the woman; actually old men sometimes married young women, and old women occasionally married young men.

The law just mentioned prescribes punishment, not for the young men and women who fail to marry, but for their parents who fail to marry them. The young people had nothing to do with the matter, and apparently marriages were arranged in much the same way at an earlier date. At all events they could not be arranged by the principal persons concerned. The *Book of Poetry* says repeatedly: 'In taking a wife how does one proceed? Without a go-between it cannot be done.'[2]

We have no way of knowing the marriage customs of the common people, but regarding those of the aristocracy we have some information in the *Book of Poetry* and a full description in the *I Li*. The father of the man sent a wild goose to the father of the girl, symbolizing the proposal of marriage. If it was acceptable, they divined to get the approval of the spirits, and to fix the day for the wedding. On the appointed day the bridegroom set out from his home in a carriage, going to that of the bride, who awaited him with her own carriage ready. After some ceremonial greetings, the bride and her duenna mounted the bride's carriage, while the bridegroom mounted to the driver's seat and drove it for three revolutions of the wheels. Then he went to his own carriage and returned home in it, that of the bride following. Arrived at the home of the bridegroom, the couple shared a ceremonial meal and retired to the bridal chamber. The next day the bride met her parents-in-law, gave them a ceremonial feast, and in turn was given one by them. From that time she became a member of their household, and stood to them in the same relation of almost absolute obedience as their own children. After three months the bride was presented to the ancestors of her husband's house, and took part in his sacrifices for the first time; then, and only then, she was considered to become a wife in the full sense of the word.[3] Up to this time she was, as it were, on trial, and might be returned to her parents if she was found unsatisfactory.

Once she had taken part in her husband's sacrifices, the marriage was normally to endure until the death of one of the couple. Death released either party, who could remarry. If the wife had borne him a son, the father was supposed to respect her memory by waiting for a time, while there was evidently a certain amount of sentiment against a widow's remarrying

PLATE XIII

A SQUARE BRONZE *I* OF SHANG TYPE

IT CONTAINS A TYPICAL SHANG INSCRIPTION OF TWO CHARACTERS. SIMILAR VESSELS HAVE BEEN EXCAVATED BY THE NATIONAL RESEARCH INSTITUTE AT ANYANG.

Reproduced by courtesy of Mr. P. C. Huang.

at all. There is not, in so far as I know, any instance of the later custom whereby the wife often committed suicide on her husband's death, but we find widows objecting strenuously to attempts to remarry them, and referring to themselves as 'merely waiting for death.' Nevertheless women not only remarried, but sometimes were taken from one husband and given to another while the first was alive. A woman of an official family of Lu was given to one man as wife, taken from him and given to an officer of another state, and when her second husband died sent back to the first man. It is not to be thought that she did not resent such treatment bitterly, but she was used as a political pawn, as many another woman has been in other times and other places.

There was divorce in the older period, but there is no information as to the grounds on which it was considered to be justified, or the manner in which it was carried out. Apparently it could be done by the husband alone, without reference to any tribunal. The divorced woman returned to the home of her parents. A later work lists seven reasons for divorce: disobedience to her parents-in-law, barrenness, adultery, jealousy (of her husband's other women?), disease, talking too much, and stealing. But she was not to be divorced in three cases: if there was no ancestral home for her to go to; if she had worn mourning for three years for one of her husband's parents; if her husband, poor at the time of marriage, had since become rich.

It was customary among the aristocracy for one or more bridesmaids to accompany the bride to her new home, and to assume the position of secondary wives along with her. It appears that this custom goes back even to the days of the Shang dynasty, but the specific regulations by which the number of such women was fixed probably grew up gradually, the whole matter being subject to great variation in our period. Sometimes the bridesmaid was a younger sister of the bride, sometimes cousins acted in this capacity. When the ruler or heir to the throne of a state married his bride was accompanied by women from other ruling families. The *Tso Chuan* says that such women must be of the same surname as the bride,[4] but in practice this rule was not always observed. Later works tell us that the ordinary *shih* married two women at once, the great officer three, and the ruler of a state and the king nine. But we have no way of knowing how early such rules were formulated. These secondary wives from great families were called *ch'ieh*, but their status was naturally much better than that of the ordinary female servant called by that name. The status of the common servile *ch'ieh* was so low that the principal wife might put her to death without consulting her husband. Upon the death of the principal wife one of the women who had accompanied her at the time of marriage might take over her functions, but was not supposed to be given her position—though this, like most other forbidden practices, was done by those who wished to and had the power. It is sometimes said that after this single marriage to two or several women husbands were not supposed to marry again, or to take other women, but the fact is that they did so in many cases of which we have record.

One naturally wonders how the wife proper felt about this polygamy. It is often said that Chinese women to-day are used to it; to be sure, they have had several thousand years to become so. A foreign woman whom I know ventured to ask a Chinese woman friend this question: 'How do most Chinese women feel about concubines?' The eyes of the Chinese woman snapped as she replied, 'How would you feel about a concubine?' Descendants of the original Mormons say that even the followers of Brigham Young admitted that the abolition of polygamy brought much greater peace and happiness to their community. Human nature seems to be very similar everywhere, and it was not different in early Chou China. The jealousies and intrigues bred by putting a number of women in more or less seclusion in a harem, as competitors for the regard, the goods, and the power of a single man, were responsible for an incalculable amount of disorder and war, and occasioned immeasurable unhappiness to the human beings directly involved.

Eunuchs are mentioned but rarely in the early Chou literature. Undoubtedly they were used, as later, to guard the women's quarters for the wealthy and powerful, though I know of no passage which says so. And they seem at times to have enjoyed considerable power and favour with the rulers, as they often did with such calamitous results in later periods. It has been argued, since our first mention of eunuchs is in Chou literature, that they must have been introduced for the first time in the Chou period. But we have no pre-Chou literature, save the oracle inscriptions, and there is no reason whatever for eunuchs to be mentioned in them, whether they existed or not. It is, therefore, quite impossible to determine when eunuchs were first used in China on the basis of our present evidence.

In the following verse a wife laments that she has been supplanted by a new favourite:

> 'You feast with your new wife,
> And think me not worth being with. . . .
> You cannot cherish me,
> You even count me as an enemy.
> You disdain my virtues—
> A pedlar's wares which do not sell. . . .
> Cavalierly and angrily you treat me;
> You give me only pain.
> You do not think of the former days,
> And are only angry with me.'[5]

Yet a wife was not completely helpless, if her own family was powerful. A wife was supposed to be treated with respect, and if her husband failed in this she could complain to her family. Tung Shu, a great officer of the State of Chin in the latter part of the sixth century, married a woman of the Fan family. Before the wedding his friend Shu-hsiang remonstrated with him, pointing out that since the Fan family was very wealthy the match was hardly suitable. Tung Shu replied that that was the very reason he was marrying; he wished to become connected with this wealthy family in order to 'get up in the world.' But after he was married his wife told her brother that he did not treat her with the proper respect. The brother responded by having Tung tied up and suspended from a tree in the court, open to the public gaze. Shu-hsiang happened to pass that way, and the dangling benedict begged him to intercede for him. 'Why,' his friend asked, 'should I do that? You wanted to "get up in the world"—and there you are!'

When marriage was arranged by the families and polygamy in one form or another was common, we hardly expect to find a great deal of romantic love in marriage. Yet there are many recorded cases of sincere attachment between husband and wife. 'I will hope to grow old with you' is a phrase often on the lips of wives in the *Book of Poetry*. The same work includes many laments of widows and of wives torn by circumstances from their husbands.

'My husband is away on service,
And I know not when he will return.
Where is he now?
The fowls roost in their holes in the walls,
And in the evening of the day,
The goats and cows come down from the hill.
But my husband is away on service;
How can I but keep thinking of him?

My husband is away on service,
Not for days merely, or for months.
When will he come back to me?
The fowls roost on their perches,
And in the evening of the day,
The goats and cows come down and home.
But my husband is away on service;
Oh if he be but kept from hunger and thirst!' [6]

If the opportunities for courtship before marriage were sometimes limited, it seems occasionally to have taken place after the wedding. Certainly there was a good deal of love-making before marriage, as the *Book of Poetry* proves, but whether the inclinations of young people in this respect were ever followed in arranging marriages is not certain. As to the common people we have, as has been said, little information. Most writers on ancient China hold that an almost unlimited sex licence was granted to youthful plebeians following certain religious ceremonies in the spring. This may well be true, but there is almost no evidence concerning it in the authentic materials which date from the early period.

It is difficult to say how much of the *Book of Poetry* deals with the aristocracy and how much with the commoners, but many of the love verses must come from the upper classes. Had women always been so secluded as they were at some times and in some places, love affairs would have been virtually impossible, but obviously they were not.

> 'I pray you, Mr. Chung,
> Do not come leaping over my wall;
> Do not break my mulberry trees.
> Do I care for them?
> But I fear my brothers.
> You, O Chung, are to be loved,
> But the words of my brothers
> Are also to be feared.
>
> I pray you, Mr. Chung,
> Do not come leaping into my garden;
> Do not break my sandal trees.
> Do I care for them?
> But I dread the talk of people.
> You, O Chung, are to be loved,
> But the talk of people
> Is also to be feared.'[7]

Sometimes the lady made it unnecessary for her swain to go to her home for his wooing.

> 'How lovely is the retiring girl!
> She was to await me at a corner of the wall.
> Loving and not seeing her,
> I scratch my head and am in perplexity.' [8]

But courtship was sometimes possible without resort to clandestine meetings.

> 'The Chên and Wei
> Now present their broad sheets of water.
> Ladies and gentlemen
> Are carrying flowers of valerian.
> A lady says, "Have you been to see?"
> A gentleman replies, "I have been.
> But let us go again to see.
> Beyond the Wei,
> The ground is large and fit for pleasure."
> So the gentlemen and ladies
> Make sport together,
> Presenting one another with small peonies.' [9]

The above poem is said to concern a spring festival in connection with which there was great licence and dissipation. This may be true; on the other hand, this interpretation may be the result of the same puritanism which makes it a crime, punishable by law in some parts of China to-day, for a man and a woman to walk together on the public street.

Certainly there was licence and wickedness and seduction in ancient China. We find gallants who boast of the number of highly placed women with whom they have had affairs, and women who, being mistress to many men in turn, ruin them and sometimes throw the states they rule into turmoil. There was lewdness, incest, adultery enough to satisfy the most avid. But there was also a great deal of the light-hearted courtship natural to young people burdened neither with wickedness nor puritanism.

> 'If you, Sir, think kindly of me,
> I will hold up my lower garments and wade across the
> Wei.
> If you do not think of me,
> Is there no other gentleman (to do so)?
> You foolish, foolish fellow!'[10]

And there was the perennial anxiety of the unmarried woman who sees youth slipping from her.

> 'Dropping are the fruits from the plum-tree;
> There are only seven-tenths of them left.
> For the gentlemen who seek me,
> Now is the fortunate time!
>
> Dropping are the fruits from the plum-tree;
> There are but three-tenths of them left.
> For the gentlemen who seek me,
> Now is the time!
>
> Dropped are the fruits from the plum-tree;
> In my shallow basket I have collected them.
> Would the gentlemen who seek me
> Only speak about it!'[11]

There was not a little of admiration which went beyond mere physical attraction, and love which was based on the qualities of heart and mind.

> 'The modest, retiring, virtuous young lady—
> For our prince a good mate is she. . . .
> Waking and sleeping he sought her,
> He sought her and found her not.
> And waking and sleeping he thought about her.
> Long he thought; oh! long and anxiously;
> On his side, on his back, he turned, and back again.'[12]

Another sings of his bride:

> 'In her proper season that well-grown lady,
> With her admirable virtue, is come to instruct me.
> We will feast, and I will praise her.
> "I love you, and will never be weary of you."
> Although I have no good spirits
> We will drink what I have, and perhaps be satisfied.
> Although I have no good viands,
> We will eat what I have, and perhaps be satisfied.
> Although I have no virtue to impart to you.
> We will sing and dance.'[13]

Since the consent of parents was absolutely necessary for marriage, it was inevitable that young women should sometimes elope with suitors who were not approved. In the following story of such an elopement, note the mention of a double standard of morality for men and women.

> 'A simple-looking lad you were,
> Carrying cloth to exchange it for silk.
> But you came not to purchase silk—
> You came to make proposals to me.
> I convoyed you through the Ch'i,
> As far as Tun Ch'iu.
> "It is not I," I said, "who would protract the time;
> But you have had no good go-between.
> I pray you not to be angry,
> And let autumn be the time."
>
> I ascended that ruined wall,
> That I might see you returning through the pass;
> And when I saw you not,
> My tears flowed in streams.
> When I did see you coming,
> I laughed and I spoke.

MARRIAGE

You had consulted, you said, the tortoise-shell and the
  reeds,
And there was nothing unfavourable in their response.
"Then come," I said, "with your carriage,
And I will remove with my goods."

Before the mulberry tree has shed its leaves,
How rich and glossy are they!
Ah! thou dove,
Eat not its fruit.
Ah! thou young lady,
Seek no licentious pleasure with a gentleman.
When a gentleman indulges in such pleasure
Something may still be said for him;
When a lady does so,
Nothing can be said for her.

When the mulberry tree sheds its leaves,
They fall yellow on the ground.
Since I went with you,
Three years have I eaten of your poverty;
And now the full waters of the Ch'i
Wet the curtains of my carriage.
There has been no difference in me,
But you have been double in your ways.
It is you, Sir, who transgress the right,
Thus changeable in your conduct.

For three years I lived as your wife,
And thought nothing of my toil in your house.
I rose early and went to sleep late,
Not intermitting my labours for a morning.
Thus on my part our contract was fulfilled,
But you have behaved thus cruelly.
My brothers will not know all this,
And will only laugh at me.
Silently I think of it,
And bemoan myself.

I was to grow old with you—
Old, you give me cause for sad repining.
The Ch'i has its banks,
And the marsh has its shores.
In the pleasant time of my girlhood, with my hair simply gathered in a knot,
Harmoniously we talked and laughed.
Clearly were we sworn to good faith,
And I did not think that faith would be broken.
I did not think that faith would be broken—
And now, it is ended!'[14]

But there is no satisfying human nature. Another lady tells us in verse that, when besought to forsake the path of rectitude and run away with a 'handsome gentleman,' she resisted temptation and held fast to virtue. Having done so she should, one supposes, have been rewarded by being perfectly happy. But she concludes by saying, 'Now I repent that I did not go with him!'[15]

CHAPTER XXII

THE FAMILY

THE traditional Chinese family, ancient and modern, is a group very different from the one which we know by that name. We think of a family as being composed of a man and a woman and their unmarried children. The Chinese family includes several generations occupying the same dwelling, living under the authority of the eldest generation, and holding goods and property more or less in common. We have no exact data on the constitution of the family prior to 600 B.C., but it appears to have been substantially of this sort.

The authority of the father was virtually absolute. He was the monarch of his family. In handing down a decision King Hsiang declared: 'No appeal by a subject can be made over the head of his immediate superior. For if such an appeal against the authority of one's immediate superior could be made, we should then have sons litigating against their fathers, and there would be no proper discrimination of superiors and inferiors.' It was handled much more simply; the father's orders were final. Down to the establishment of the Chinese Republic, in the present century, a father held the power of life and death (subject, however, to certain restrictions) over his children. An incident in the *Tso Chuan* makes it appear that a father had to get the permission of his ruler to put his son to death, but in this case the son was an official of the state, which may have made a difference. The eldest son was his father's normal successor, but the father could set him aside if it pleased him; he might even appoint a son of a concubine to be his heir, if he thought the boy more able, or if his mother were sufficiently attractive and teased him to do so.

Concubines continually plotted to this end, because it put them into a position of honour and authority.

The authority of the mother was second only to that of the father. If her husband were dead the dowager of the eldest generation reigned almost supreme. The authority of the old woman of position in China is a thing which defies definition. It has been said that the strongest title to a piece of land in China is that of an old woman occupying it who refuses to get off. Almost anyone else can be dispossessed, but the combination of the dowager's actual helplessness with the veneration given to age, plus the virtual omnipotence of public opinion in China, make it almost impossible to dispossess her. Such old women do practically as they please.

A great officer of Lu, Wên-po by name, gave a feast for some of his colleagues, at which turtle was served. But the turtle was small. This niggardliness angered the principal guest who, after looking at it, said, 'Gentlemen, let us wait for this turtle to grow up before eating it!' and, turning on his heel, went out. When the mother of Wên-po heard of the affair she, too, was angry. She drove that dignitary out of his own house, and kept him out for five days. Then she only let him return because the Duchess of Lu interceded for him.

But if the authority of parents was despotic, they did not always use it harshly. The *Book of Poetry* says:

> 'O my father, who begat me!
> O my mother, who nourished me!
> You indulged me, you fed me,
> You held me up, you supported me,
> You looked after me, you never left me,
> Out and in you bore me in your arms.
> If I would return your kindness,
> It is like great Heaven, illimitable.'[1]

Nor did children obey their parents only from compulsion, as many incidents show. Duke Hsien of Chin made Li Chi, a captive barbarian woman, his principal wife, in spite of unfavourable responses from divination. When a son was born to her, she started plotting to have him made heir to the state, in place of the rightful heir. In 656 B.C., while the duke was away, she used a ruse to get the heir to sacrifice to his dead mother, after which he sent some of the sacrificial flesh and liquor to the palace for the duke, according to custom. Li Chi poisoned them, and when the duke arrived gave them to him. He poured out a little of the liquor on the ground in sacrifice, and it rose in a small mound. This made him suspicious, and he fed some of the flesh to a dog and to a servant. Both died, whereupon Li Chi declared that this was an attempt of the heir to murder him. The heir, warned, fled to another city. Someone advised him to lay the whole matter before his father, who, he said, would certainly discern the truth. But he replied: 'Without the lady Chi my father would not rest or enjoy his food. If I explain, she will be condemned. The duke is getting old; if this happened, I could not be happy either.'[2] Whereupon he hanged himself. More than once we find sons willingly facing death rather than disobeying their parents or making them unhappy. But even more frequently, of course, we find them fleeing to find asylum in other states—especially the scions of noble families who are involved, innocently or otherwise, in intrigues.

Filial piety is the chief of Chinese virtues. It is at once the social, the political, and the religious duty of every individual. For the family is the unit of society, and filial piety is its bulwark. The father is the prototype of all political authority, and disobedience to him would threaten the foundations of the state. The relation of the child to his parents and grandparents is like their relation to their deceased ancestors, and the service and support which he gives them are like the worship and sacrifices which they pay to the dead. It is possible that the word *hsiao*, 'filial piety,' originally meant 'sacrifice,' and so stood primarily for obedience and devotion to the spiritual ancestors. As we shall see, the distinction between the dead and the living in ancient China was at best not sharply defined, so that duties to the two blended easily. A Chinese proverb current to-day says: 'It is more meritorious to care properly for one's father and mother who are living than to burn incense to ancestors who are dead.'

Filial conduct and its reverse were not merely the business of the individuals and the family directly concerned. It was a virtue lauded even in a king, as in the poem:

> 'Men loved him, the One Man,
> And responded to him with a docile virtue.
> Ever thinking how to be filial,
> He brilliantly continued the work of his fathers.'[3]

Failure in filial duty was universally condemned by public opinion and might even be punished by law. State documents dating from the very beginning of the Chou dynasty lay much stress on the duties of the young to their parents and elders, and one of them goes so far as to say:

'The king says, "Fêng, such chief criminals are greatly abhorred, and how much more detestable are the unfilial and unbrotherly —the son who does not reverently discharge his duty to his father, but greatly wounds his father's heart; the father who can no longer love his son, but hates him; and the younger brother who does not think of the manifest will of Heaven, and refuses to respect his elder brother, so that the elder brother . . . is very unbrotherly to his junior. . . . You must deal speedily with such offenders according to the penal laws of the Accomplished King, punishing them severely and not pardoning."'[4] It will be noted that the duties here prescribed are reciprocal; the junior must love and respect his senior, but the senior must also be worthy of such regard.

It was but natural that loyalty reached its highest point in the family. One who was disloyal to his kin not only lost their assistance, but was regarded as more than dubious by all other persons, since he could not get on with his own family. He could not trust others, because they were, after all, members of other family groups, which claimed their first loyalty.

> 'Of all the men in the world
> None are equal to brothers. . . .
> Brothers may quarrel inside the walls,
> But they will oppose insult from without. . . .
> Loving union with wife and children
> Is like the music of lutes;
> But it is the accord of brothers
> Which makes harmony and happiness lasting.'[5]

We find instances of fraternal loyalty which go even to the point of death. But here as elsewhere we are dealing with human beings, and the fact of relationship did not always hinder those who plotted for the possession of power. Especially among rulers of states, blood seems to have been scarcely thicker than water.

The supreme duty of family loyalty was that of blood revenge. If one's father or elder brother were killed by, or by the order of, another it was one's duty to exact a life in return—that of the killer, if possible, if not then that of any near relative of the killer who could be reached. Such a one was considered an enemy; in such case, as it is said in the *Discourses of the States*, 'He who sees his enemy and does not kill him is not a man!' Revenge as a duty was upheld even by moralists and philosophers.

It is probable that more of ancient China has survived to the present in connection with the family system than with any other institution. Even the tradition and the tolerance of blood revenge are not wholly dead. The following article is a Reuter's dispatch which appeared in the *Peiping Chronicle*:

'Nanking, 14th March [1933].—The government to-day formally issued a mandate pardoning Cheng Chi-cheng, the man who killed General Chang Tsung-chang, former Tupan of Shangtung, on Tsinan railway platform.

'The mandate says that, in consideration of the fact that Cheng committed murder to avenge his uncle and father, he should be exempt from serving the sentence passed on him of seven years' imprisonment.'

Whether or not there is, as some say, more in this matter than meets the eye, such a statement would not have been issued if the idea of blood revenge were a dead letter in the public mind.

What if one's father were killed by his ruler? Which loyalty came first, that to state or to family? This is a question which is constantly being thrashed out, and never finally answered. In the sixth century B.C., when the armies of Wu invaded the State of Ch'u, its prince had to flee to a city ruled by one of his vassals. Now it happened that the father of this prince, coveting his possessions, had caused the father of the vassal to whose city he had fled to be put to death. The younger brother of the vassal wished to kill the prince to avenge his father, but the elder demurred. 'Revenge,' he declared, 'can only be spoken of as between equals. . . . If not, then there could be no such thing as superiors and inferiors. . . . It may not be done.' But his brother replied, 'I cannot consider that; I am thinking of our father!' Because he feared for the safety of his prince, the elder brother helped him to remove to another city. When the invasion was over and conditions had returned to normal, the prince rewarded both brothers, which caused great surprise. Rather, he was told, he should have rewarded the elder and put the younger to death. 'No,' he replied, 'both of these men acted properly, the one toward his father, the other toward his ruler. Was it not just, then, to reward them both?'

Such chivalry, while certainly admirable, had in it more than a little of the quixotic. Had it been widely emulated it must have ended in destroying all authority. We may be very sure it was not. The custom of exacting vengeance made it very difficult to punish the members of powerful families with safety, even though they might be guilty of criminal acts. The result was inevitable. When such persons were killed it was not unusual to wipe out their whole clan along with them. It was ruthless, but there was little else to be done. To leave survivors was like sowing so many dragon's-teeth to become avengers later on. This made things very dangerous for the members of powerful families, who might be wiped out at any time for a crime of which they personally were quite innocent, or for an affair of which they were entirely ignorant. But it had one good effect from the point of view of the government. It made it necessary for every man who wished to keep his head to be his brother's keeper in a very definite sense, and to try to see that no member of his family made trouble. If he could not, he had one other recourse, though I know of only one case in which it was used, and it is later than our period. In the fifth century B.C. a minister of the State of Chin, head of the Chih family, chose as his heir a son of whom another member of the family, Chih Kuo, did not approve. Chih Kuo warned him that disaster to the family would result if this son was put in power, but his protest went unheeded. Chih Kuo therefore went to the Grand Recorder and had his surname changed from Chih to Fu. A few years later the Chih family was wiped out, as he had foreseen, and Fu Kuo alone escaped because of his foresight.

Occasionally we find a protest against the visitation of punishment upon the relatives of the criminal along with him. But to understand the situation we must realize that in a sense each family was a state within itself, and that the ruler of the larger state dealt with it very much as such. Individuals within the family were to be controlled by its head, and if they were not so controlled that was the fault of the family, just as it was the fault of a state if rebellion occurred within its borders.

Aristocratic families had their own retainers, and the principle was stated in one place that if such retainers had served a family for three generations it was their duty to support it even in opposition to the ruler of the state. The family of a minister of the State of Chin in the sixth century is said to have possessed wealth equal to half the state treasury, and to have maintained an army of retainers equal to half the state troops.

In war each clan fought together as a unit. Certain offices were hereditary in certain families, being filled from their members for generations. The individual was merged, if not submerged, in the family. The truest patriotism was shown on its behalf. Self-sacrifice for the feudal state, and even at times for China as a whole, was not rare, but the greatest heroism for the sake of family or clan was an everyday occurrence. To lay down one's life for the preservation of one's family was considered good fortune. To be sure, there was an element of selfishness in this. For one's life on this earth is in any case brief, but death is long. And after death, if one's posterity were extinguished, he would have no sacrifices.

Aristotle's definition of the state as 'a union of families and villages' rather than of individuals fits the Chinese situation very well. Theoretically, just as every family had its retainers so the aristocratic families of lower rank were loyal retainers of the family of their lord, and the rulers of states were the family dependants of the king. But actually it did not work out so simply. Family loyalty was reinforced by familiarity and by the institution of ancestor-worship, so that it often vied with that due to the state. And innumerable problems arose. The ruler was supposed to give the best offices in his bestowal to his relatives; if he failed to treat his relatives with special consideration, he was giving a bad example to his subjects, which might lead to disorder. But did this mean that he must endanger the state by employing his relatives, though incompetent, and refusing to use others who might be gifted? When the call of the state to military duty interfered with the care due to one's parents, what attitude should he take? If one's relatives did rebel against constituted authority, should one aid them or not? The choice was sometimes made one way, sometimes another.

Confucius was one of the staunchest upholders of the authority of the state, yet: 'The Duke of Shê said to Confucius, "Among us there are some who are truly upright in their conduct; if the father has stolen a sheep, the son will bear witness to it." Confucius replied, "In my part of the country, the upright are different from this. The father conceals the misconduct of the son, and the son conceals the misconduct of the father. It is in this that uprightness lies."'[6] This is a problem which exists, of course, at all times and in all countries. But it is a greater problem in China because the number of those who are considered close relatives is much greater than in most places.

In all of this there is little scope left for the individual as such. Seeing the gregariousness of the Chinese, who seem to delight in living in large family groups, with a degree of group familiarity unknown to persons of like class in the West, one sometimes wonders if they never have the desire to be completely alone, free of other human beings and especially of relatives, which comes to the rest of us on occasion. Here again the *Book of Poetry* provides an answer.

'In the low, wet grounds is the carambola tree;
Soft and pliant are its branches,
With the glossiness of tender beauty.
I should rejoice to be like you, (O tree), without consciousness.

In the low, damp grounds is the carambola tree;
Soft and delicate are its flowers,
With the glossiness of tender beauty.
I should rejoice to be like you, (O tree), without a family.

In the low, damp grounds is the carambola tree;
Soft and delicate is its fruit,
With the glossiness of tender beauty.
I should rejoice to be like you, (O tree), without a household.'[7]

CHAPTER XXIII

THE BUSINESS OF LIFE

LAND was the chief form of wealth in early Chou China and almost the sole source of income apart from that produced by one's own exertions. To become rich without owning land was said to be quite impossible.

In theory all land belonged to the king, who gave it to his vassals in return for service. They gave lands to still lesser vassals, who might parcel it out still further. The king had the right to take back any land from any of his vassals and give it to another, and we can see from bronze inscriptions and from the literature that he sometimes did this in the early days when he was powerful. But just as in medieval Europe, the powerful vassals soon ceased to look upon their title to lands as provisional. At first, when such a noble died it was considered necessary for the king to appoint his heir to succeed him, and to give his estates to the heir, but this soon degenerated into a mere form, if it was maintained at all. In practice the vassal looked upon his territory as his by inherited right, and it was necessary to wage war to displace him. As lesser vassals grew in power, and possessed private armies, the same situation grew up all along the line, so that if land changed hands it ordinarily did so either as a result of sale or exchange, or with the accompaniment of violence.

Each individual who held land as a fief from a superior was commonly expected to turn over to that superior a portion of the revenues which he received from it as tribute. At the lower end of the scale was the aristocrat who, as a sort of gentleman farmer, supervised directly the work of agriculture. This supervision was delegated to the chief among his household servants, and the actual field labour was done by peasants, serfs, or slaves.

We have no statistics from this period as to the average size of individual holdings of land, the yield of grain per acre, and so forth, but we do have what is far more interesting to most of us—vivid pictures of the agricultural life of the time preserved in the *Book of Poetry*.

'They clear away the grass and the bushes;
And the ground is laid open by their ploughs.
In thousands of pairs they remove the roots,
Some in the low wet lands, some along the dykes.
There are the master and his eldest son;
His younger sons, and all their children;
Their strong workmen and the helpers.
How the noise of their eating the viands brought to them resounds!
(The husbands) think lovingly of their wives (who have brought them food).
(The wives) keep close to their husbands.
Then with their sharp plough-shares
They set to work on the south-lying acres.
They sow their different kinds of grain,
Each seed containing in it a germ of life.
In unbroken lines rise the blades,
And well-nourished the stalks grow long.
Luxuriant looks the young grain,
And the weeders go among it in multitudes.
Then come the reapers in crowds,
And the grain is piled up in the fields,
Myriads and hundreds of thousands and millions (of stacks);
For liquor and for sweet liquor,
To offer to our ancestors, male and female,
And to provide for all ceremonies.
Fragrant is their aroma,

Enhancing the glory of the state.
Like pepper is their smell,
To give comfort to the aged.
It is not only here that there is this abundance;
It is not only now there is such a time—
From of old it has been thus.'[1]

The *Book of Poetry* contains a number of such poems, and some of them contain the same couplets. These repeated verses are possibly quoted from songs which the labourers themselves sang in the fields, to lighten their toil and give it rhythm.

In these poems, and in the literature generally, there is very little mention of domestic animals, except as being used in sacrifice. They had the ox, sheep, pig, and dog, all of which were used for food on occasion, but there is no indication that they were raised in large numbers. We have definite evidence that in some parts of the country at least they were kept in enclosures, not allowed to range over the countryside in herds.[2] Hunting was one of the chief sports of the aristocracy, but it does not seem to have been very important in providing food. In one place the term 'flesh-eaters' is used to mean 'high officials';[3] this, like everything else, indicates that this was a predominantly agricultural period in which meat as food was of decidedly minor importance.

When the poem quoted above refers to 'thousands of pairs' of field labourers we need not take it literally, but it is evident that farming was carried on on a large scale. There are many references to the overseers, who directed the activities of the labourers. Whether there were any small farmers who were left entirely to their own direction, planting what they pleased and cultivating as they pleased, merely giving a fraction of the produce to the landlord, it is not possible to say. There is some reference to 'private fields,' but just what they were is obscure.

Works on ancient China commonly make much of a system of farming, mentioned by the philosopher Mencius, by which square plots of territory were divided, checker-board fashion, into nine fields of equal size. Each of the eight fields around the sides of the square was cultivated by a family for its own living, while the field in the centre was cultivated by these eight families in co-operation, its produce being the share which went to the noble who owned all the land. But it is possible that this was simply an ideal scheme in Mencius' own mind, which was never put into practice. At all events, the bronze inscriptions and the literature show that in the early period such a system was practised very little if at all; we have no real evidence that it existed.

If we try to form an orderly picture of the financial arrangements under which farming was carried on, basing it on the books and inscriptions which actually date from our period, we find it almost impossible. Here the landlord seems to take all of the produce, giving back to the labourers for their support as much as he sees fit to. There he appears to take only a share of their crop, but in one place that share is larger and in another smaller. We have to remember that within ill-defined limits the master of the land could do exactly as he pleased. General practice was probably influenced by different customs in different localities, and always varied by the character of the men who held the power. Some of them took all they could get, grinding their underlings down until they drove them to despair, flight, and rebellion. Others, moved alike by humanitarian motives and an intelligent selfishness, sought to found the security of their position on the prosperity and contentment of their subjects. Especially when war threatened, and the loyalty of the people was of particular importance, we find rulers courting popularity by lightening or remitting taxes. But even a light and regularized system of taxation would not have guaranteed the people against this kind of oppression. For just as in medieval Europe they were liable at any time to be forced to wall cities, build roads and palaces, and go on military expeditions, with little or no compensation.

Of one thing we may be quite sure—this was not the type of

economy in which the ruler, as a benevolent despot who owns everything, makes himself responsible for the welfare and the support of each of his subjects. There were government relief measures in times of famine and disaster, it is true, but it was quite possible for individuals to be in the direst poverty and even to starve. The *Book of Poetry* pictures this for us too.

> 'The people now have no maintenance,
> For Heaven is pounding them with its calamities.
> The rich may get through.
> But alas for the helpless and solitary!'[4]

Poverty evidently existed even in good times.

> 'There shall be young grain unreaped,
> And here some sheaves ungathered;
> There shall be handfuls left on the ground,
> And here ears untouched—
> For the benefit of the widow.'[5]

But the submerged were not always unmurmuring.

> 'You do not sow or reap—
> How do you get the produce of those three hundred farms?
> You do not follow the chase—
> How is it that we see badgers hanging up in your courtyards?
> Ah! the true aristocrat
> Would not eat the bread of idleness!'[6]

The political, social, and economic structures dovetailed in the fact that the people in general were divided into those who worked the land and those who governed them. Literature and scholarship had not, in our period, separated themselves from this scheme of things. The production of books was almost entirely the work of officials. Teachers and scholars were the dependants of nobles, having a place in the political hierarchy, and so were most of those who discharged religious functions. Confucius, in the latter half of the sixth century B.C., is considered to have been the first private teacher, gathering his own circle of disciples rather than teaching as an official. But two groups fell outside the system. These were the merchants and the artisans.

Of the status of artisans in the early period we know very little. Obviously a considerable number of them would have been needed to make the weapons and utensils, chariots and fine clothing, which were used by the aristocratic classes. They lived in cities, close to the aristocrats for whom they worked. How they were paid we cannot tell with certainty, but in some cases at least they did not hold any land, but were paid directly for their toil. Whether they were paid according to the value of the articles which they produced, or whether they received a regular living in return for which they were expected to do whatever was required of them is not clear; the latter method seems more probable. They must have enjoyed a much better standard of living than that of the peasants. A very late section of the *I Li* says that when a diplomatic mission arrived from another state, the officers of lowest rank among the guests were quartered on artisans and merchants;[7] these two classes must, then, have had homes far above the level of those of the peasant population.

There were others whom we cannot class as government officials nor yet as artisans in the ordinary sense. Physicians are such a group. There were apparently a good many of them, with not a little of medical theory. It was complicated by much admixture of religious and metaphysical ideas, but food and stagnant water were recognized as sources of disease and even of epidemics. Drugs were administered, but there appears to have been scepticism with regard to internal medicine even at the beginning of the Chou period. The *Book of Changes* mentions a case of illness, but predicts recovery—if no drugs are used![8]

Another class which obtained its living outside the usual

methods were the robbers. Not the robber barons, of course; as everywhere, they occupied a respected place in the social scale. But it is mentioned, among the regular measures taken in preparation for a visit by an important personage, that the minister of justice put known criminals under special surveillance.

Merchants also were outside the usual scheme. They carried on their trade with little restriction, save that they had to pay taxes and tariffs. There is a theory, based upon the fact that the character Shang which is the name of the dynasty also means 'merchant,' that many of the Shang nobles, shorn of their lands by the Chou conquest, went into trade; whether there is any truth in it would be hard to say. We do know, however, that trade over considerable distances was carried on from the very beginning of the Chou period.

Merchants sometimes became very rich, but they were not allowed to hold rank in our period. Later on the government, in need of funds, hit upon the plan of selling titles, which has been much used since in China as elsewhere.

The goods which merchants carried must have been chiefly luxuries, such as articles of clothing and food, which could not be procured everywhere with equal ease. Salt, fish (dried, undoubtedly), furs, cloth of various kinds, and silks are named as articles of trade. Tariffs were collected at the borders of each feudal state, but the State of Ch'i abolished these charges in order to stimulate trade at the time when its duke was the actual ruler of China.

Both bronze inscriptions and books show that there were a number of roads. They were kept in repair, and sometimes planted with trees. Rest-houses and inns were provided by the government for travellers, at least for those who went on official business. These roads were guarded by the feudal states through which they passed, so that when the power of the king declined even his own messengers had to ask permission to use them. Merchants, ranging from one end of China to the other, and even venturing out among the barbarian tribes to trade, had unparalleled opportunities to gather information, and more than once they were used as spies by the states of their residence.

The problem of a satisfactory medium of exchange was not solved in the early Chou period, although steps were taken toward a solution. Much trading was done by means of bartering goods of one sort for those of another. This was not a bad system for the merchant who, loading his carts with the special products of his own district, could carry them elsewhere, trade, and return home laden with foreign goods. Late books tell us that tribute was largely paid in terms of such goods as grain, silks, varnish, and ivory, depending upon the nature of the district rendering it.

Cowry shells were extensively used as gifts, and apparently as money, in early Chou times. Many bronze inscriptions tell us of 'punitive' expeditions against the barbarians of the east and south-east, whose chief crime seems to have been that they possessed cowries which they did not give to the Chinese for nothing. These raiders returned rich with plunder, when they were successful. The use of cowries gradually declined, possibly due to an over-supply which reduced their value. Furthermore, they possessed no intrinsic value like that of metal.

Metal, especially copper, was always in demand, for making weapons, sacrificial vessels, and other articles of bronze. Having a high value, being transportable with comparative ease, and being virtually imperishable, it was inevitable that it should come to be used as a medium of exchange. Bronze inscriptions from the opening century of the Chou dynasty mention gifts of metal, which was almost certainly copper, and sometimes measure it in terms of the unit known as a *lieh* or *huan*, literally a 'double handful.' This was apparently a unit of weight, which later sources tell us was equal to six Chinese ounces (at present a Chinese ounce is equal to about one and one-third of ours). This was used as a monetary unit, although there is no evidence that coins or even ingots of that weight were made up at that period, for use as money, as they were later. Bronze inscriptions mention gifts and transactions involving from five to three hundred of these *lieh*, but it is impossible to form even an estimate of its value as money. Taxes and fines for criminal offences were sometimes taken in metal. One book included in the *Document Classic* gives an elaborate schedule of fines, up to one thousand *lieh*, but it cannot be taken seriously; it is obviously much later than the date to which it is attributed, and is probably a complete forgery.

The beginning of coinage in China is commonly ascribed to the latter part of the fifth century B.C. There is, however, a passage in the *Discourses of the States* which not only says that coins were made in 524 B.C., but clearly implies that they were very common at that date and had been well known for a long time. But whether or not this passage is authentic is a doubtful question.

CHAPTER XXIV

THE ENJOYMENT OF LIFE

WHILE it is true that we know little of the life of the common people of this early period, we know quite enough to be sure that it was not devoid of happiness, full though it might be of toil. The records of a slightly later time tell us of many festivals, chiefly of a religious nature, which must have been very ancient.

The *Book of Poetry* gives us several accounts of harvest festivals.

'In the tenth month they sweep clean their stack-sites.
The two bottles of liquor are enjoyed,
And they say, "Let us kill our lambs and sheep,
And go to the hall of our prince,
There raise the cup of horn,
And wish him life for ten thousand years, without end." '[1]

There was apparently a good deal of more or less spontaneous merry-making.

'There are the white elms at the east gate,
And the oaks on Wan Ch'iu;
The daughter of Tzŭ-chung
Dances about under them.

A good morning having been chosen
For the plain in the south,
She leaves twisting her hemp,
And dances to the market-place.

The morning being good for the excursion,
They all proceed together.
"I look on you as the flower of the thorny mallows;
You give me a stalk of the pepper plant." '[2]

This period in Chinese history is most nearly comparable to the feudal age in Europe, which came something more than fifteen hundred years later. If we compare the life of the aristocrats of the two periods, it seems to me that the Chinese must have had much the more interesting existence of the two. Among a list of the chief amusements available to the European noble there is included the delight of 'standing at a window and watching the snow fall'; one can hardly imagine a Chinese being reduced to spending much of his time on this diversion, fascinating though it must have been. For one thing, he was much better educated than was his European counterpart. Moreover, the poetry with which members of the upper class were expected to be familiar shows a love and appreciation of flowers, scenery, and nature generally such as seems not to have been present in the European to the same degree.

The religion of the Chinese undoubtedly did more to add to his enjoyment of life than did that of the medieval baron. The piety of the European noble was frequently open to grave question; whatever one may think of the religious practices of the ancient Chinese, they were usually sincere and assiduous in carrying them out. And whereas the religious ceremonies of medieval Europe were carried on to a very large extent by a special class of men set aside for the purpose, the Chinese aristocrat had himself to preside over and take part in frequent and colourful rituals which were a part of the life of his household.

The houses of the ancient Chinese, apparently much like those of the present, were certainly inferior to the medieval castle from the point of view of their ability to stand a siege. But in comparison to those gloomy piles of stone, with mere slits for windows, they must have been veritable corners of paradise to live in. And nobles who were rich enough delighted in building pavilions and pleasure parks to add to the attractiveness of their surroundings.

Medieval nobles had their jesters and minstrels. Chinese

rulers had jesters too, and dancers, whose functions seem to have been partly religious and partly theatrical. The following poem is by such a dancer.

> 'Easy and indifferent! Easy and indifferent!
> I am ready to perform the ten thousand dances,
> When the sun is in the meridian,
> In that elevated place.
>
> With my large figure,
> I dance in the ducal courtyard.
> I am strong as a tiger;
> The reins in my grasp are like ribbons.
>
> In my left hand I grasp a flute;
> In my right I hold a pheasant's feather.
> I am red as if I were rouged;
> The Duke rewards me with a cup of liquor.'[3]

Hunting and war were two sports indulged in by the Chinese and the medieval noble alike. We have already had occasion to consider the manner of hunting in Chou times, and the fact that it was used as a means of training the army. Since war was a chief duty of the aristocrat, he naturally indulged in games and matches which kept him in trim for fighting. In Europe the tournament, matching knights against each other in the use of their principal weapons, filled this place. In China the chief weapon was the bow, and archery contests were therefore an important ceremony for the Chinese nobility. There were schools for training the young aristocrats in shooting; one bronze inscription tells of the appointment of the master of such a school by the king, probably in the ninth century B.C. The king himself sometimes gave prizes for prowess in archery. But although it was recognized as an accomplishment of the most serious value, archery was also a sport, engaged in for the fun of the thing. Kings frequently took part themselves. A bronze, probably from the ninth century B.C., tells us that on one occasion the king, returning from a military expedition to the south, stopped at the seat of one of his nobles on the way. The vassal, eager to entertain the king, gave him a feast. After that the king and the vassal had a round of shooting at the targets, followed by a round of drinking. The king was so pleased with the entertainment provided that he gave his vassal several presents, including four horses. In addition to these incidental matches, there were official archery contests of various sorts, in which many persons of more or less rank and office took part. The *I Li* describes the ceremonial to be used in some of them, with the greatest detail. Just how early these official contests, with their elaborate fixed ritual, came into existence we cannot tell. They were commonly held in one of the schools for archery mentioned above.

A peculiarly happy method was used for scoring. The element of competition was utilized to give point and zeal to the efforts of the contestants, while at the same time it was impossible for any individual to be pointedly humiliated by failure. The shooters were paired, and each pair shot together, one at the left-hand and one at the right-hand target. Each shot was scored, not for the individual, but for the total tally of the right or the left. Thus one-half of the contestants vied with the other half, but no one person could feel the entire onus of defeat. One is tempted to see in this an early example of a Chinese characteristic which is very prominent to-day, that is, an intense aversion to subjecting any individual to public humiliation—what is commonly called the desire to preserve 'face,' for others as well as for oneself. Special care was taken to preserve the prestige of reigning nobles who might take part in the affair. The master of archery stood behind the noble and corrected his aim before he shot, and some shots which counted as misses for others, were counted as hits for him. After the score had been determined the forfeit was paid by

PLATE XIV

BRONZE CHARIOT FITTINGS WHICH PROBABLY DATE FROM THE SHANG PERIOD

NOTE THE HUB-CAP IN THE CENTRE.

Reproduced by courtesy of the William Rockhill Nelson Gallery of Art, Kansas City.

the losing side, each one of the losing half of the company advancing in turn and draining a cup of liquor. A feast, with music and drinking, preceded or followed or both. The *Book of Poetry* gives us a vivid picture of such an occasion.

> 'When the guests first approach the mats,
> They take their places on the left and the right in an orderly manner.
> The dishes of bamboo and wood are arranged in rows,
> With the sauces and kernels displayed in them.
> The liquor is mild and good,
> And they drink, all equally reverent.
> The bells and drums are properly arranged;
> And they raise their pledge-cups with order and ease.
> (Then) the great target is set up;
> The bows and arrows are made ready for the shooting;
> The archers are matched in classes.
> "Show your skill in shooting," (it is said).
> "I shall hit that mark," (it is responded),
> "And pray you to drink the cup." '[4]

Eating always has been and no doubt always will be one of the principal pleasures of man, and the ancient Chinese did not neglect this department, as many bronze inscriptions, the *Book of Poetry*, the *I Li*, and other sources assure us. Not merely the archery contests, but also sacrifices and other ceremonies frequently ended in feasts. The *I Li* describes a sort of banquet said to have been given by the chief official of a district to all the important men in it, every three years.[5] Other banquets were given on many official occasions. They were given to rulers and nobles by their inferiors, and were given by superiors, as a special honour, to persons of inferior rank. Diplomats of the present day who complain that they have to attend too many dinners would not have gained by being born in ancient China, for the banquet was a chief tool of diplomacy then as now.

The ritual to be followed at these banquets, diplomatic and otherwise, is most exacting. Each guest has his place, determined by his rank, and there is an elaborate ceremonial, involving much sacrificing, much bowing and yielding of precedence, to be gone through. Music accompanies the ceremony, the pieces to be played being prescribed by formula. One comes to wonder whether there could have been any pleasure in such a procedure. But finally: 'the dainties are served; they drink, no account being taken of the number of cups; and music is played without any restriction of the number or order of the tunes.'[6]

In eating they did not sit on chairs, but reclined on mats, using low stools as arm-rests. Like the modern Japanese they did not wear shoes on these mats. Chopsticks were not, I believe, invented until shortly after our period. There is a story to the effect that the last ruler of the Shang dynasty used ivory chopsticks, but this appears to be pure legend. In so far as I know, no chopsticks have been excavated from this time, and we know that meat was sometimes served in great pieces which it would have been impossible to manage with such utensils. It appears that they ate by means of spoons, a knife, and their fingers—utensils which sufficed our own ancestors until quite recently indeed.

One fact which impresses the reader of accounts of their feasts is the amount of washing which was done. Among the regular articles laid out in preparation for a meal was a jar of clean water for washing, which was ladled as it was needed into basins, and a receptacle to receive used water. The guests washed their hands, with some ceremony, before the meal. During the meal, when liquor was drunk, the cup was washed, if not after each using very nearly so. And the person who washed the cup, who was a participant doing it as an honour to the next drinker, washed his own hands before washing the cup. This cleanliness was not merely a matter of ceremony. A late section of the *I Li* prescribed that in entertaining foreign diplomats and members of their suites, facilities should be provided for general ablutions every three days, and a full bath every five.[7]

Not all feasts were official, however. Relatives and friends, in groups large and small, were entertained simply or lavishly as desire and circumstances permitted.

> 'Look at that bird,
> Bird as it is, seeking with its voice its companion;
> And shall a man
> Not seek to have his friends?
> Spiritual beings will then hearken to him;
> He shall have harmony and peace. . . .
> I have strained off my liquor in abundance;
> The dishes stand in rows,
> And none of my brethren are absent.
> The loss of kindly feeling among people
> May arise from faults in the matter of dry provisions.
> If I have liquor I strain it, do I;
> If I have no liquor I buy it, do I;
> I make the drums beat, do I;
> I lead on the dance, do I.
> Whenever we have leisure,
> Let us drink the sparkling liquor.'[8]

From the amount of ceremony and drinking one might suspect that food had little place in these dinners, but he would be mistaken. The ancient Chinese appreciated the culinary art—so much so that in two places the *Book of Poetry* lists the Chief Cook of the ruler as among the most important officials of the state.[9] Unfortunately no cook-books from those times have survived to us, but we have the names of a number of foods and dishes which they served. The following list is compiled from the literature. Since food is mentioned only incidentally, we cannot suppose that the menu was limited to those dishes which happen to be named in the literature. It is possible that a few of the items listed here were not used until rather late, since they appear only in the *I Li.* Also, while every attempt has been made to secure accuracy, it is very difficult indeed to be absolutely sure in every case of the signification of the names of fruits and vegetables found in ancient books. It will be understood, therefore, that the following list is to be considered as nothing more than a suggestion, though in general an accurate one, of the diet of the early Chou Chinese.

Cereals

Wheat
Rice dumplings
Rice porridge
Panicled millet porridge
Glutinous millet
Boiled hempseed

Vegetables

Celery (?)
Mustard
Bamboo sprouts
Ferns (two varieties)
Duckweed
Pondweed
Taro hash
Beans
Pickled mallows
Scallion pickle
Pickled leeks
Pickled leek-flowers
Pickled rush roots
Salted vegetables

Miscellaneous

Relishes
Sauces
Salt

Fish

Sturgeon
Bream
Carp
Mudfish
Turtle
(Various other fish not easy to identify)

Meats

Beef broth
Mutton broth
Pork broth
Broth with vegetables
Beef (broiled, sliced, minced)
Pork (in gravy; with mustard sauce; roasted)
Mutton (broiled, sliced)
Dog
Tripe and cheek
Dried meat (plain and spiced)
Snail hash
Pickled snails
Elk flesh hash
Deer flesh hash
Pheasant
Hare
Quail
Jay

Fruits

Wild Grape	Fruit of the Jujube Tree, called the Chinese Date (raw and stewed)
Peach	
Plum	
Pomelo	Chestnuts (raw and cooked)
Orange	Melons (raw and pickled)

We have seen that meals were accompanied by drinking. Some of the drinks provided appear to have been non-alcoholic, or of very slight alcoholic content, made from various infusions of grains or of fruit juices. The liquor commonly used, for sacrifice and for drinking both with meals and at other times, was made of millet, probably a sort of millet beer. Its alcoholic content must not have been very large, since they drank considerable quantities of it and then proceeded to shoot in archery contests.

The history of the use of liquor in early Chou times is rather interesting. The first Chou kings appear to have been prohibitionists, or at least strong advocates and even enforcers of temperance. Early Chou books, and a bronze inscription, tell us that the Shang people, toward the end of the dynasty, were besotted with drink from their ruler down, and that that was why the Chous were given the divine command to conquer them. We might suppose that this was only a part of the propaganda which always accompanies war, and I think that it was, in part. But it appears to be true, also, that the Chous, as a ruder, less civilized people, used liquor less than did the Shangs. Coming in contact with the urban luxury of the Shang aristocrats, the Chous looked upon it as sinful and decadent.

This provided the Chous with a good argument to help justify their invasion on moral grounds, when such justification came to be needed. Also, there was good reason why the Chou rulers should have sought to restrict the use of liquor by their own followers during the conquest and in the critical years when they were trying to make their holdings secure. Ancient

Chinese history has several instances in which battles were lost because generals were too drunk to direct their men.

Out of this situation we have the *Announcement Concerning Liquor*, a decree now found in the *Document Classic*, which was apparently written by the original Duke of Chou about a decade after the Chou conquest. It was addressed to his brother, who was put in charge of a large portion of the conquered Shang people, as ruler of the State of Wei. It declares that liquor was originally used only for sacrifices, but that later it was abused, and became the ruination of states and people. In fact, it asserts, disorders may always be traced to liquor, and it was because of this evil that Shang lost its place of sovereignty. The Accomplished King was zealous in opposing the excessive use of liquor. Drinking should be limited to sacrifices, and to certain stated occasions, after duties have been fully performed, when it is permissible to feast and to drink to the full. The utmost vigilance is necessary to keep the people from falling into drunkenness. Lenience is to be exercised toward the former people of Shang, for they have long been corrupted; they must, if possible, be gradually reformed. But as for the Chou people, 'If you are told that there are companies who drink together, do not fail to apprehend them all, and send them here to Chou, where I shall put them to death.[10]

A bronze known as the *Ta Yu Ting*, which was probably cast only a few years after the writing of this proclamation, also ascribes the fall of Shang to liquor, and says that the early Chou kings did not allow excessive drinking.

These measures were like American prohibition in the fact that they allowed the use of liquor in religious ceremonies, but condemned it otherwise. The death penalty for social drinking was a little more stringent than anything enforced in the United States, however. But if these measures ever really operated in ancient China they were of short duration, for the Chous soon became as fond of luxury and the flowing bowl as the Shangs ever could have been. Even simple meals were accompanied by liquor, while at banquets it flowed unceasing. To be sure, every meal was attended by some sort of sacrifice, corresponding to the saying of 'grace,' but if this be said to have made the drinking religious it can be counted as nothing more than an excuse. In poems and rituals, time after time, we read that the expansive host commands: 'Let there be none who do not drink to the full!' This drinking did not always go to the point of drunkenness, but the following verses from the *Book of Poetry* show what often happened:

'When the guests first approach the mats,
They take their places on the left and the right in an orderly manner.
The dishes of bamboo and wood are arranged in rows,
With the sauces and kernels displayed in them.
The liquor is mild and good,
And they drink, all equally reverent. . . .
When the guests first approach the mats,
All harmonious are they and reverent.
Before they have drunk too much,
Their deportment is carefully observant of propriety;
But when they have drunk too much,
Their conduct becomes light and frivolous—
They leave their seats and go elsewhere,
They keep dancing and capering.
Before they have drunk too much,
Their deportment is cautious and grave;
But after they have drunk too much
It becomes indecent and rude—
Thus, being drunk
They lose all sense of orderliness.

When the guests have drunk too much,
They shout and they brawl,
They disorder the dishes,
They keep dancing in a fantastic manner.

Being drunk
They become insensible of their errors.
With their caps on one side, and like to fall off,
They keep dancing and will not stop.
If, when they had drunk to the full, they went out,
Both they and their host would be happy;
But remaining after they are drunk
Is what is called doing injury to virtue.
Drinking is a good institution
Only when there is good deportment in it.

On every occasion of drinking,
Some get drunk, and some do not.
An inspector is appointed,
With a recorder to assist him.
But those drunkards, in their vileness,
Are ashamed of those who do not get drunk.
These have no opportunity to speak,
And prevent the others from proceeding to such great abandonment.
(They might say), "Do not speak what you ought not to speak.
Do not say what you have no occasion to say.
If you speak, drunk as you are,
We will make you produce a ram without horns.
With three cups you lose your memories—
How dare you go on to more?" '[11]

Among the pleasures enjoyed by the ancient Chinese aristocrat, music was not the least. There were professional musicians, but it was also customary for individuals to play an instrument for their own pleasure. The instrument chiefly used for this purpose was stringed, played by plucking; its notes are described as 'quiet and pleasant.' It was considered an appropriate companion to both joy and sorrow.

Music was played as an accompaniment to ceremonies of all sorts, as well as to feasts. It held a very important place in connection with sacrifices, hymns of praise being played and sung as a part of the ritual. Even in archery contests the shooting was done in time to music, and shots not loosed in accord with the rhythm were not counted.

The musicians were commonly blind. They were treated with honour, holding official positions. At feasts they were given food and liquor, in their turn, like other guests. At banquets and similar functions music was furnished by groups of two sorts. One was a quartet, which sang to the accompaniment of string instruments played by two of its members. Music of another kind was provided by a band of players equipped with a type of reed-organ, which had a number of pipes and was played by blowing upon it.

For sacrifices and more important occasions an orchestra of many pieces played. It was composed of drums, bells, and musical sounding stones, each of many varieties, and wind instruments.

Some of the pieces of music played were tunes composed to accompany verses in the *Book of Poetry*, while others were purely instrumental, without words. All have been lost. We are unable even to form a general picture of the music of ancient China with any assurance that it is accurate. Nothing could be less correct than the supposition that the music of modern China, and especially the percussive symphonies of the modern Chinese theatre, give any adequate idea of classical Chinese music.

There was a great deal of ritualism connected with music in the early period. Certain pieces were to be played at certain times, certain songs were used when the principal guest entered, others when he left, and so on. But the elaborate system of metaphysical ideas which surrounded music at a later time does not appear in the books of the period before 600 B.C. Later, we find elaborate theories linking music with numerology, magic, and government. It was said that the morals and even the future of a state could be known by examining its music, so that the king might use this means of learning whether his vassals ruled their territories well or ill. But all this appears to be the philosophical elaboration of a later day.

CHAPTER XXV

RELIGION

THE most searching questions which can be asked about a religion are not 'What are its deities?' and 'What are its beliefs?' but 'What are its aims?' and 'How are they attained?' To understand this aspect of a culture we must first learn what are the needs and desires which the people hope to satisfy through religion, and then examine the means by which they seek to satisfy them. For the Shang period our information was too little to allow of this, but for early Chou times the picture is relatively complete.

Especially in the bronze inscriptions we get a very good cross-section of the desires of those who made them. The casting of a large bronze vessel was an event in the life of even a wealthy and powerful individual. If it was intended for sacrificial purposes he believed that it would help him to obtain from the all-powerful gods those things which he most desired, and he frequently went to the trouble of stating them explicitly. Since these vessels were expected to endure for 'ten thousand years' and more, their inscriptions do not, unfortunately, express the specific desires of their makers for success in this or that business of the moment; they are couched in general terms.

Analysis of the three hundred and thirty-two inscriptions covered by my notes shows that the most universal prayer is: 'May my sons and grandsons for ever treasure and use this vessel.' The real meaning of this is, of course, that he wishes his line to continue, and his descendants to sacrifice to his spirit for ever. This is the chief desire, and it helps to explain why individuals are sometimes ready to sacrifice their individual lives and even the welfare of the state as a whole for the sake of the continuation of their families.

Next to this comes the desire for long life. On the Western Chou bronzes it is sought in only about eight per cent. of the inscriptions, but more than one-half of the Eastern Chou pieces pray for longevity. The desire for long life is very strong among the Chinese to this day, and it is not easy for us, who sometimes feel that the best we could ask is to die after passing our prime, to understand. One hears even young Chinese women wish that they were old, and young and blooming foreign women are sometimes shocked, on the Chinese streets, to hear beggars address them as 'aged dame'; it is a compliment. A part of the reason for this is the veneration paid to age in China, and the place of the old in the family system. A man is almost a minor in China until his father dies, no matter how old he may be. Custom still obliges him to render a large measure of obedience during all his father's lifetime, and this was backed by law until the advent of the republic. Parents and grandparents must not only be supported, but must be given the best of everything and treated with the greatest honour. Old persons are in authority and may be tyrants if they like; the young, among the old-fashioned at least, have very little recourse. In such a system it is ordinarily not until one is old that one can begin to enjoy life fully, and to be a person of consequence.

Prayers for 'blessings' or the 'assistance' of the spirits in general terms are naturally frequent on the bronzes. Sometimes it is asked that the spirits shall 'protect my person,' or grant 'good fortune.' The Chinese equivalent of 'give us this day our daily bread' is not lacking. A desire quite understandable to all who find satisfaction in their work is expressed by officials: 'May I long assist the Son of Heaven in the administration of government.' 'Children without limit' are requested, and some ask that after living a long life they may 'come to a good end.' All of these fall more or less into the class of material things, but we find occasional petitions for such 'spiritual' blessings as tranquillity and wisdom.

Like the men of Shang times, these people were eager to know the future, and we find them seeking to read it in a variety of ways. The old method with the tortoise-shell was still used, as well as the method which involved the *Book of Changes*. Dreams, the songs of boys, and persons gifted with special ability in that direction were all used to roll back the curtain of the future. Not merely kings, but people of all sorts —couples planning an elopement, wives of soldiers longing for their husband's return—besought the oracles.

Sacrifice, sometimes accompanied by prayer, was the method by which they sought to obtain blessings from the spirits. Not all sacrifices needed to be accompanied by prayer. Some offerings were made regularly, as much a matter of course as the food given to an aged father, and the constant aid and protection given by the spirits to their worshippers were as much to be expected as the care exercised by a father over his son. But when the worshipper was confronted by some unusual difficulty or faced by some special need, then he had to make it known to his deity in the form of a prayer. It is probable that this was usually written, read aloud at a sacrifice, and then burned. Such prayers, made on all sorts of subjects, were especially important for war. As with us, both sides prayed for victory, and it was felt that the prayer had no little effect on the outcome.

The things which were sacrificed were in general the same as in the Shang period. But it will be remembered that the Shangs sacrificed no products of agriculture except liquor. The Chous sacrificed grain from the beginning of the dynasty, and their ancestors deigned even to eat cooked vegetables. The things to be sacrificed varied according to rank, down to the common people who are said to have sacrificed fish to their ancestors. Animals given to the spirits had to be perfect. If a bull, selected for sacrifice and accepted by divination, later had one of its horns nibbled by a mouse, it could not be offered.

Some information concerning sacrifice in the Chou period is furnished by the excavations at Hsün Hsien. We have already seen that there is only one case of what appears to be human sacrifice, which contrasts greatly with what was found at Anyang. One pit, about thirty feet square and twenty feet deep, is especially interesting, for it was apparently used for the offering of a large 'chariot sacrifice.' No human remains were found in it. At the bottom of the pit were seventy-two horses, twelve chariots, and eight dogs. The horses were evidently hitched to the chariots, at the time of interment, but the wheels had been removed from the chariots. Each of the dogs had a bell hung about its neck. Earth was probably thrown in from the north side, for the horses were all at the south side, in the greatest confusion as if something had frightened them and caused them to run that way. The dogs were found at the base of the south, east, and west walls, where they were obviously trying to climb out as the earth was thrown in upon them. After the dogs and horses were covered with earth the wheels of the chariots were thrown into the pit, and it was filled up to the ground level.

There were many different sorts of sacrifices, at many different times. Some were made only for a particular occasion, as to celebrate a victory, or as part of a diplomatic mission. Others, like those of spring and of autumn, were connected with agriculture and the calendar. The dead were sacrificed to very frequently when they had first died, but were gradually fed less often, apparently with the idea that they became accustomed to their status as spirits and required less nourishment. A little bit of any food or drink partaken of was poured out for the spirits at every meal.

An interesting figure in the sacrifices to ancestors was the 'personator' of the ancestor sacrificed to. This was a descendant, who was considered for the time being to be possessed by the spirit honoured in the ceremony. He ate and drank of the food and liquor offered, and then told the descendant making the sacrifice that his offerings were acceptable, and pronounced a blessing upon him. In a case of necessity the personator might be a child or even a baby who had to be held in arms and assisted in the performance of these duties.

The ancestral temple was the centre of the life and affairs of the family. Not only sacrifices, but the other ceremonies connected with important events in the family life took place there. The proposal of marriage was received by a girl's father in the ancestral temple, and after she was married she was not fully wed until the time when, three months after she entered her husband's family, she was introduced to its ancestors and took part in sacrifices in its temple.

But the ancestral temple was more than a family centre in the narrow sense of the word. In the temple of the ordinary aristocrat, not only his affairs but those of all his dependants were centred, and his retainers assisted him in its ceremonies. The temple of the ruler of a state was the centre of its activities, and he was assisted there by men who were masters in their own temples. The king's ancestral temple was the centre of affairs for all of China, and when he was powerful the rulers of states acted as his assistant in its rites.

All of the most important activities of the state took place in the ancestral temple of its ruler. Here the new heir assumed his position. Military expeditions set out from the temple, and returned to it to report and celebrate victory upon their return. The business of diplomacy, and state banquets, took place there. Officials were appointed to office and given rewards, and vassals were invested with territories, in this same hall. Apparently sacrifices not only to the ancestors but also to heaven were sometimes offered here; whether heaven was also sacrificed to in the open air, in this early period as it was later, is not clear.

The ancestral temple symbolized the state in so far as the state was conceived as the estate, the patrimony, of its ruling family. But the state was also considered as a territorial entity, a 'fatherland,' and in this sense it was symbolized by the *shê*, the so-called 'altar of the land.' Originally this was simply the soil, the giver of crops, to which sacrifices were offered for an abundant harvest; in time of drought it was thought that sacrifices to the land could produce rain. It was not easy to sacrifice to the soil without some symbol, and this symbol was found in a mound which may have been natural at first. But such mounds came to be thrown up in every village, and since they symbolized the land of the little district they became centres of religious activity in each community. Nobles who held lands comprising many villages had larger mounds, representing all of their territory, and the same was true of the rulers of states and even the king himself.

This *shê* is a very old deity. As we saw, it already existed in Shang times. In the early Chou period it was still recognized to be an agricultural deity, and it was sacrificed to for rain and for good harvests. In this period it was frequently called *shê chi*, 'land and grain' or 'the altar of land and grain.' But it was also recognized as a religious and symbolic centre of the state. Commanders of military expeditions had not only to receive their orders in the ancestral temple, but also to take part in certain ceremonies at this mound, before they could set out on an expedition. And certain state activities, especially the execution of some criminals, were carried out here. The *shê* of the late Manchu dynasty is still to be seen, just west of the imperial palace in Peiping.

The importance of the ancestral temple and the *shê* as twin centres of the spiritual influences guarding the state is shown by the fact that when a state or a dynasty was extinguished it was considered necessary to destroy them. Only in this way could the spirits protecting the former ruler be enfeebled, and their enmity be made less dangerous.

In addition to these two places where sacrifices were performed, other offerings were made in the suburbs of the capital and at various places in the open air, according to the nature of the deities being honoured and their rites.

There was not a priesthood in our sense of the word. There were officials, retainers, and servants who specialized in religious functions. They had charge of keeping up the temples, they composed and recited prayers, and they were skilled in ritual and often assisted and even guided their lords in performing the prescribed ceremonies. But they were always of lesser rank and status than the person who took the chief part in the ritual; in lesser aristocratic families their functions were performed by men who were not of aristocratic standing, or even by slaves. They had little or no real authority in religious matters. There was no conflict of church and state, because there was no church except as it was identified with those who wielded the political power.

There was, to be sure, still another class of persons who claimed to be in direct communication with spirits, even to be possessed by them. They were both male and female, and we may call them wizards and witches. They called up spirits, communicated with them, and performed various acts of a more or less magical sort, including prophecy. Their claims were believed in very widely, but they were not held in very good repute. Occasionally one of them, by gaining influence over some ruler, came to a temporary position of great power, but they were generally regarded as of questionable respectability. It was not the thing to be in relations of too much intimacy with spirits, any more than it was dignified for one in an inferior position to flatter his ruler and become a favourite. The statement of Confucius, that one should 'Respect the spirits, but maintain the proper distance in relations with them,'[1] covers the case perfectly. To fail in one's duties to them was impious and dangerous, but to fawn upon them with excessive attentions was equally blameable.

Spirits, and especially the spirits of ancestors, were extremely important. Wooden tablets, inscribed with their names, were set up in the ancestral temple, and when a military expedition went forth one of these was carried with it. The spirits did not dwell in the temple at all times, but were summoned to it on ceremonial occasions. Mats and arm-rests were provided for them at such times, just as if they had been living men. To honour them with a sacrifice and to honour an esteemed person, still living, with a feast, were called by the same terms; sometimes the same ritual vessels were used for both purposes.

In general the spirits of the dead, from kings to the humble, seem to have been conceived of as living in the heavens. But there was another idea, frequently mentioned in later books, that the dead lived under the earth at a place called the 'Yellow Springs.' I know of only one reference to it in the early period. Duke Chuang of the State of Chêng had a younger brother whom he treated very indulgently, with the result that he wished to rob him of his state. Their mother was partial to the younger brother, and agreed to aid him in his plot. It was discovered and foiled, in 722 B.C. Duke Chuang, very angry with his mother, swore that he would not see her again 'until we reach the Yellow Springs,' that is, after death. But in time good nature and filial piety made him repent of his oath, and a resourceful subject suggested a means of evading it. The Duke had two tunnels digged under the earth, meeting in the centre; he entered at one end and his mother entered at the other; they met underground and the conditions of the oath were considered fulfilled.[2] This suggests that the Yellow Springs was simply a term denoting the abode of the dead underground in the grave, like the Sheol of the Hebrews.

The power of ancestral spirits was not believed in by their descendants only. In 660 B.C. the Ti barbarians defeated the armies of the State of Wei very decisively, and pressed on to take the capital. They captured two high officials of Wei, who told them, 'We have charge of the sacrifices of the state; if you do not allow us to precede you, it will be impossible to take the city.' On this the captured officials were allowed to go ahead and warn the inhabitants.[3] Chinese themselves acted similarly. More than once, if we may believe the records, states which had been vanquished and might have been annexed were spared because of the fear of the anger of their ancestors. The State of Lu, home of Confucius, endured to the end of the Chou dynasty, although it was small and weak during most of its history, while larger and more powerful states fell all about it; undoubtedly this was partly due to the prestige of the Duke of Chou, its founder.

It was not only by the general exercise of protection or punishment that the spirits of the dead manifested themselves. At times they took possession of unfortunate individuals, and sometimes they appeared as ghosts, rewarding benefits or taking revenge for past injuries. It is related that King Hsüan was shot by a ghost. King Mu is said to have been the son, not of his mother's husband, but of an ancient and mischievous ghost who carried on an intrigue with her.

One of the most typical ghost stories has to do with the troubled times of the State of Chin. It may be recalled that Shên-shêng, the heir apparent of Duke Hsien, unwilling to take the barbarian woman who delighted the aged Duke from him, succumbed to her plotting and killed himself. At the same time the other sons of the Duke fled the state, and lived abroad. Thereafter various other states plotted to put this or that scion on the throne, as their own protégé. On the death of Duke Hsien, two of his sons took his place in succession, in the same year, 651 B.C. Both were murdered. A third became Duke Hui. He is generally acknowledged to have been a man of no character, placed in power by the State of Ch'in because he was expected to be a useful puppet. He soon proved arrogant and treacherous. Later, when Hu T'u, former charioteer of Shên-shêng who committed suicide, was driving through the country, he saw the ghost of Shên-shêng, who got into the chariot and rode with him, saying, 'I-wu [Duke Hui] has violated all propriety. I have had a request granted by Ti [that is, Shang Ti, the chief deity]. The State of Chin is to be given to Ch'in, and Ch'in will continue the sacrifices to me.' Hu T'u replied to him: 'Your servant has heard that spirits do not enjoy sacrifices made by those who are not their kindred, and that people only sacrifice to the dead of their own family. Will not my lord's sacrifices really be extinguished in that case? And what is the guilt of the people of Chin? I ask that my lord consider before he causes them to be wrongly punished, and his own sacrifices to be cut off.' Shên-shêng replied: 'Very well, I will change my request. Seven days hence, on the western side of the new city, there will be a wizard through whom you may communicate with me.' Hu T'u agreed, and the prince vanished. At the time and place agreed upon Hu T'u was told: 'Ti has granted that only the guilty person shall be punished. He shall be defeated in Han.'[4]

Hungry ghosts, wandering about without sacrifices, made trouble. Sometimes they stole the sacrifices of other spirits; sometimes they made people ill until they were fed. For them to cross one's path was dreaded, but greatest of all was the fear that one might himself become one of them after death. This was a tremendous moral force. If a subject attempted rebellion, it was not merely his own life which would be forfeit if he failed; there was a considerable probability that his whole family would be wiped out, and with it would go his sacrifices.

Invisible spirits were all about.

> 'Do not say, "This place is not public;
> No one can see me here."
> The approaches of spirits
> Cannot be calculated beforehand,
> But the more should they not be slighted.'[5]

Not only the ghosts of the dead but various spirits of water and forest were to be dealt with. Offerings were made to various minor powers, such as the path and the cross-roads. Mountains and rivers were especially important. The Yellow River was a spirit who had special power to give victory in war to those who sacrificed to it. It liked precious jades and fine clothes. Its habit was to appear in dreams and make known to mortals what it wanted. Woe betide him who failed to cast the coveted article into its waters!

Shang Ti, the 'highest ruler' whom we met in the Shang period, here figures as the chief deity. He is apparently a sort of ruler of the heavens. The former kings are 'at the left and right of Ti,' and he seems to function as the president of the great spirits. But we find Shang Ti also called by another name—Heaven. There is no question that in the Chou period these are commonly used as two names for the same deity. On the other hand, we find that on early Chou bronzes Heaven is mentioned very commonly, while Shang Ti occurs but rarely. But Heaven, as the name of a deity, does not occur once in all of the thousands of Shang oracle inscriptions that are known. What apparently happened is that the Chou people had a chief deity, called Heaven, before they came into close contact with the Shangs. When they took over many aspects of Shang culture they found that Shang Ti filled a place something like that of their Heaven, and identified the two. This is a familiar process in the history of religions. The Romans identified several of their deities with Greek gods, Juno with Hera, Venus with Aphrodite, and so on.

The origin of Heaven as a deity among the Chou people is very difficult to trace. The Chinese word is T'ien 天; its form in early Chou times was , which is clearly the figure of a man. After some years of study of its use in literature and on bronze inscriptions, and of the development of the character in comparison with the development of other characters, I have evolved the following theory: The original meaning of this word was simply 'a great man,' that is, a man of power,

PLATE XV

A BRONZE CEREMONIAL VESSEL OF THE TYPE *TING*, CAST DURING THE MIDDLE CHOU PERIOD

THIS IS AN UNUSUALLY BEAUTIFUL EXAMPLE OF THAT DATE. IT IS INSTRUCTIVE TO COMPARE THIS PIECE WITH THE FRONTISPIECE AND OTHER PLATES OF SHANG RITUAL VESSELS. THERE WAS A GRADUAL DEGENERATION OF THE ART OF BRONZE CASTING FROM SHANG TO MIDDLE CHOU TIMES, A GRADUAL DECREASE IN DELICACY, SUBTLETY, AND SOPHISTICATION. THIS *TING* IS NOW IN THE CHINESE NATIONAL PALACE MUSEUM.

Photograph by courtesy of Professor Jung Kêng.

prestige, and importance. As such it applied especially to rulers and to kings. From this it was applied to the same men after death, when, as spirits, they became still greater; here then we have it as meaning the 'Great Spirits,' that is, the spirits of the former kings and great personages of the past, considered as a body. By an easy transition it was used also to mean 'the abode of the Great Spirits,' that is the heavens, the sky. Here, then, we have the idea of Heaven as a vague symbol of the vast power of the great spirits and the place where they dwell. Since Chinese does not commonly distinguish singular and plural, it was easy to think of this vague, over-ruling power as a single person, and thus, from the 'Great Spirits,' we get the idea of a single 'Great Spirit,' Heaven, a vast, somewhat impersonal over-ruling deity.

The proof for all this is, of course, much more complicated than this statement. But there are many passages which cannot be explained satisfactorily on any other basis, and I believe that it is sound. While it cannot be said, as yet, to be more than a theory, it has already been published in Chinese and accepted by a number of Chinese scholars who are thoroughly familiar with the evidence on which it is based.

In this connection it is interesting to note that the title by which the Chou kings were commonly known was T'ien Tzŭ, 'the Son of Heaven.' If Heaven originally meant the former kings considered as a group, then it is altogether fitting that the reigning king should be known as their descendant. But this can hardly be called a final proof of this theory, since we find elsewhere kings said to be descended from gods who were never mortals. We have seen that the title *wang* 王, 'King,' which was later considered to be the exclusive possession of the ruler of all of China, was originally merely a name for a territorial chieftain. From bronze inscriptions we can see that the Chou kings themselves seem to have tolerated use of this title by certain of their loyal vassals. But this is not the case with the title 'Son of Heaven.' Of such there could be only one, and to assume this title was to avow one's intention of making himself master of all China. It was definitely linked with the imperial sway, and lesser rulers did not dare to usurp it; they were prevented, no doubt, by religious awe as well as practical policy.

Everywhere that we find a growing spirit of humanitarianism and an expansion of social conscience we also find in religion a corresponding increase of emphasis on ethics, accompanied, perhaps, by a lessening of the stress laid on purely ritual practices. We find this in China during the Chou period, and many of the scholars and statesmen who champion the new point of view remind us strikingly of the Hebrew prophets. Virtue, they declare, is far more important than sacrifices in getting the favour of the gods. For one who is in the wrong to lead an army to battle is to go to certain defeat. Especially, they insist, is it impossible for a ruler who oppresses his people to enjoy the prosperity which comes from heaven, no matter how plentiful the grain or how fat the animals which he may sacrifice. And the sacrifice of human beings, which was common in Shang times and not unusual in the early days of Chou, is condemned with growing vehemence. The sanctity of human life, even of the lives of very unimportant persons, becomes a principle in the ethics and the religion of the official class.

The problem of evil was vexing, in this as in every other religion. It was staunchly declared that evil actions invariably found their punishment, in misfortune, disgrace, or untimely death, on this earth. In native Chinese religion there was no punishment of evil after death, except the punishment which came to a man whose sacrifices were cut off because his family had been extinguished. But unless his posterity had ceased, the spirit of the evil-doer was sacrificed to along with the good, and if the line was destroyed the good ancestors suffered with the bad. This was not very satisfactory. And there were cases, of which everybody knew, in which men who had lived thoroughly wicked lives enjoyed them up to the very end, when they died full of years and surrounded by luxury, and thereafter enjoyed uninterrupted sacrifices for many generations. But even so such a one could not be sure of escaping misfortune, if we may believe the *Discourses of the States*. For after one such hardened malefactor had been buried, smoke was seen to issue from his grave. His coffin had burned up. His sins had followed him even into the tomb, and found him out at last.

CHAPTER XXVI

LAW

UNTIL the establishment of the Republic in 1912 the government of China functioned without a written constitution. There are, however, various important books and documents which, taken together, might be said to contain the fundamental laws and doctrines on which the Chinese state has been based. If we were to gather together such a body of literature, we should find it to be composed very largely of documents written during the Chou dynasty or very shortly thereafter. And if we made a list of the various principles and doctrines which made up the Chinese constitution of former years we should find that a disproportionate number of them came to something much like their present form during the Chou dynasty.

If we look into ancient books which set out the forms and procedure of Chinese government, such as the *Ceremonial of Chou* and the *Ceremonial Records*, we find elaborate institutions of a complexity and a nicety of organization which surprise us. Some scholars, both Chinese and foreign, have made the mistake of supposing that these elaborate schemes give us a faithful picture of the machinery through which the early and powerful Chou kings ruled. But it is abundantly evident, from contemporary records, that no such far-flung bureaucracy could have exercised its well-regulated sway in those times. As we have seen, government was very largely farmed out to individual feudal lords who were given territories which they might rule as they saw fit, so long as they gave to their immediate superior, whether the king or another feudal lord, military service and such tribute as was expected of them. Only if they came into conflict with other nobles or if their people were oppressed to the point of actual rebellion was interference in local affairs by the superior to be expected. In such conditions wide variations in methods of administration were inevitable.

Whence, then, come the books containing elaborate if not altogether practical schemes of a far-flung supervision by a central government? They are not difficult to account for. We have seen that after 771 B.C. the power of the Chou kings virtually ceased. Instead there ensued a long and sanguinary struggle for power between the various states, bringing conditions which no thinking person could find satisfactory. By contrast the earlier and in many ways cruder times of Western Chou, when the Chou kings did exercise some degree of sovereignty over all of the China of their day, seemed ideal. The officials and philosophers, building on the basis of fact, proceeded to work out an ideal system of government, which they declared had actually been practised formerly. The result was that, while it had never previously existed, as much of it as was practicable was taken over at various times by later Chinese governments. Even some of the recently created government of 'Manchukuo' is said to be based on 'usages of the Chou dynasty,' which in reality means upon these idealized books.

But if the China of early Chou times had no written constitution, and if the elaborate schemes of government which later scholars attributed to this period do not actually go back so far, it does not follow that there was no law and no basis of government in those times. Everywhere custom is the basis and the forerunner of written law, and there is no country in the world in which custom and tradition have been revered and observed more faithfully than in China.

Not only do the Chinese now respect antiquity, but they did so even in very ancient times. The exhortations to 'study and follow the ways of the wise kings of old' and to 'pattern yourself after the ancients' are among the most usual motifs of the literature even of the very beginning of the Chou period.

The *Document Classic*, the *Book of Poetry*, bronze inscriptions and other sources join in showing this.

> 'I think of the men of old,
> That I may be kept from doing wrong . . .
> I think of the ancients,
> And find what is in my heart.'[1]

Time after time we find enunciated the doctrine that custom, and the example of former rulers, is binding as against the wish or whim of the ruler of the moment. Naturally this doctrine was resisted by the rulers, and often with success. But they could not entirely disregard it, and those who did so too stubbornly sometimes lost their power and even their lives as a result.

About 601 B.C. Duke Ling of the State of Ch'ên exhausted the resources of his territories to build a marvellous pleasure pavilion for his mistress. The people were compelled to construct it with forced labour. Their crops were neglected, and the state was generally left to go to ruin while its ruler's tastes were pandered to. But the worst of the criticisms which were levelled against him, from the point of view of the times, was that 'he has departed from the laws of the former kings.'

It must be remembered that many things beside mere inertia made for adherence to tradition. The former rulers were ancestors of the present ruler; not to conform to their ways was to be scarcely filial. Even more important, the former rulers were powerful spirits; to flout their example was to run the risk of making enemies before whom any mere mortal might quail. On the other hand, the force of tradition was not absolute. 'To follow an erroneous example,' declared King Ch'êng of Ch'u, 'is to aggravate the error.' And one could find more than one tradition on any important question; sometimes these were mutually contradictory, so that it was impossible to follow all of them. In this case it was recognized that one must select and follow the most worthy precedents.

Tradition had, then, much of the force of law. But if we seek to prove the existence of written codes of law in early Chou times we have a difficult task. We have, it is true, in the earliest and quite authentic literature passages which have been translated as 'the punishments will be determined by the regular laws of Yin (i.e., Shang),'[2] etc. In the *Book of Poetry* we have:

> 'The Accomplished King said, "Alas!
> Alas! you Yin-Shang.
> It is not that Shang Ti has caused this evil time,
> But it arises from Yin's not using the old ways.
> Although you have not old experienced men,
> You have still the ancient statutes and laws." '[3]

The term here translated as 'statutes' definitely refers to books.

The section in the *Document Classic* known as 'The Harangue at Pi,' is a speech made by a feudal noble to his army at the launching of a military expedition. In the course of the address he says:

> 'When the horses and cattle are seeking one another, or when your followers, male or female, abscond, presume not to leave the ranks to pursue them. But let them be carefully returned. I will reward you who return them according to their value. But if you leave your places to pursue them, or if you who find them do not return them, you shall be dealt with according to the regular punishments. And let none of you dare to rob or detain (vagrant followers or animals), to jump over enclosures and walls to steal away horses or oxen, or to decoy away servants or female attendants. If you do so, you shall be dealt with according to the regular punishments.'[4]

This certainly infers that there was a definite and generally understood body of military law, and we get the impression from other passages that there was such a body of law for application to criminal offences by the civil population. But were these, or were they not, written codes? This is a hard question. It seems difficult to suppose that they were not, in a civilization so fond of writing as that of early Chou China.

On the other hand, we find ourselves at a loss if we seek to bring any definite evidence of such written codes. There is a book in the *Document Classic* called 'The Punishments of Lü,' which is traditionally ascribed to the first half of the tenth century B.C. Here we might expect to find a code, but actually we have nothing of the sort. It opens with some general and highly dubious statements concerning the origins of criminal law, continues with a disquisition on the impartiality to be observed in trying cases, and becomes specific only in setting forth an elaborate schedule of fines to be applied in place of various punishments. It presupposes a highly refined and elaborate schedule of criminal law.

'Of crimes that may be redeemed by the fine in lieu of branding there are one thousand, and the same number of those that would incur cutting off the nose. The fine in lieu of cutting off the feet extends to five hundred cases, that in lieu of castration to three hundred, and that in lieu of death to two hundred. Altogether, set against the five punishments there are three thousand crimes.'[5]

If we could accept this document as coming from our period we should certainly have to believe that there was a very detailed criminal code in existence. But comparison of this book with other early literature shows that it was written long after the end of our period.

In so far as I know, there is not, in all of the literature of the early Chou period, a single statement that a specific crime legally calls for a specific punishment. It would seem that the 'laws of the former kings' which are so frequently spoken of were certain general maxims of conduct and statements of principle, while it was left to the individual ruler to take what steps he found necessary to ensure the practice of these principles by those under his power. The earliest reference to a specific code which I know is that of the *Tso Chuan*, which says that in 536 B.C. the criminal code of the State of Chêng was cast, presumably on one or more bronze vessels. When this event took place, an official of Chin sent a letter of protest to the minister responsible for it. This letter is worth quoting because it shows the attitude of the time concerning law. It reads, in part:

'Formerly I considered you as my model, but I have ceased to do so. The former kings reached their decisions in criminal cases after careful deliberation on the particular circumstances of the case in hand; they did not set up general laws because they feared that this might give rise to a contentious spirit among the people. But as crimes could not be prevented, they set before them the barrier of righteousness, sought to bring them to rectitude, caused them to act in conformity with right, maintained them with good faith, and cherished them with benevolence. They also instituted places of salary and position to encourage them to conform, and strictly laid down punishments to awe them from excesses. Fearing that these were insufficient, they taught them loyalty, urged them by their conduct, instructed them in what was most important, employed them in a spirit of harmony, came before them in a spirit of seriousness, met exigencies with vigour, and gave their decisions with firmness. And in addition to this they sought to have sage and wise persons in the highest positions, intelligent discriminating persons in all offices, leaders of loyalty and sincerity, and teachers of gentle kindness. In this way the people were successfully dealt with, and disasters and disorders did not arise.

'But when the people know what the exact laws are, then they do not stand in awe of their superiors. And they come to have a contentious spirit, and make their appeal to verbal technicalities, hoping thus to be successful in their argument. They can no longer be managed. When the government of Hsia had fallen into disorder the penal code of Yü was made;

under the same circumstances in Shang times they set up the code of T'ang; and in the Chou period the decay of the government led to making the code of the nine punishments.'[6]

The three codes mentioned here have not come down to us; that they ever existed is highly questionable. But the point of view expressed here is clear, and it seems to represent that of ancient China. It is based on the theory that general laws can never meet specific cases satisfactorily, and that the setting forth of a general code actually invites wrongdoing, by proclaiming that any action, no matter how anti-social, may go unpunished so long as its perpetrator is clever enough to stay within the limits set by the laws. Certainly this ancient Chinese protest against the defeating of justice by recourse to legal technicalities is one which we to-day can well understand. But if one does not choose to set up a code of laws, the only alternative is to leave complete discretion in the hands of the judge, who must also decide who is to be prosecuted, what punishments are to be inflicted, and in what manner. All of these functions were performed, in ancient China, by the ruler himself or by officials to whom he delegated his power.

Such a system could be completely satisfactory only under two conditions. In the first place, the number of persons under the rule of each individual in authority must be so small that he could easily keep himself acquainted with their activities. Within limits, this condition did exist in ancient China. Each petty aristocrat was the unquestioned arbiter even of the life and death of the people under his authority. He in turn was similarly subject to the noble above him. But the people under the lesser noble were not the concern of his superior. In each case, the immediate overlord had the final decision, without right of appeal. Thus we have a sort of pyramid system in which the actual number of people directly under the jurisdiction of a single individual was not unduly large. Furthermore, it was the case in ancient China as it is in modern that many conditions which would for us be matters of public law were taken care of within the family. The family or clan group has until very recently, and perhaps in some places still does, inflict even capital punishment upon its members if it is deemed necessary.

A second condition is necessary for the satisfactory functioning of a system which places legislative, judicial, and executive powers in the hands of one individual. He must be very wise and perfectly honest. Our records indicate that the men of ancient China were about as wise and about as honest as those of modern China, or Europe, or America, which means that the system sometimes worked very well and sometimes worked very badly. Bribes of various sorts, including beautiful women, were presented to officials and even to the king to influence their decisions in legal cases.

Superiors did not ordinarily interfere with or overrule the decisions made by their vassals in specific cases, but the Chous were wise enough to realize that unless they could give to the people of their territories a reasonable degree of justice, resentment against their newly established power would reach dangerous proportions. Therefore we find in the early literature, and even on bronzes, constant exhortations to their vassals to deal justly, and to be cautious, even lenient, in delivering sentence. They were instructed to distinguish clearly between intentional and unintentional acts. The early kings sought to prevent their vassals from becoming drunk with power by reminding them that they exercised only a delegated authority.

'It is not you, Fêng, who inflict a severe punishment or death upon a man; you may not of yourself so punish a man or put him to death.'[7]

In the early literature we find the following punishments mentioned: the stocks; the cangue; cutting off the toes, the feet, the ears, or the nose; capital punishment by various methods, including boiling alive. Fines, sometimes in terms of metal and sometimes in terms of goods such as arms or armour, were exacted. The penalties under military law were especially severe. Even in time of peace the driver of a chariot might be put to death if his vehicle got out of line in manœuvres.

In a late work it is said that 'punishments do not go up to the great officers.'[8] This no doubt expresses a pious hope on the part of the official class; nevertheless, persons of all ranks were compelled to submit to punishments of all sorts on occasion. But it is true that men of power and position were punished less often than common men, for the very good reason that it was more difficult to punish them. Every man of considerable position had something of a private army to protect him, and a family to avenge him. Therefore he was not punished unless the aggravation was severe and the opportunity good; in this case not only the offender might be put to death, but as a precautionary measure his relatives were frequently killed or enslaved. We have one bronze inscription in which the maker boasts that it was found impossible for the king's officials to fine him.

Civil law had to do only with disputes between persons of more or less equal rank. Between superior and inferior there could be no litigation—the superior was right, automatically, if he was really superior in power as well as in name. Disputes between equals were heard by the noble who was the superior of both parties, or by an official appointed by him for the purpose. Several such disputes are recorded in bronze inscriptions and in the literature. For the most part they have to do with quarrels over lands, but in one case we find a review of a commercial transaction. Naturally it is in connection with cases of this type that we hear most of bribery, for the parties concerned were well able to pay for a favourable decision.

It is clear, then, that there was not a little of legal procedure, punishment of crime and trying of lawsuits, at this time. Yet one ingredient of what we mean when we speak of 'law' was lacking. An offence was an offence because some person in authority chose to treat it so. The killing of a human being was not necessarily a crime in itself; it became so because someone in a position of sufficient power condemned and punished it. There did not exist, in a word, that concept of 'the law,' which acts impersonally on all, high and low, rich and poor, seeming to punish almost automatically without the volition of human individuals. Of course it only seems that this is the case, even now, and it does not even seem so in the myriad cases of gross miscarriage of justice which still occur. But at least we have such a theory, and it hardly existed in early China—or in the rest of the world prior to 600 B.C.

Human life as such was held very cheaply. This is well illustrated by a particularly cold-blooded story in the *Discourses of the States*. A minister of the State of Chin, Chao Hsüan-tzŭ by name, used his influence to have Han Hsien-tzŭ appointed to a post giving him control of military discipline. Wishing to determine whether Han was worthy of the appointment, Chao waited his opportunity and then, during a battle, ordered one of the charioteers under his command to break ranks. The charioteer obeyed, whereupon Han promptly had him arrested and executed, in accordance with military discipline. Chao then praised Han for his uprightness, in that he dared to punish the retainer of the man who had recommended him. But of the charioteer whose life was deliberately sacrificed nothing is said—he was a pawn in the game.

When food was suspected of being poisoned it was fed to a dog and a servant; if they died, it was declared unsafe. On one occasion a maidservant (perhaps a concubine—this is not wholly clear) reported to the wife of the future ruler of Chin a conversation by her master which she had overheard. To keep the content of the conversation from spreading further, her mistress had the girl killed at once. Eunuchs, then as later, were persons of some little power. But when the chief eunuch of Duke Li of Chin treated one of the ministers with disrespect, the minister killed him on the spot. It is recorded that this irritated the duke.[9]

Such killings were not mere matters of persons of a high caste despising and oppressing the plebeians. Commoners could be dispatched without formality; persons of standing were killed similarly, but it made more trouble. But assassination was frequently practised to remove troublesome ministers and vassals too, and even to get rid of rulers who were disliked for one reason or another. For this we need not look with any special horror on the ancient Chinese. Political assassination has been a favourite weapon in the Occident until very recently, and at the present day with the increasing reign of dictatorships it is returning to favour and practice.

CHAPTER XXVII

THE OFFICIAL CLASS

THE Chou dynasty was founded by military conquest, and its government was based on military domination. Territories were parcelled out to various military chieftains, who became the great feudal lords, and they in turn gave out fiefs to such of their followers as distinguished themselves on the battle-field. The chief honours were bestowed for military exploits, and might was, in a very large proportion of cases, right. The common people, and all those who were without military backing, lived in a status not very far different from that of slavery. Their rulers, secure in the possession of armies, ruled and taxed and confiscated and exacted forced labour at will.

Yet within a few centuries of the beginning of the Chou dynasty we find a very different theory, and to some extent fact, of government in vogue. Government is held to be the privilege not of the man who has an army at his back but of him who is able to govern for the greatest benefit of the people. And the important posts in the government are occupied, not primarily by warriors, but by scholars, men educated according to the ideas of the day for the career of civil servants.

This is a remarkable change, and one which seems almost impossible until we examine its inner workings. It looks as if the ancient Chinese had suffered a change of heart, and the rulers, or some of them, had said, 'We are wrong. We should not oppress these people, seeking only our own luxury. The only just basis of government is that it shall bring about the welfare of the governed. We will, therefore, turn the administration of government over to men educated for governing, who will decrease our revenues but benefit the people.' It may seem that the hard-headed and pleasure-loving feudal rulers of early Chou times had such thoughts, but this will not appear very plausible to anyone well acquainted with human nature. The change had no such sentimental background. It was born of grim necessity, and of the uses to which that necessity was put by the members of the official class.

The tradition of the Chinese official class goes into the misty background of Chinese history. Its members, some of whom are still alive, claim that it goes back even beyond the Shang dynasty. We can trace it to the beginning of the Chou. It is no exaggeration, then, to say that it is by far the longest tradition of its sort in human history. It continued until the end of the Manchu dynasty; with the revival of sacrifices to Confucius by the Nanking government in 1934 it might even be claimed that it persists into the present.

There is more than a superficial resemblance between the tradition of this Chinese official class and that of the incomparably younger British civil service. As in Britain, its posts have often been filled for successive generations by members of families which specialized in government service. It is said that this family tradition has given to the British civil servant an integrity not often found elsewhere; the same thing has been true of the Chinese. On the other hand, in both Britain and China posts have seldom been filled on the basis of heredity alone; ability and training have been the prime qualifications.

There is an interesting similarity between the British and the Chinese education given to those destined for governmental careers. As far back as our period in China, just as in modern Britain, the curriculum gave a large place to 'classical' subjects, leaned heavily on tradition, and was very much like what we know as a 'humanistic' education. Neither curriculum gives much place to 'vocational' training as such.

We still have, preserved in the *Discourses of the States*, the curriculum prescribed by a member of the official class for the heir-apparent of the State of Ch'u at the end of the seventh century B.C. It gives a very large place to history, poetry, and other literature, especially the literature of antiquity. Government documents and law are among the subjects to be studied. All these are branches of learning considered appropriate for the student at Oxford or Cambridge who is destined for a government career. The Chinese also studied ceremonial and etiquette, which for the Englishman would be considered extra-curricular, but necessary. The Chinese education was broader than the English in that it included music, according in this respect with the educational ideals of the time of Plato.

Is such an education practical? Of the record of the Chinese there is this much to be said, that those who have continued this tradition have maintained it, and have successfully governed one of the largest empires on the globe through a longer period than any other has persisted without fundamental change. Time after time representatives of other systems have taken the reins in China, only to fail. Men like the founder of the Han dynasty, uneducated rustics who looked down on the Confucian scholars as impractical bookworms, have come to the throne. Tribes from outside the sphere of Chinese culture have conquered the celestial kingdom and established themselves as its masters. But one and all they have been glad after a time to call in the scholars to continue the government of China in the time-honoured way. The system has been charged with impracticability. Its adherents can reply that it has accomplished more, in practice, than any other.

That there should have been in ancient China rulers who were oppressive, short-sightedly self-seeking, following policies which could only end in ruin, is not very remarkable, nor unusual in world history. Nor is it remarkable or unusual that there should have been, at the same time, men of broad vision, proposing policies for the good of the people as a whole on the broad platform of peaceful and enduring government. But the difficulty is to get them together, to persuade the rulers to put power into the hands of such men and deliberately to reduce the luxury of their courts and the arrogance of their rule for the sake of security, prosperity, and the good of the people as a whole. Ordinarily this has proved possible only through bloody revolution, and the defect of revolution is that it seldom leaves those best fitted to rule in power. In ancient China a revolution in governmental policy did take place, but it came silently and without bloodshed. The manner of its coming is most interesting. The scholars who triumphed appeared to have everything against them, while the powerful rulers and military men who opposed them seemed to hold all the trump cards.

One of the keys to the success of the scholars in their struggle is found in a phrase which begins many early Chou documents, 'The King agrees in saying . . .' This means that the decree was written, not by the king (or other noble) himself, but by a member of his secretariat, at his order. The wishes expressed were those of the king, but the language was that of the scholar. And into the longer decrees we frequently find written little sermons on ethical conduct, put there by the scribe in the name of the king. The king himself could hardly fail to be flattered at having such high-sounding phrases put into his mouth, and he could regulate his own conduct according to these precepts or not as he pleased. But for his son or his grandson they became a problem. If such a descendant wished to act in a manner which his ministers considered unwise or immoral, here were the statements of his own ancestor which could be quoted against him. If he refused to comply with them, he was guilty of unfilial conduct. Worse, he might give offence to the powerful spirits of his ancestors, who could send down the most fearful punishments if they chose.

Another strong weapon of the scholars, which aided them in getting control of the reins of government, was their monopoly of education. Unlike the situation in medieval Europe, a knowledge of books was not something for an aristocrat to be ashamed of in ancient China. Kings and nobles did not wish their children to grow up as ignoramuses, and the only tutors to be had were men more or less inoculated with the scholarly tradition. It is perfectly natural, then, that the princelings should have been taught the ethics of the official class along with its books, and should in many cases have been glad to employ its disciples as their ministers later on.

But the chief reason for the triumph of the scholars was that their doctrines really worked out in practice. They said that honesty was the best policy, and they proved it when they were given a chance to do so. They declared that oppression and tyranny on the part of a ruler were sure to bring his downfall, and they could point to an impressive number of cases in which it did just that. They claimed that their policies, if put into operation, were capable of bringing the largest measure of success in the long run, and they demonstrated that it was true.

The most famous individual of this group during our period was Kuan Chung, who lived in the seventh century B.C. He was apparently not born into the aristocracy, and it is certain that he was poor in his youth. But he rose to the position of adviser to the Duke of Ch'i. It will be recalled that after the collapse of the Chou dynasty in the west the kings moved eastward and ceased to rule in anything but name. Several large states started appropriating all of the territory they could from their weaker neighbours, and any of them would have been glad to found a new dynasty, displacing the Chous. But no one state was strong enough to oppose a combination of all the others. The result was a 'balance of power' in which each state eyed every other with suspicion, and there was no central authority in China. This gave the barbarians on the borders just the opportunity they wanted, and they invaded even to the heart of Chinese territory without meeting united opposition. Thus the policy of unrestrained conquest by individual states threatened to end in the extinction of Chinese culture.

Kuan Chung advised Duke Huan of Ch'i to reverse this

policy. If Ch'i wished to become the supreme power in China it must first, he declared, return to the neighbouring states all of their territory which Ch'i had won by conquest. This sounded like madness, but it left Ch'i surrounded by friends instead of enemies, free to send its armies abroad to repulse the barbarians and to 'punish' those states which were not submissive to the Chou king; this really meant not submissive to Ch'i, which took the leadership in the name of the king. In 667 B.C. the king recognized the position of Duke Huan as 'First Noble,' and even before that time he had actually been the nearest thing to a ruler which the China of his day knew. Kuan Chung's advice, that the best way to gain control of territory was to give up the fruits of conquest, was thoroughly vindicated, and it is recognized that he is very largely responsible for saving Chinese culture from the fate which threatened it in his day.

In the code of the official class there are several ingredients. One is the personal devotion of a retainer to his lord. This is very strong. The Chinese are great hero-worshippers, capable of any amount of self-sacrifice for the sake of a leader to whom they are devoted. In the early period especially it was felt that the retainer or minister of a feudal lord must protect his person or die in the attempt, and the only honourable course for the follower of a noble who had been killed by his enemies was death in battle or suicide. Likewise the minister who failed in his mission or in any way brought disgrace on his lord frequently committed suicide in order to redeem his honour. This ancient Chinese tradition of personal devotion to the lord lies behind the tradition of the Japanese *samurai*, and the modern devotion of the Japanese to his emperor. The ancient Chinese custom of suicide to redeem disgrace is a part, at least, of the origin of the Japanese *hara-kiri*.

This personal devotion to the ruler is just what we should expect in a feudal society. But as we find it in the tradition of the official class it did not produce servile acquiescence in every command of the superior. It was the duty of the official to advise, and to insist upon, not what the ruler wished but what would be the wisest and most beneficial course for him to pursue in the long run. To be a 'yes man' was considered worthy only of contempt. Yet to be otherwise sometimes took real courage. One duke had a minister who remonstrated with him to the point of making himself bitterly disliked. Finally the duke warned him that one more remonstrance would mean death. He replied that he was perfectly willing to die for the good of his lord. More than one minister was quietly assassinated for making himself too troublesome. And many, of course, chose the easiest course of agreeing in every scheme of their masters.

We sometimes find the chief duty of the minister interpreted as being due, not to the ruler personally, but to the state considered as a territorial unit. Patriotism as a feeling for a particular piece of territory has played a much smaller place in China than in most parts of the world, yet we do find it cropping up occasionally in the ancient period.

Most of all, however, we find the conception that the duty of the minister is to aid and to influence the ruler to govern in such manner as will bring about the welfare of the people as a whole. This is a remarkable fact, and one which at first seems almost unaccountable. The people as a whole, that is those below the aristocracy, were completely subject to the dictation of the ruling classes. Many of them were slaves and serfs. They did not even have a 'vote' to make it worth while for politicians to become sentimental over them. Was it merely out of the goodness of their hearts that the members of the scholarly class, who were not, after all, very humble themselves, championed them? Was it solely from the benevolence of their natures that the kings allowed themselves to be influenced in their behalf? One may doubt it.

Indeed, the whole talk of solicitude for the welfare of the people is so difficult to account for that one is at first tempted to disbelieve it entirely, and to think that it has been written into the ancient books by Confucian scholars of later years, as a matter of propaganda. But this is not the case. We not only find such sentiments expressed in early and authentic books which have come down to us, but even in early bronze inscriptions, which can hardly have been tampered with.

I suggest three main reasons for this humanitarianism which is a fundamental plank in the platform of the Chinese official class. The first is the fact that the people had a great deal of power if they chose to use it. The armies were not, for the most part, professional; they were composed of levies of the peasants and common people, officered by the aristocrats. And the most common arm was the powerful reflex bow, which was able to pierce the best armour worn by the aristocrats. This meant that the aristocracy was not in the position of the medieval knights of Europe, who could don their armour, bestride their mailed chargers, and go out against any number of armed peasants or foot soldiers and laugh at them. Even dukes and kings in ancient China were frequently wounded by arrows. These facts lead to two conclusions. First, whenever the populace became really disaffected it could and in fact frequently did simply desert the ruler in the face of the enemy, and he was left powerless. Second, if the people were oppressed to the point where resentment was universal, they possessed the power to revolt, and the aristocrats could not stand against their united opposition. Unlike the war lords of modern China, they had no machine-guns with which a handful of mercenaries could mow down thousands of peasants. For this reason, then, it was essential that the people should be kept contented or at least below the line of active resentment against their superiors.

Secondly, it was the profession and the interest of the scholars who built the tradition of the official class to govern. For the most part they were not military men, and they were not primarily interested in enlarging the territories of their rulers. Such enlargement meant war, and war meant hardship for the people, murmuring against the government, and conditions which generally interfered with stable and orderly rule. Therefore we find the official class opposing territorial aggrandizement and war in general. Likewise, however much the nobles might find splendour and luxury to their liking, these things meant little to their ministers, and the high taxation which they necessitated had a tendency to weaken the state and to create resentment which at the least made administration more difficult and at the worst might provoke rebellion. To be sure, the officials themselves might and often did take an interest in piling up fortunes. But even in modern business the man who becomes keenly interested in his work places the success of the institution which he is building even higher than the accumulation of a great personal fortune, and many of these officials cared too much for the stability of the government which they were creating to endanger it by avarice. They were not wholly unselfish, but their selfishness had altruistic consequences. They were wise enough, and sufficiently well acquainted with history, to know that the only firm foundation for a stable and lasting government was a prosperous and contented people, and they therefore took the welfare of the people as one of their principal aims.

A third element, which cannot be neglected, is that, much as we may deny it, there is a large element of humanitarianism in the make-up of every normal human being. If we can give happiness to others as easily as not, it pleases us to do so. If they are our inferiors or dependants, so that we can feel a glow of superiority and paternalism in providing for their welfare, the tendency to do so is very strong indeed. Who could resist being called, like the Chinese emperor, 'the father and mother of his people'? There was, I suggest, a considerable element of natural human sympathy, which may not be discounted, behind the humanitarianism in the Chinese official tradition.

It is inevitable that such traditions should crystallize around the names of individuals, who sum up their principles in their lives and in quotable utterances. The founder of the Confucian tradition is commonly considered to be the Duke of Chou. Between his time and that of Confucius there are several individuals whose sayings were quoted by those who came soon after them, just as the teachings of Confucius are quoted to the present time. Confucius was only the last and most famous of such men. It is in part because he came at the end of the early development of this tradition, and summed it up, that he has become its representative *par excellence.* But by the same token he was not, as is often supposed, its founder. As a matter of fact there is very little in the philosophy of Confucius which cannot be found in the utterances of men who lived before him.

CHAPTER XXVIII

THE DECREE OF HEAVEN

THE fundamental theory of the Chinese state and of governmental authority in China is that of the Decree of Heaven. It is in China what the theory of the divine right of kings has been in Europe and the theory that 'governments derive their just powers from the consent of the governed' has been in the United States of America. This theory is as old as the beginning of the Chou dynasty. That it is still alive is shown by the fact that the revolution which ended the Manchu dynasty is known as 'the changing of the Decree.'

The essence of this theory is simple. It holds that rulers are appointed by Heaven, that is, the supreme deity, for the purpose of ruling the world so as to bring about the welfare of men. The ruler may legitimately rule only so long as he does so in the interest of his subjects. The moment he ceases to bring about the welfare of the people, it is the right and the duty of another to revolt and displace him, taking over the appointment of Heaven and administering the government for the public good. There is no question here of voting by the people, except as they vote by supporting the previous government or the rebel. Heaven chooses the ruler, and Heaven chooses the man to displace him, but 'Heaven does not speak.'[1] The issue must be decided by war and bloodshed.

It will be seen that an integral part of this theory is the flat statement that the king is no more than a public servant, the steward of Heaven appointed for the purpose of promoting the public good. The statement attributed to Louis XIV, 'I am the state,' is impossible in the face of such a conception of the place of the ruler. According to this Chinese theory the king is, indeed, no more than one cog in the machinery of the state, and a cog which is to be thrown away and replaced by a new one the moment it ceases to work properly.

It is difficult to imagine such a theory being brought forward by the kings or those near to them. One would naturally suppose that it must have been the production of the scholars, the members of the official class mentioned in the last chapter. We should expect that it had gradually gained favour during the early centuries of the Chou dynasty, as that class grew in influence. But the fact is that this theory, in all of its essentials, was full blown during the very first years of the Chou rule, and was apparently developed by persons close to, perhaps members of, the royal house.

In order to investigate the way in which this rather remarkable occurrence came about, let us first look at the orthodox picture of Chinese history, built around the theory of the Decree of Heaven, which has been painted by traditional Chinese scholarship. This is the official version of Chinese history, still accepted by the vast majority of Chinese scholars, and until very recently accepted by virtually all of them. It has also been accepted, until very recently, by a large number of foreign scholars, with more or less of reservations.

This legendary history takes us back to very remote antiquity indeed, but it starts to become specific at a period somewhat earlier than 2500 B.C. At this time, or a little later, China was already united, we are asked to believe, under the beneficent rule of a sage emperor. There was little warfare, for even the barbarian tribes submitted willingly to his rule. And there were no laws and no lawyers and no punishments, for the people lived harmoniously together in a state of uncorrupted goodness. A number of these emperors did not leave their thrones to their sons, but instead picked out the most virtuous and able man in the whole world and designated him to be the next emperor. But such conditions were obviously too good to last. The people learned to do evil (from the barbarians—here is a shrewd stroke at the foreigner!) and punishments had to be instituted. And the hereditary principle of succession to the throne was established, resulting in the Hsia dynasty (traditionally dated 2205-1766 B.C.). Since rulers were no longer selected on the basis of their ability to rule, but merely by heredity, it was inevitable that unworthy kings should come to the throne. And with increasing luxury the dynasty gradually went downhill, by that process known so well in monarchies the world over, until finally the function of the monarch as the servant of the people and the guardian of their welfare was entirely forgotten. Heaven then looked about for someone to take over the throne, and the choice fell on T'ang, known as 'the Successful,' of the Shang line. He attacked and defeated the degenerate last sovereign of Hsia, and established the Shang dynasty. The career of this dynasty repeated that of the Hsia, until the last king of the Shang line gave himself over to luxury, cruelty, debauchery, and women. He neglected the affairs of government, oppressed the people, and failed even to render the proper sacrifices to his ancestors and the other deities. Heaven again looked for a candidate to take his place, and the choice fell on the Chous, with what result we know.

This is a very interesting version of Chinese history, and one which has played a rôle of the greatest importance. But as cold-blooded fact it has a number of defects. In the first place, many things show that the accounts of the early emperors are little more than legend. Early versions of the stories concerning them disagree on the most important points, and even on the number and the order of these rulers. And the Hsia 'dynasty' as such is in little better case. Apparently there was a State of Hsia, but it did not rule all of China. The version of their history given by the descendants of the Shang kings in the *Book of Poetry* claims that the Shangs ruled all of China, at the same time when the orthodox history says that the Hsias ruled it. Both are wrong. There was no single rule over China until much later.

In the second place, Shang tradition seems to be entirely ignorant of the fact that the last Hsia king was wicked, and that the founder of the Shang dynasty was appointed by Heaven to punish and displace him on that account. Apparently the idea of the Decree of Heaven was not familiar to the Shang people in this sense. They merely recount, in their traditions, that T'ang the successful conquered a number of states or tribes, of which Hsia was one.

Thirdly, we have no reason to believe that previous to the Chou conquest any single ruler or group controlled anything like so large a territory as that of the Chou dynasty. But the idea of the Decree of Heaven carried with it the idea of a single rule over all China—ideally, over all the world. It is difficult to suppose that such an idea could have existed prior to the dream, at least, of such wide empire. But we know that the Accomplished King who planned the Chou conquest had such a dream, so that his son could say, 'We must go on . . . to complete the work of the Accomplished King, until it has spread everywhere, and from the corners of the sea and the rising sun there shall be none who is disobedient to our rule.'[2] Also, though this is a detail, it is worth noting that the term Heaven in the sense which is used here is the name of a deity which seems to have come in only with the Chous.

Nor have we any evidence which supports the Chou contention that the last Shang king was a degenerate, given over to wild debauchery. Whether we have any oracle inscriptions from his reign is a point on which experts differ; there is evidence on both sides. If we do, then we can say that the king personally attended to divination, was zealous in the performance of his religious duties, and does not appear to have been at all as the Chous painted him. Whether we do or not, it is altogether probable that the Chou story of the wickedness of the last Shang king was merely another example of that propaganda which always has been and always must be associated with war.

If we look at the whole theory of a 'Decree of Heaven,' as a mandate to rule China handed down from one dynasty to another, it is difficult to see how it could have existed earlier than the Chou conquest. On the other hand, we know that it did exist within a few years of the completion of that conquest. I am convinced that this theory was originated, or at least chiefly developed, by the Chous themselves as a part of their effort to bring the whole sphere of Chinese culture into willing subjection to their rule. It was a peaceful, psychological conquest which sought, with a large measure of success, to make permanent the gains of the original military conquest.

Let us consider the situation of the Chous and the tribes allied with them after the military conquest. They themselves tacitly admitted that they were of an inferior culture, for they turned toward Shang traditions for their standards. Many of the people whom they conquered must have considered them uncouth barbarians. Their armies, perhaps taking advantage of temporary weakness on the part of the Shangs, had defeated them in battle. But it was one thing to carry everything before them in the first flush of conquest, and quite another to enlist the loyalty and co-operation of the population, which could alone make possible a stable and prosperous rule over the wide empire which they hoped to establish. Experience has shown time and again that it is impossible to rule a hostile people permanently by means of garrisons of soldiers, and this is especially the case when the soldiers do not have weapons which are decisively superior to those which the population can get possession of. 'Who lives by the sword by the sword shall die.' The Chous knew this, and they realized that it was essential to make their position legitimate, founded on something more than military force which could be annulled by an armed revolt. The danger of their situation was impressed upon them by the uprising of the Shang people, a few years after the conquest, which almost unseated them.

I do not suggest for a moment that the chief counsellors of the Chou kings called a meeting at which someone said, 'What we need is the theory of the "Decree of Heaven." Let us devise and promulgate it.' Such an idea would be absurd. Nor do I think that the Chous were not sincere in the matter. Every nation which sets forth to conquer the world or a portion of it sincerely believes that it is engaged in carrying out a divine command. The elements of the theory undoubtedly existed in their own and in Shang traditions, and the theory itself came into being, beyond doubt, almost unconsciously. But it was developed and used by the Chous enthusiastically, for the very good reason that it met perfectly the needs of their situation.

This theory changed the Chou conquest from a looting raid by a band of barbarians to a holy crusade carried on, somewhat reluctantly, at the express command of the highest deity. It made the Chous not the conquering oppressors of a subjected populace, but the champions of the people, liberating them from the tyrannical sway of a degenerate king rejected by men and gods alike. And it made them and their allies not a band of uncouth barbarians who threatened, in their crude military strength, to destroy the bright flower of Chinese culture, but rather the champions of that culture, coming with knightly devotion and sacred wrath to cleanse the seats of the mighty and allow the torch of Chinese civilization to burn with the clear pure flame of former days. This theory represented the Chou kings and feudal lords, not as hateful tyrants gorging themselves on the spoils of war and the sweat of an enslaved population, but as benevolent monarchs sent by Heaven for the one purpose of restoring to the people the blessings of justice, peace, and prosperity.

All of Chinese history was written by men of whom every one believed that the theory of the Decree of Heaven was as old as Chinese culture. We can hardly expect, therefore, to find left after three thousand years any very plain evidence that it was an innovation or largely an innovation of the beginning of the Chou period. Nevertheless, some indications of this fact do still exist.

One would suppose that the Chous could hardly have expected to make the officials of the vanquished Shang dynasty themselves believe that their downfall was the righteous retribution caused by their great wickedness. This propaganda, for that is exactly what it was, must have been intended chiefly to win over the peoples who had been friendly or subject to Shang, but not the Shangs themselves. But we also find it stated, in the baldest possible manner, in the speeches of the Duke of Chou addressed to the Shang officials, exhorting them to be loyal to their conquerors and warning them of the punishment to be feared if they persist in rebellion. He tells them that the action of the Chous, in conquering them, has a perfectly good precedent in the course of the founder of their own dynasty. 'You know,' he said, in the address called 'Many Officers,' 'that your forefathers of the Yin [i.e. Shang] dynasty had books and archives showing how Yin superseded the decree of Hsia.'[3] He says that their 'forefathers' had such records. Why does he not say that they themselves have such records? Apparently because, as we can see from other sources, the Shangs did not have any such tradition—until it was created for them by the Chous.

There are several books in the *Document Classic* which are supposed to date from Shang times, and which are permeated with the theory of the Decree of Heaven. Some of them, ascribed to Shang nobles, denounce the last Shang king and his government in the most virulent terms, going so far as to declare that 'Among the Yin [Shang] people there are none, small or great, who are not given to highway robberies, villainies and treachery. The nobles and officers imitate one another in violating the laws; all are guilty, and there is no certainty that offenders will be apprehended. The lesser people rise up and treat one another as enemies. Yin is now sinking in ruin. . . .'[4] These books contain various discrepancies, and it is not difficult to determine that they are almost certainly forgeries of the Chou period, probably perpetrated as a part of the same campaign of propaganda which has been mentioned.

Indeed, there is reason to believe that the Chous carried their activities farther than merely composing new books, embodying their own political doctrines, and ascribing them to Shang authors. It looks as if they may even have gone to the length of wiping out genuine books of the Shang period which were in existence. This may sound fantastic, but let us consider the evidence. We know, from the oracle bones, that there were regular books, apart from the bone inscriptions, in Shang times. There are many references to books of the Shang and even earlier periods in early Chou literature. But not a single genuine work from a period earlier than the Chou has come down to us. On the other hand, we have numerous genuine documents from the very beginning of the Chou period—eight books of the *Document Classic*, the original text of the *Book of Changes*, and parts of the *Book of Poetry*. This is a remarkable fact, which justifies at least the suspicion that it is not due to pure accident.

In the beginning the theory of the Decree of Heaven was of the greatest possible assistance to the Chou kings. It did succeed, in very large measure, in throwing over their reign a mantle of legitimacy which aided greatly in the task of changing the people of their vast territories from conquered enemies to loyal subjects. And it played a considerable rôle in developing the Chinese official class which from that day to the present century has been the backbone of Chinese government. But it proved to be a two-edged sword, if not indeed a boomerang.

For it saddled the Chinese monarch with such a responsibility as no other individual in the world has ever had to carry. Compared with his cares, the *noblesse oblige* of the Occident is scarcely a gesture. In the first place, he was completely to blame for everything which went wrong in China. As the theory was developed it was not only his fault if the people were poverty-stricken, or if rebellion raised its head, but he was even responsible for droughts, floods, and plagues. And some of the most pathetic passages in any literature are those in which the more conscientious Chinese emperors, accepting in full the responsibility for some great catastrophe yet unable to discover in what they have erred, plead with Heaven to send its punishment on them alone, but to spare the innocent people.

According to this theory the one excuse for the existence of the emperor was that he should bring about the welfare of the people, and this was his one claim to his title. If he failed or ceased to do this, he ceased in fact to be emperor, although he might continue obstinately to occupy the throne. So long as he could justify himself by the general prosperity of the people, his person was sacred, but so soon as this was not the case it became the right and even the duty of another, who felt himself charged with the Decree of Heaven, to displace him as a usurper and rule in his place. The effect of this has been to give a perfect excuse to anyone who wished to start a revolution at any time.

It has had another effect. It has made the Chinese ruler in theory, and sometimes in fact, a tremendously earnest individual. Anyone who really believed that the weight of such responsibility rested on his shoulders would be earnest, of course. And most Chinese kings have had this theory drummed into them by tutors, steeped in the official tradition, from infancy. It is not remarkable that some of them have reacted violently against the whole thing, and resorted to frivolity, but not all of them have done so. And the same seriousness, to an even greater extent, has manifested itself in the official class. In so large a group of people there have always been insincere individuals, but there has been a larger measure of selfless devotion to the task of administration than one might expect.

A new conception of the world came in, in all probability at the same time as the idea of the Decree of Heaven. We have seen that until the time of the Chou dynasty the territory even of north China was split up between various small states or tribes. And it is probable that there had not yet been born the conception of a single, Heaven-ordained ruler, governing all the world as the earthly counterpart of the supreme deity. But the Chous did dream of such a rule, and they succeeded in bringing about a unification of all the peoples who were thoroughly impregnated with Chinese culture. All of the people who were outside their state were barbarians, who lived on the borders. They were negligible people, who ought to be subject to the 'middle country' but who, not being completely human, were not intelligent enough to acknowledge its authority save vaguely. And there grew up the idea of Chung Kuo, the Middle Country, from which the Chinese still name their land.

This name means exactly what it says. According to the ancient theory, still believed by most Chinese, China is the centre of the whole world, geographically, politically, and culturally. We read in ancient books that men exiled to the border countries saw a gradual decline in culture as they left the Chinese capital and approached the periphery of the Flowery Kingdom. Finally, after they had travelled for some days, they were 'surprised to see anything which resembled humanity.' Europeans and Americans, it must be remembered, are nothing more than barbarians from the outer darkness according to this theory. And it must also be remembered that a comparison of Chinese and Occidental culture a scant two centuries ago did much to support the Chinese theory. Many learned and informed Europeans of the fourteenth to the eighteenth centuries frankly looked up to Chinese culture as superior. It is said that prior to 1750 more books had been published in Chinese than in all other languages combined. At any rate, true or not, the theory of the supremacy of Chinese culture has been and still is largely held by the Chinese, and this belief is one of the important factors in the Chinese situation.

By the end of our period, roughly 600 B.C., all of the fundamental elements of China had come into being. For China is not merely a section of the world's surface, not merely a group of people, not merely a culture. It is a group of people occupying a particular territory, sharing a common culture, held together by a common history based on certain ideas. Without those ideas which bind them together we could have the people, the territory, even the shared culture, but no China. Those ideas, which brought and which have held the Chinese together, are fundamentally three: First, that the government of China is a divinely ordained institution, ideally governing the whole world but necessarily, save for brief interludes of disorder, governing all civilized people, that is, all those who share in Chinese culture. Second, that the one end of the Chinese government is to secure the welfare of the people, and that when the government fails to do this it is the right and duty of the people to rebel, supporting him who is appointed by Heaven to bring a rebirth of virtuous rule. Third, that in order to rule properly the monarch must call to his assistance the most able men in the country, men of character who have fitted themselves for the task of governing by profound study of history, who can bring the lessons of the past to bear upon the problems of the present.

These basic ideas are what have made China, as such, and they had come to a large measure of maturity by 600 B.C. China was born. But these ideas did not find concrete expression in a unified government until perhaps the second century B.C. We might say that at this latter date China came of age.

There is a general impression among people who know little about China, and among some people who know a good deal, that China has remained virtually unchanged, has made no advance, since Han times. This is completely untrue. But it has seemed to many people to be true for two reasons.

In the first place, foreigners who have studied China up to the present time have studied the period between the sixth century B.C. and the second century A.D. more than all the rest of Chinese history put together. There is good reason for this. It was an important period, formative of many elements of Chinese culture. And the Chinese themselves, firm believers in a classically grounded education, have studied this period exhaustively and made it easier to study than any other.

The second reason why foreigners, looking at Chinese history, think that there has been no change in two thousand years, is that they compare it with European culture and forget to consider certain facts (which are not very complimentary to us Westerners) in making the comparison. China, it must be remembered, came of age about the second century B.C. and *stayed of age*. She did not have, after that time, a period in which the continuity of her culture was broken, so that the structure had to be begun again almost from the bottom. She had worked out a cultural and governmental system which enabled her, even when she was conquered by barbarians, to absorb them into her cultural and political system so that it remained virtually intact. She was not, like Europe, shattered and thrown into the Dark Ages.

China had her Dark Ages, perhaps, in the early part of the Chou dynasty, and her feudal period in the middle and latter days of that dynasty, much more than a millennium before the same circumstances took place in Europe. Even in China's dark ages the standard of culture and literacy among the aristocracy was far higher than it was among the European aristocracy of like, and far later, periods. And when China was through with these things she was through with them. China has had her periods of trouble and disunion, but when it is considered that China is as large as Europe it must be admitted that she can show a far better record of peace and unity than Europe can.

There seems to be a limit to the culture and sophistication to which human beings can attain. Those who soak themselves in the ancient literature of any cultured people, Greeks, Romans, or Chinese, commonly testify to the conviction that the best minds of two thousand years ago and more seem to be as keen, as fully aware of and able to cope with the most important problems of human life, as urbane and as thoroughly sophisticated as—how many people living to-day? If Mencius, Ssŭ-Ma Ch'ien, Plato, Epictetus, Cicero and Shakespeare came back to-day and were shown the things on which we base our claim to greatness, would they be lost in admiration or in amusement?

China reached a high standard of culture in the second century B.C., and she has never completely receded from it. She has changed, but only gradually and by a process of evolution, not cataclysmically. Yet some Chinese philosophers of recent centuries differ more thoroughly in their approach to problems from the approach of Confucius' day than the philosophies of Bergson, Whitehead and Dewey differ from the theories of Plato's time. Chinese art has made tremendous strides through the centuries, and so has literature. In the physical sciences China has nothing to compare with recent Western progress, but it must be remembered that most of this is very recent.

When we speak of the cultural progress of the modern Occident, we are not comparing our present with the great days of antiquity. We are comparing it rather with the cultural abyss to which Europe had sunk prior to the Renaissance. But if we compare the Athens of Pericles and the Rome of Augustus with the New York, London, Paris, or Berlin of our own day, can we honestly say that we have advanced, culturally? Yes, in certain respects. And in certain respects, and to an equal degree, Peiping, the cultural capital of present-day China, represents an advance over the capital of the Han dynasty.

On the other hand, Peiping of the twentieth century does not represent the advance over the Chinese capital of the thirteenth century which the London of to-day can show over the London of that time. But is it just to say that the Chinese are backward because they have never sunk so low that they might, by contrast, show a meteoric rise?

The beginnings and the early history of Chinese culture are eminently worthy of study. This is especially true because, in China, early cultural gains have not been lost, so that study of the early and classical periods is especially important and necessary if one wishes to understand the later history. But we should never forget that in Chinese culture we are dealing with a living, not a dead civilization, and that the chief reason for studying its past is that we may better understand its present and its future.

SELECTED BIBLIOGRAPHY

I.—THE STONE AGES

ANDERSSON, J. GUNNAR.

(1) *Children of the Yellow Earth* (London, 1934).

(2) 'Cave-deposit at Sha Kuo T'un in Fengtien, The.' *Palæontologia Sinica*, Series D, Vol. 1, Fasc. 1 (Peking, 1923).

(3) 'Early Chinese Culture, An.' *Bulletin of the Geological Survey of China* (1923), 5, 1.

(4) 'Preliminary Report on Archæological Research in Kansu.' *Memoirs of the Geological Survey of China*, Series A, Number 5 (Peking, 1925).

ARNE, T. J.

'Painted Stone Age Pottery from the Province of Honan, China.' *Palæontologia Sinica*, Series D, Vol. 1, Fasc. 2 (Peking, 1925).

BISHOP, CARL WHITING.

(1) 'Beginnings of North and South in China, The.' *Pacific Affairs* (1934), 7, pp. 297-325.

(2) 'Neolithic Age in Northern China, The.' *Antiquity* (1933).

(3) 'Rise of Civilization in China with Reference to its Geographical Aspects, The.' *The Geographical Review*, 1932, Vol. 22, Number 4, pp. 617-631.

BLACK, DAVIDSON.

(1) 'Human Skeletal Remains from the Sha Kuo T'un Cave Deposit in Comparison with those from Yang Shao Tsun and with Recent North China Skeletal Material, The.' *Palæontologia Sinica*, Series D, Vol. 1, Fasc. 3 (Peking, 1925).

(2) Note on the Physical Characters of the Prehistoric

Kansu Race, A.' *Memoirs of the Geological Survey of China*, Series A, Number 5 (Peking, 1925).

(3) 'Study of Kansu and Honan Æneolithic Skulls and Specimens from Later Kansu Prehistoric Sites in Comparison with North China and Other Recent Crania, A.' Part I. 'On Measurement and Identification.' *Palæontologia Sinica*, Series D, Vol. 6, Fasc. I (Peking, 1928).

LI CHI.

西陰村史前的遺存(清華學校研究院叢書第三種)(1927)

LI CHI, LIANG SSŬ-YUNG, and TUNG TSO-PIN, editors. 城子崖,中國考古報告集之一, Ch'êng-tzŭ-yai, *Archæologia Sinica*, Number I. With a summary in English by Liang Ssŭ-yung (Nanking; published 1935, dated 1934).

LIANG SSŬ-YUNG.

'New Stone Age Pottery from the Prehistoric Site at Hsi-yin Tsun, Shansi, China.' *Memoirs of the American Anthropological Association*, Number 37, 1930.

LICENT, TEILHARD DE CHARDIN, and BLACK.

'On a Presumably Pleistocene Tooth from the Sjara Osso Gol.' *Bulletin of the Geological Society of China* (1927), 5.

PALMGREN, NILS.

'Kansu Mortuary Urns of the Pan Shan and Ma Chang Groups.' *Palæontologia Sinica*, Series D, Vol. 3, Fasc. I (Peking, 1934).

PEI, W. C.

'Preliminary Report on the Late Palæolithic Cave of Choukoutien, A.' *Bulletin of the Geological Society of China* (1934), 13, 3.

TEILHARD DE CHARDIN and LICENT.
'On the Discovery of a Palæolithic Industry in Northern China.' *Bulletin of the Geological Society of China* (1934) 3, 1.

TEILHARD DE CHARDIN and C. C. YOUNG.
'Preliminary Observations on the Pre-Loessic and Post-Pontian Formations in Western Shansi and Northern Shensi.' *Memoirs of the Geological Survey of China*, Series A, Number 8 (Peking, 1930).

WEIDENREICH, FRANZ.
'Sinanthropus Population of Choukoutien (Locality 1), with a Preliminary Report on New Discoveries, The.' *Bulletin of the Geological Society of China* (1935), 14, 4.

II.—SHANG AND CHOU EXCAVATIONS

安陽發掘報告 (*Preliminary Reports of Excavations at Anyang*) (Four volumes, 1929-1933).

成立三週年工作概況及第二次展覽會展品說明 (1935).

III.—ORACLE BONE INSCRIPTIONS

鐵雲藏龜，劉鶚編 (1903).

契文舉例，孫詒讓著 (1904).

殷商貞卜文字攷，羅振玉著 (1910).

殷虛書契前編，羅振玉編 (1912).

殷虛書契菁華，羅振玉編 (1914).

鐵雲藏龜之餘，羅振玉編 (1915).

殷虛書契後編，羅振玉編 (1916).

Oracle Records from the Waste of Yin, by James Mellon Menzies (Shanghai, 1917).

殷卜辭中所見先公先王考，及續考，王國維著（遺書初集卷九）(1917).

殷周制度論，王國維著（遺書初集卷十）(1917).

戩壽堂所藏殷虛文字，姬佛陀編 (1918).

戩壽堂所藏殷虛文字考釋，王國維著 (1919).

簠室殷契類纂，王襄編 (1920).

龜甲獸骨文字，林泰輔編 (1921).

殷虛文字類編，商承祚類次 (1923).

殷契鉤沈，葉玉森著（學衡第二十四期）(1923).

說契，揅契枝譚卷甲，葉玉森著
（學衡第三十一期）(1924).

鐵雲藏龜拾遺，附攷釋，葉玉森編著(1925).

簠室殷契徵文，王襄著(1925).

增訂殷虛書契考釋，羅振玉著(1927).

甲骨文斷代研究例，董作賓著
（慶祝蔡元培先生六十五歲論文集）(1933).

甲骨學文字編，朱芳圃編著(1933).

殷契佚存，商承祚編纂(1933).

殷契卜辭，容庚瞿潤緡合著(1933).

殷虛書契續編，羅振玉著(1933).

福氏所藏甲骨文字，商承祚編纂(1933).

殷虛文字存真，徐敬參著 (1933).

卜辭通纂，郭沫若著 (1933).

甲骨文編，孫海波譔集 (1934).

IV.—INSCRIPTIONS ON BRONZE

歷代鐘鼎彝器款識法帖，
薛尚功編 (Sung dynasty; reprinted 1633).

積古齋鐘鼎彝器款識，阮元編 (1804).

攈古錄金文，吳式芬撰 (1895).

愙齋集古錄，吳大澂編 (1896).

周金文存，鄒安編 (issued serially, 1916 and later).

殷文存，羅振玉類次 (1917).

金文編，容庚撰集 (1925).

殷周青銅器銘文研究，郭沫若著 (1931).

貞松堂集古遺文，羅振玉撰集 (1931).

貞松堂集古遺文補遺，羅振玉撰集 (1931).

兩周金文辭大系，郭沫若撰集 (1932).

兩周金文辭大系圖錄，郭沫若編 (1934).

貞松堂集古遺文續編，羅振玉撰集 (1934).

V.—HISTORICAL TEXTS AND CRITICISM.

十三經注疏：

周易

尚書

毛詩

儀禮

春秋左傳

國語韋氏解

史記集解索隱正義合刻本

今文尚書經說攷(皇清經解續編卷千七十九至卷千百十六)陳喬樅著 (1862).

尚書孔傳參正，王先謙著 (1904).

古史辨，第一至第五冊，顧頡剛編著 (1926-1935).

漢石經碑圖，張國淦編 (1931).

VI.—TRANSLATIONS.

LEGGE, JAMES.

(1) The Chinese Classics:

Vol. I, *Confucian Analects*, *The Great Learning*, and *The Doctrine of the Mean* (2nd ed., Oxford, 1893).

Vol. II, *The Works of Mencius* (2nd ed., Oxford, 1895).

Vol. III, *The Shoo King*, or *The Book of Historical Documents* (London, 1865).

Vol. IV, *The She King*, or *The Book of Poetry* (London, 1871).

Vol. V, *The Ch'un Ts'ew*, with *The Tso Chuen* (London, 1872).

(2) *The Yi King*, *Sacred Books of the East*, Vol. XVI (Oxford, 1882).

STEELE, JOHN.

The I-li; or, *Book of Etiquette and Ceremonial* (London, 1917).

NOTES

CHAPTER I

[1] III Menzies, p. 4. (For title of book, see bibliography. The roman numeral indicates the section of the bibliography in which it will be found.)

CHAPTER II

[1] II *An Yang Fa Chüeh Pao Kao* (Preliminary Reports of Excavations at Anyang).
[2] *Ibid.*, pp. 677-680.
[3] That of the *Annals of the Bamboo Books*. On this system see Carl Whiting Bishop, 'The Chronology of Ancient China,' in *Journal of the American Oriental Society* (1932), 52, pp. 232-247.

CHAPTER III

[1] See Berthold Laufer, 'Some Fundamental Ideas of Chinese Culture,' in *The Journal of Race Development* (1914), Vol. 5, p. 161.
[2] I Andersson, 1, pp. 94-126.
[3] I Weidenreich, pp. 436-440.
[4] I Andersson, 4, pp. 46-47.
[5] I Andersson, 4, p. 23.
[6] Cf. I Palmgren, p. 4.
[7] Andersson, 'Der Weg über die Steppen,' in *Bulletin of the Museum of Far Eastern Antiquities*, Stockholm (1929), 1, pp. 152-153.
[8] I Andersson, 1, p. 209.
[9] I Black, 3, p. 81.

CHAPTER IV

[1] VI Legge, 1, Vol. III, p. 417.
[2] VI Legge, 1, Vol. IV, pp. 438-440.
[3] VI Legge, 1, Vol. IV, pp. 303-305.
[4] VI Legge, 1, Vol. IV, p. 646.
[5] VI Legge, 1, Vol. I, p. 179.
[6] VI Legge, 1, Vol. V, p. 310.

CHAPTER V

[1] VI Legge, 1, Vol. IV, p. 129.
[2] VI Legge, 1, Vol. IV, pp. 288-290.
[3] VI Legge, 1, Vol. IV, pp. 291-292.
[4] VI Legge, 2, p. 139.
[5] I Bishop, 2, p. 396.
[6] VI Legge, 1, Vol. V, p. 290.
[7] Berthold Laufer, 'Some Fundamental Ideas of Chinese Culture,' in *The Journal of Race Development* (1914), Vol. 5, pp. 167-170.
[8] I Andersson, 1, pp. 242-243.

NOTES

CHAPTER V—continued

[9] VI Legge, 1, Vol. III, pp. 371-372.
[10] VI Legge, 1, Vol. III, p. 374.
[11] VI Legge, 1, Vol. IV, pp. 307-309.
[12] I Anderson, 1, pp. 335-336.
[13] I Bishop, 2, p. 395.
[14] VI Legge, 1, Vol. IV, pp. 228-229.

CHAPTER VI

[1] I Anderson, 1, p. 194.
[2] I Anderson, 1, p. 215.
[3] VI Legge, 1, Vol. III, p. 555.
[4] VI Legge, 1, Vol. III, pp. 115, 121.

CHAPTER VII

[1] II *An Yang Fa Chüeh Pao Kao* (Preliminary Reports of Excavations at Anyang), pp. 677-680.
[2] M. Rostovtzeff, *The Animal Style in South Russia and China* (Princeton, 1929), p. 70.
[3] M. Rostovtzeff, *The Animal Style in South Russia and China*, pp. 73-74.

CHAPTER IX

[1] M. Rostovtzeff, *A History of the Ancient World*, Vol. I (Oxford, 1926), p. 27.
[2] *Li Chi*, translated by James Legge, *Sacred Books of the East*, Vol. XXVII (Oxford, 1885), p. 323, Vol. XXVIII (Oxford, 1885), pp. 285, 467.

CHAPTER X

[1] VI Legge, 1, Vol. IV, p. 404.
[2] VI Legge, 1, Vol. IV, p. 619
[3] VI Legge, 1, Vol. I, p. 160.
[4] VI Legge, 1, Vol. I, p. 203.
[5] Berthold Laufer, *Chinese Clay Figures*, Part I (Chicago, 1914), Plate XI.
[6] VI Legge, 1, Vol. V, p. 397.
[7] I Andersson, 1, p. 249.
[8] VI Steele, Vol. II, p. 82.
[9] VI Legge, 1, Vol. III, p. 622.
[10] VI Legge, 1, Vol. V, p. 320.
[11] VI Legge, 1, Vol. V, p. 345.
[12] VI Legge, 1, Vol. V, p. 183.

CHAPTER XI

[1] W. A. Mason, *The History of the Art of Writing* (New York, 1920), p. 177.

CHAPTER XIII

[1] F. A. Larson, *Larson, Duke of Mongolia* (Boston, 1930), p. 102.
[2] Chuang Tzŭ, *Mystic, Moralist, and Social Reformer*, translated from the Chinese by Herbert A. Giles (2nd ed. Shanghai, 1926), p. 217.
[3] VI Legge, 2, pp. 147, 150.
[4] VI Legge, 1, Vol. V, 213.

NOTES

CHAPTER XIV

[1] VI Steele, Vol. II, p. 7. (This passage belongs to a section of the *I Li* which is obviously a late interpolation.)
[2] VI Legge, 1, Vol. V, p. 177.
[3] VI Legge, 1, Vol. V, p. 629.
[4] VI Legge, 1, Vol. V, p. 635.
[5] VI Legge, 1, Vol. V, pp. 225, 352, 606.
[6] VI Legge, 1, Vol. IV, pp. 199-200.
[7] *Li Chi*, translated by James Legge, *Sacred Books of the East*, Vol. XXVII, pp. 181-182.
[8] I Andersson, 3, pp. 16-17.

CHAPTER XV

[1] VI Legge, 1, Vol. IV, p. 437.
[2] VI Legge, 1, Vol. III, p. 390.
[3] VI Legge, 1, Vol. III, p. 386.
[4] VI Legge, 1, Vol. III, p. 386.
[5] VI Legge, 1, Vol. III, p. 438.

CHAPTER XVI

[1] VI Legge, 1, Vol. III, p. 485.
[2] VI Legge, 1, Vol. III, pp. 371-374.

CHAPTER XVII

[1] VI Legge, 1, Vol. V, p. 140.
[2] VI Legge, 1, Vol. IV, pp. 354-355.

CHAPTER XIX

[1] VI Legge, 1, Vol. III, pp. 474-486.
[2] VI Steele, Vol. I, pp. 189-191.
[3] VI Legge, 1, Vol. III, p. 264.
[4] VI Legge, 1, Vol. IV, pp. 263-264.
[5] VI Steele, Vol. II, p. 50.
[6] VI Legge, 1, Vol. I, p. 278.
[7] VI Legge, 1, Vol. V, p. 105.
[8] VI Legge, 1, Vol. V, p. 609.
[9] VI Legge, 2, p. 140.
[10] VI Legge, 1, Vol. IV, p. 540.
[11] Berthold Laufer, 'Some Fundamental Ideas of Chinese Culture,' in *The Journal of Race Development* (1914), Vol. 5, p. 170.
[12] VI Legge, 1, Vol. I, p. 265.
[13] The translation of the *Discourses of the States* published by C. de Harlez in 1893-1895 is only partial and not altogether satisfactory; it has not been used in the preparation of this book. All translations from the *Discourses of the States* are my own, made from the Chinese text directly. As was stated in the preface, none of the research upon which this book depends was based on translations; they have been used solely in the process of laying passages which it was desired to quote before the reader. In one or two cases I have retranslated entirely, so that the wording of the translation referred to in the note differs entirely from that found in the text of this book. In every case the note is to be considered primarily as a locating of the passage in the text, rather than a statement of a source which has in all cases been literally copied. Nevertheless, the changes made in translations have been relatively slight in most instances.

NOTES

CHAPTER XX

[1] VI Steele, Vol. II, p. 82.
[2] VI Legge, 1, Vol. IV, pp. 377, 378.
[3] VI Steele, Vol. I, p. 164.
[4] *Li Chi*, translated by James Legge, *Sacred Books of the East*, Vol. XXVII, p. 90.
[5] VI Legge, 1, Vol. IV, pp. 306-307.
[6] VI Legge, 1, Vol. IV, p. 562.
[7] VI Legge, 2, p. 154.
[8] VI Legge, 1, Vol. V, p. 151.
[9] VI Legge, 1, Vol. V, p. 332.
[10] VI Legge, 1, Vol. IV, pp. 163-164.
[11] VI Legge, 1, Vol. IV, p. 88.
[12] VI Legge, 1, Vol. IV, p. 561.

CHAPTER XXI

[1] *Li Chi*, translated by James Legge, *Sacred Books of the East*, Vol. XXVII, p. 365. (The force of this reference cannot be appreciated from the translation; it must be compared with the Chinese text.)
[2] VI Legge, 1, Vol. IV, pp. 157, 240.
[3] VI Steele, Vol. I, pp. 18-41.
[4] VI Legge, 1, Vol. V, p. 368.
[5] VI Legge, 1, Vol. IV, p. 56-58.
[6] VI Legge, 1, Vol. IV, pp. 112-113.
[7] VI Legge, 1, Vol. IV, pp. 126-127.
[8] VI Legge, 1, Vol. IV, p. 68.
[9] VI Legge, 1, Vol. IV, p. 148.
[10] VI Legge, 1, Vol. IV, p. 140.
[11] VI Legge, 1, Vol. IV, pp. 30-31.
[12] VI Legge, 1, Vol. IV, pp. 1-3.
[13] VI Legge, 1, Vol. IV, pp. 392-393.
[14] VI Legge, 1, Vol. IV, pp. 97-101.
[15] VI Legge, 1, Vol. IV, p. 141.

CHAPTER XXII

[1] VI Legge, 1, Vol. IV, p. 352.
[2] VI Legge, 1, Vol. V, pp. 141-142.
[3] VI Legge, 1, Vol. IV, p. 459.
[4] VI Legge, 1, Vol. III, pp. 392-393.
[5] VI Legge, 1, Vol. IV, pp. 250-251.
[6] VI Legge, 1, Vol. I, p. 270.
[7] VI Legge, 1, Vol. IV, p. 217.

CHAPTER XXIII

[1] VI Legge, 1, Vol. IV, pp. 600-603.
[2] VI Legge, 1, Vol. III, p. 623.
[3] VI Legge, 1, Vol. V, p. 596.
[4] VI Legge, 1, Vol. IV, p. 320.
[5] VI Legge, 1, Vol. IV, p. 381.
[6] VI Legge, 1, Vol. IV, p. 170.
[7] VI Steele, Vol. I, p. 234.
[8] VI Legge, 2, p. 111.

NOTES

CHAPTER XXIV

[1] VI Legge, 1, Vol. IV, p. 233.
[2] VI Legge, 1, Vol. IV, pp. 206-207.
[3] VI Legge, 1, Vol. IV, pp. 61-62.
[4] VI Legge, 1, Vol. IV, pp. 395-396.
[5] VI Steele, Vol. I, pp. 51-73.
[6] VI Steele, Vol. I, pp. 68, 111-112.
[7] VI Steele, Vol. I, p. 234.
[8] VI Legge, 1, Vol. IV, pp. 253-255.
[9] VI Legge, 1, Vol. IV, pp. 322, 533.
[10] VI Legge, 1, Vol. III, pp. 399-412.
[11] VI Legge, 1, Vol. IV, pp. 395-400.

CHAPTER XXV

[1] VI Legge, 1, Vol. I, p. 191.
[2] VI Legge, 1, Vol. V, pp. 5-6.
[3] VI Legge, 1, Vol. V, p. 129.
[4] VI Legge, 1, Vol. V, p. 157.
[5] VI Legge, 1, Vol. IV, p. 515.

CHAPTER XXVI

[1] VI Legge, 1, Vol. IV, p. 42.
[2] VI Legge, 1, Vol. III, p. 391.
[3] VI Legge, 1, Vol. IV, p. 509.
[4] VI Legge, 1, Vol. III, pp. 623-624.
[5] VI Legge, 1, Vol. III, pp. 605-606.
[6] VI Legge, 1, Vol. V, p. 609.
[7] VI Legge, 1, Vol. III, pp. 389-390.
[8] *Li Chi*, translated by James Legge, *Sacred Books of the East*, Vol. XXVII, p. 90.
[9] VI Legge, 1, Vol. V, p. 405.

CHAPTER XXVIII

[1] VI Legge, 1, Vol. II, p. 355.
[2] VI Legge, 1, Vol. III, p. 485.
[3] VI Legge, 1, Vol. III, p. 460.
[4] VI Legge, 1, Vol. III, p. 275.

INDEX

INDEX

INDEX

INDEX

INDEX

INDEX

INDEX

SKETCH MAP OF CHINA

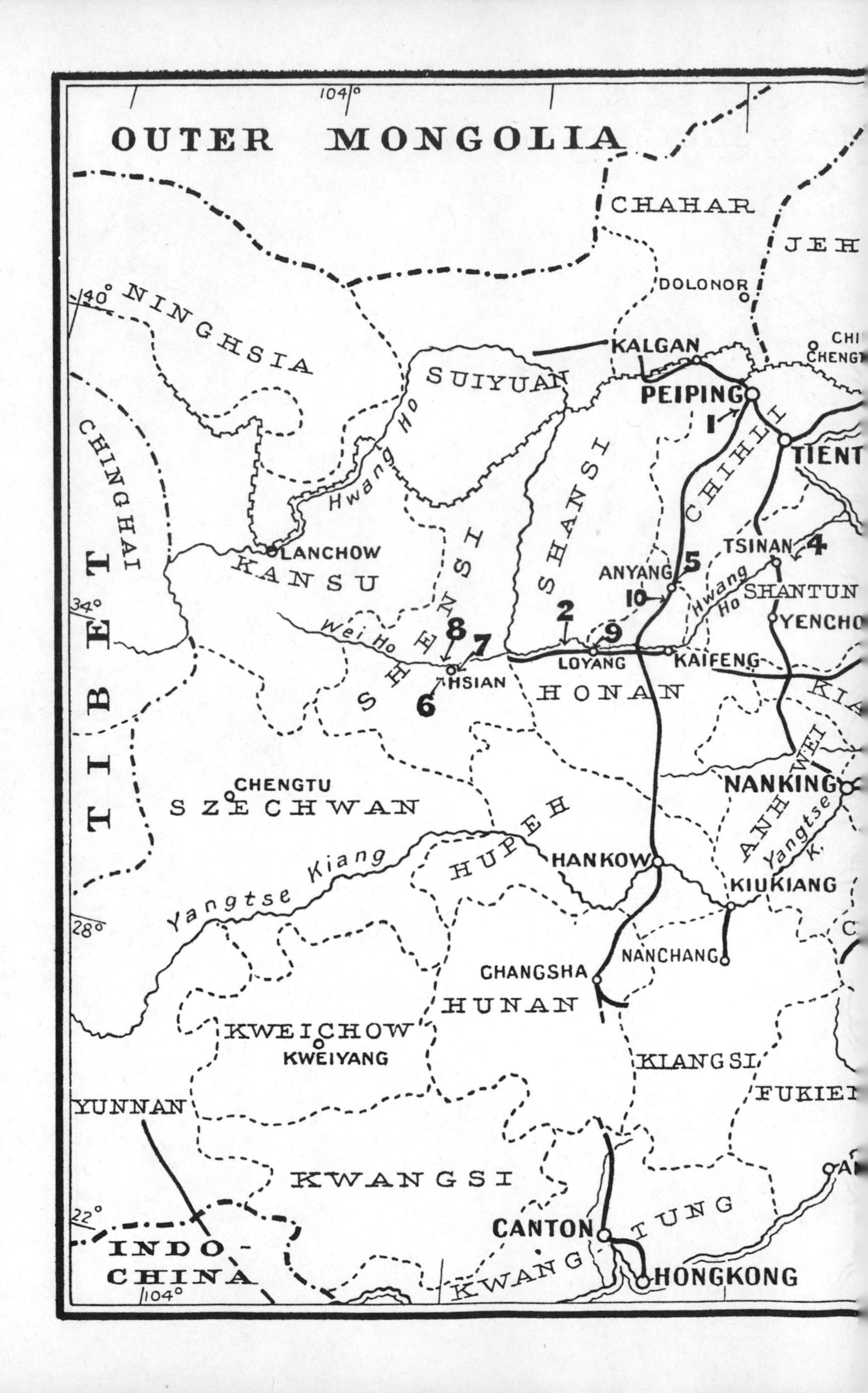
OUTER MONGOLIA
104°
CHAHAR
JEH
DOLONOR
NINGHSIA
40°
KALGAN
CHI
CHENG
SUIYUAN
PEIPING
1
TIENT
CHINGHAI
Hwang Ho
SHANSI
CHIHLI
SHENSI
TSINAN
4
LANCHOW
KANSU
ANYANG
5
10
Hwang Ho
SHANTUN
YENCHO
34°
Wei Ho
8
7
2
9
LOYANG
KAIFENG
HSIAN
6
HONAN
TIBET
ANHWEI
NANKING
CHENGTU
SZECHWAN
HUPEH
Yangtse K.
Yangtse Kiang
HANKOW
KIUKIANG
28°
NANCHANG
CHANGSHA
HUNAN
KWEICHOW
KWEIYANG
KIANGSI
FUKIEN
YUNNAN
KWANGSI
22°
CANTON
KWANGTUNG
INDO-CHINA
HONGKONG
104°

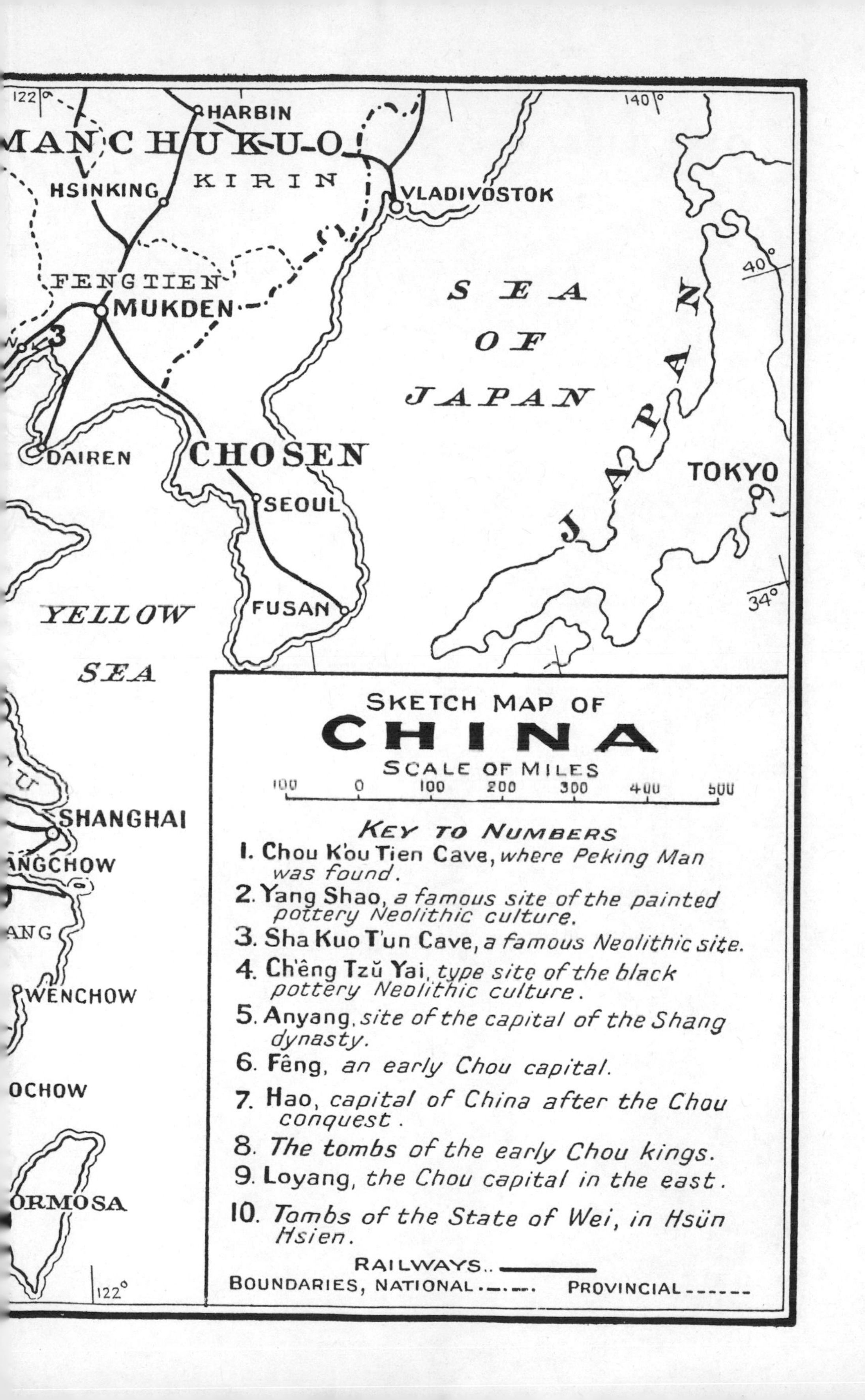

122°
HARBIN
MANCHUKUO
KIRIN
HSINKING
VLADIVOSTOK
140°
FENGTIEN
MUKDEN
3
SEA
OF
JAPAN
JAPAN
40°
DAIREN
CHOSEN
TOKYO
SEOUL
34°
YELLOW
SEA
FUSAN
SHANGHAI
ANGCHOW
ANG
WENCHOW
OCHOW
ORMOSA
122°
SKETCH MAP OF
CHINA
SCALE OF MILES
100 0 100 200 300 400 500
KEY TO NUMBERS
1. Chou K'ou Tien Cave, where Peking Man was found.
2. Yang Shao, a famous site of the painted pottery Neolithic culture.
3. Sha Kuo T'un Cave, a famous Neolithic site.
4. Ch'êng Tzŭ Yai, type site of the black pottery Neolithic culture.
5. Anyang, site of the capital of the Shang dynasty.
6. Fêng, an early Chou capital.
7. Hao, capital of China after the Chou conquest.
8. The tombs of the early Chou kings.
9. Loyang, the Chou capital in the east.
10. Tombs of the State of Wei, in Hsün Hsien.
RAILWAYS
BOUNDARIES, NATIONAL
PROVINCIAL